Collector's
Guide to

DOLLS

Identification & Values

of the
1960s
and
1970s

Cindy Sabulis

COLLECTOR BOOKS
A Division of Schroeder Publishing Co., Inc.

The current values in this book should be used only as a guide. They are not intended to set prices, which vary from one section of the country to another. Auction prices as well as dealer prices vary greatly and are affected by condition as well as demand. Neither the author nor the publisher assumes responsibility for any losses that might be incurred as a result of consulting this guide.

On the cover:

1960s Dolls: First row, left to right: Baby Small Talk by Mattel, Heidi by Remco, Penny Brite by Deluxe Redding. Second row: Tressy by American Character, Tammy by Ideal, Mary Poppins by Horsman. Third row: Chatty Cathy by Mattel, Pebbles by Ideal.

1970s Dolls: First row, left to right: Love by Hasbro, Lilac Rock Flower by Mattel, Kookie Flatsy by Ideal, Dancing Dawn by Topper, Live Action Barbie by Mattel, Crissy, Velvet, and Tiffany Taylor by Ideal.

Catalogs pages reprinted in this book are courtesy of the following companies:
Sears, Roebuck and Co. Archives, Hoffman Estates, Illinois
J.C. Penney and Co.
Montgomery Ward and Co.
Mattel, Inc.

Any corrections to information printed within this book or contribution of photos for future use can be sent to the author c/o Toys of Another Time, L.L.C., P.O. Box 642, Shelton, CT 06484. Submissions are gratefully appreciated, however, no letters or photos can be acknowledged or returned.

Cover design by Beth Summers
Book design by Joyce Cherry
Photographs by Cindy Sabulis

Searching For A Publisher?

We are always looking for knowledgeable people considered to be experts within their fields. If you feel that there is a real need for a book on your collectible subject and have a large comprehensive collection, contact Collector Books.

Collector Books
P. O. Box 3009
Paducah, KY 42002-3009
www.collectorbooks.com

Copyright © 2000 by Cindy Sabulis

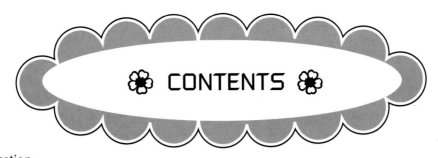

CONTENTS

🌸 DEDICATION 🌸

To Patty, my friend and my sister, who shares my passion and excitement for collecting.

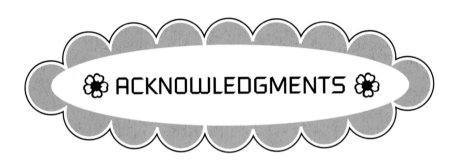

🌸 ACKNOWLEDGMENTS 🌸

Even knowing a little about a lot of different dolls, I still didn't know enough to write this book alone. It was with the help of many doll friends that I was able to gather information and find out values for dolls that were beyond my expertise. Many thanks to those who provided information included within the text of this book. A big thank you also to those who loaned dolls to be photographed or spent time photographing their dolls for me to include. The following contributors were very generous in sharing information and/or photos of their dolls:

Michelle Andrews
Patty and Greg Andrews
Laura Coplen-Miller
Carla Marie Cross
Gayle Davisson
S. DeDivitis
Mala Drzewicki
Robin Englehart
Marcia Fanta
Jeri E. Fowler
Pamela Grimes
Karen Hickey
Phyllis Janowski, Alice's Dolls
Joedi Johnson
Juliana Johnson
Cathy Kidney-Bremner

Janet and Mike Lawrence
Dal Lowenbein
Patty Massey
Nancy Jean Mong
Heidi Neufeld
Elaine McGrath
Robin Randall
Sally Seikel
Nancy Schwartz, Treasures
Pat Solzak, Golden Apple
Gloria Telep
Dawn Thomas
Kathleen Tornikoski, Romancing the Doll
Debi Toussaint-Edgar
Sharon Wendrow, Memory Lane

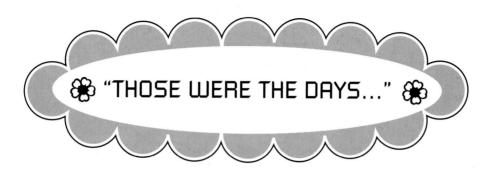

"THOSE WERE THE DAYS..."

Although many of us don't believe we collect dolls because we are trying to recapture our childhood, it is often our childhood dolls that seem to have the most emotional impact on us. So many times when I am selling at a doll show, people will see a doll on my table and exclaim, "I had one of those when I was a kid!" followed by some story about their doll. Often I hear how their doll was eventually given away, thrown away, or sold at a yard sale years ago. More times than not, if the price of the doll on my table is reasonable, the person will purchase it primarily for the memories it evokes. While it's true that most doll collectors collect many different types of dolls, there seems to be a preference among collectors for collecting the dolls they grew up with. Doll collectors who grew up in the 1930s and 1940s often have a preference for composition dolls. Those that grew up in the 1950s generally like the hard plastic dolls. And collectors who grew up during the 1960s and 1970s seem to favor the not-so-old-but-definitely-nostalgic vinyl dolls from this era.

Both new and seasoned collectors who were raised in the 1960s or 1970s have helped make dolls from these decades heavy contenders at the top of the dolls' popularity chart. Of course, what girl growing up in the 1960s and 1970s didn't play with Barbie® dolls? Prices on Barbie dolls continue to rise as grown collectors try to repurchase what they had or what they wished they had when they were children. Scores of young girls of this time owned Chatty Cathy dolls, and if they didn't own one, they were sure to have had friends who did. How could anyone growing up in the '60s not remember Patti Playpal, Thumbelina, Kissy, Tressy, Tammy, or Liddle Kiddles? The "mod" years of the 1970s brought about some new and not-as-conservative dolls such as Ideal's Crissy, the World of Love dolls, Mattel's Rock Flowers, Ideal's Harmony, Topper Toy's Dawn and friends, and other hip-with-the-times dolls.

Like many other collectors I tend to favor the dolls that were available when I was a child. Although my doll collection spans from the early 1900s to the present, the ones that hold the most excitement for me are the dolls I remember having, remember seeing, or remember wanting as a child. These are the dolls of the 1960s and 1970s.

❀ INTRODUCTION ❀

❀ Using This Guide ❀

Naturally because of time and space limitations, not every doll available during the 1960s and 1970s could be included in this book. As much as possible, those dolls that were very popular at the time and that collectors love today are included. In addition, a variety of some lesser-known dolls that are not found in other doll books are included. All dolls are listed under their manufacturer with the manufacturers listed alphabetically. The dolls are not listed chronologically, for the sake of keeping all the dolls in a particular line or category together. Whenever possible, dolls are shown wearing their original outfits. If the outfit the doll is pictured in is not original, the text will say so.

❀ Doll Markings ❀

When available, markings for dolls are included as an additional means of helping the reader identify their particular doll. While not much fun to read, it does offer some aid if the reader is unsure of the doll they have. In most cases, the markings included in the text are the markings on the doll(s) pictured in the photograph, but it's not uncommon for several examples of the same doll to be marked slightly differently from each other. Markings on dolls can vary depending on the version or issue date of the doll, which mold was used, or which factory a doll came from. When a slash (/) is present in the listed markings, it indicates a new line of the doll's marking so, "1970/IDEAL TOY CORP./E9-2-H165/HONG KONG" actually would appear on the doll as

1970
IDEAL TOY CORP.
E9-2-H165
HONG KONG

❀ Sizes of Dolls ❀

The sizes of the dolls shown in the photographs are usually noted in the text. However, the manufacturing process of a doll can sometimes result in the same doll coming out in slightly varying sizes. Depending on how dolls are measured, results can be slightly different as well. For these reasons, there is often a discrepancy from one source to the next on how large or small a doll is and why your doll may measure just under or over the size given for the doll in this guide or some other source. There is really no right or wrong way to measure a doll. Some people measure a doll from the tip of the head to the tip of the toes. Others measure from head to heel. If the doll has a pointed toe, this can result in different measurements. If the doll has a bent leg, such as with a baby doll, one can measure all the way along the bent leg with a tape measure or one can straighten out the leg as much as possible and then measure. Either way, there will be a slightly different height assessment. Even something as minor as how far down a doll's head is pushed on her neck can result in different measurements of the same doll. With this in mind, understand that when size is given, it might vary slightly from the size you get when you measure a doll.

❀ Determining Values ❀

I often get calls from people wanting to know what their doll is worth simply for their own personal satisfaction. Many people tell me that they read in a price guide that their doll is worth a particular value and are looking to me for confirmation. However, determining the value of a doll is not always as simple as looking it up in a doll book. If their doll has something unusual about it that other dolls like it don't have, the doll may be valued higher than book value. If a doll has a hair cut or a large gash on its face, naturally, the value would be much lower than that listed in a book. Are the original clothes, accessories, and/or box still with the doll and in good condition? Are there any flaws on the doll, such as scratches or pinprick holes in the vinyl? Are any painted features of the doll, such as eyes, eyebrows, lip color, or hair rubbing off? Has the doll suffered any ill effects from storage over the years? These are all things that need to be considered when trying to determine value. Condition plays a big part, but it, however, is very subjective. One person may think a doll is in mint condition, while another may think the same doll is only in very good condition. Like condition, value of a doll is very subjective and will vary depending on to whom you talk or which value guide you read.

Value is the price someone might be willing to pay for an item. Dealer prices are not always indicative of the value, but they do offer a starting point. You must keep two points in mind when using dealer prices as a comparative means in determining the value of a doll. First, understand that the asking price is not always the actual selling price. Second, understand that dealers don't always know the value either. Some dealers who have never dealt with a particular doll before may not be in touch with what they can reasonably expect to get for that doll. So they either price it low in which case it will probably be snatched up fast by some lucky collector or a more educated dealer, or out of ignorance they price it too high. In the case of being priced too high, the item may sit for a long time, never moving until the price is finally lowered. The actual selling price could turn out to be only half of what it was originally. In the case of being under priced, the buyer may be able to resell it in a short period for double the original price. At a doll show if you see a $50 price tag on a doll you own, it doesn't necessarily mean your doll should be priced the same amount. If several dealers have that same doll priced in the same neighborhood, then they probably know what they can reasonably expect to get for that doll.

When it comes time to sell a doll, you might not be able to sell it regardless of price if you don't have access to the people that collect the particular doll. I once had a set of mint Madame Alexander dolls that according to value guides was worth $1,000. For two years I couldn't find a buyer for those dolls even though I priced them below book value at $600. I finally sold them through an auction and they ended up selling for $530. Was the set worth $1,000 like the "experts" said or $530, which was the actual amount the dolls sold for? In this case, it was only worth what someone was willing to pay for it.

When selling a doll, if you hope to get the value for it that is shown in doll reference books, be prepared to take your time selling it. It takes time to locate someone willing to pay top value. Experienced collectible dealers know it takes repeated exposure from many different outlets to find the right buyer willing to pay book or near book value.

This book differs from other price guides because rather than just one value I have provided a range of values. The reason for this is that there is really no single value for any collectible doll. While this may confuse some people who want to know exactly what their doll is worth, it is more realistic to have a value range. If your doll has flaws, it will be valued on the lower end or possibly below the listed value. If your doll is perfect, it would be valued on the higher end. As confusing as it seems to some people, even mint-in-box values can vary depending on how mint the box or original packaging is. A doll can still be considered mint-in-box (MIB) even if the box is squashed with the cellophane coming off as long as the doll is undamaged or unflawed. If this were the case, the doll would be valued lower then the MIB value but higher than the mint and loose value.

In your collecting travels you may encounter people selling dolls for higher or lower than the values in this book. That will always be the case. Again, I must stress there is really no one value for a doll because at different times and through various sources, people will pay varying amounts for the same items.

Unless otherwise specified, the values listed in this book are for dolls without their original boxes wearing their original clothing and in excellent condition. If a doll is in played-with condition (i.e., messed up or thinning hair, dirty, makeup paint rubbed off, scratches in plastic or vinyl) or the doll is not dressed in his or her original clothing, value would be less than listed. If a doll's hair has been cut, the value diminishes quite a bit and the doll could be worth less than half the listed value. If the original box or packaging is included with the doll, value would be higher than the listed value and can be even higher if the box or packaging is unflawed in any way. If the value listed is for a MIB (mint-in-box), NRFB (never-removed-from-box), or loose/re-dressed doll, it will say so.

All values listed in this book are based on the U.S. doll market and would vary for other countries based on supply and demand of each particular doll in that country.

❀ Doll Values and the Internet ❀

I think most collectors and dealers will agree, the Internet has had a profound impact on the collecting world. Dolls once difficult to locate can now often be found by surfing the Web. Many new collectors have started collecting after discovering childhood items on the Internet. Dealers who often couldn't get their asking price at shows or by selling items in their shop could easily find homes for their merchandise in just a short time by posting them on the Internet.

With the increased use of the Internet, the amount

of online buying and selling has made the quest for dolls even more competitive. Online auctions seem to be the hottest places for buying and selling on the Internet. While selling prices can fluctuate from one day to the next, occasionally the selling prices of some dolls jump to outrageously high and sometimes unrealistic prices in many highly competitive online auctions. Values of dolls have changed so much and so fast because of the Internet that most of the values in this guide had to be revised two or three times before it ever reached the publisher to reflect the increased interest in dolls from the 1960s – 1970s era. However, because some of these online selling prices were above the norm for similar dolls, it was difficult to factor them in the value range. I once saw a Dancerina doll sell for $300 in an aggressive online auction. The doll was loose and played with, yet at least two people wanted her badly enough to bid her ending price up unusually high for a relatively easy to locate doll. Loose and played-with Dancerina dolls often turn up at doll shows priced in the $25 – 45 price range. When the loose doll sold online for $300, I thought, is this a real-istic value for this doll? Is this the value I should report in a price guide? I eagerly watched other online auctions to see if other examples of the doll would go that high. For a while the selling prices for Dancerina dolls were higher than I had ever seen before, but as more and more online sellers put their Dancerina dolls up for sale, the ending prices started to go down. For several months after the $300 sale, I saw a mint-in-box example of Dancerina sell for $125 and a loose one with original outfit go for $15, as well as dozens of other Dancerinas selling for all kinds of prices in between. So, is a loose and played with Dancerina worth $300 while a mint-in-box one only worth $125 just because someone actually paid those prices for them? Should the value range for a loose doll be listed as $15 – $300 since dolls have sold for both the high and low prices? Ending prices of online auctions were used as one source for compiling values of dolls for this book, but when the ending bids were excessively above or below the norm, this author felt that price did not represent a realistic value to use in the value range.

❀ Hi-Tech vs. "Old-Fashioned" Doll Collecting ❀

I am a big fan of the Internet as it pertains to doll collecting. It has been an invaluable source for research, as well as for purchasing dolls that normally I would have had difficulty finding. The Internet can be great for people selling dolls and trying to locate dolls. It is ideal for those who cannot attend many doll shows or are looking for more than what is available at their local shows. The Internet has connected many collectors with similar interests and has been responsible for numerous online doll friendships.

On the down-side, the Internet has made it difficult for collectors who are not online to buy those same dolls via mail-order. A number of dealers who used to mail out lists of dolls for sale no longer do because their lists are now on Web pages. Buy-and-sell doll publications are losing subscribers to the Internet and thus are scaling back their publication. Online collectors no longer have to pay high long-distance fees or have to wait 2 – 7 days for the postal service to deliver a letter requesting information about a doll someone is selling. They no longer have to wait for the next issue of the doll publication to come out before they can find out what dolls are available. They no longer have to compete with other potential buyers who may have gotten a doll publication or a dealer's list earlier than they did. On the Internet, sellers can post an ad for a doll for sale and get a response the same day; in print, ads are usually submitted a month in advance, sometimes longer. For all these reasons, many previous subscribers no longer feel the need to buy or sell using print publica-tions since the Internet allows quick interaction between buyer and seller. Sadly, some doll publications that have been around for years are shrinking in the number of ads they contain. From past experience I have found that telephoning about a doll advertised in a publication and speaking to a live person is much more pleasant than the impersonal e-mail contact on the Internet. That personalized service is what keeps many collectors buying dolls via print publications vs. online. I am hopeful that some of the doll publications that are currently struggling can once again grow and continue to provide collectors and sellers with a place to buy and sell.

While the Internet is an exciting and marvelous place to purchase dolls, it can never replace the thrill of attending a doll show where hundreds or thousands of dolls are on display. I am amazed at the number of new collectors who started collecting dolls because of the Internet and have no idea that doll shows even exist. I encourage everyone to experience the joy of a doll or toy show where collectors can see, touch, and learn all about dolls. The Internet is a great place to purchase dolls, but it should not be the only place that collectors buy dolls.

❀ ACTIVE DOLL CORPORATION ❀

Puddins: This 10" doll has a vinyl head, vinyl arms, a plastic body and plastic legs. Her box reads, "Active Doll Corporation, Brooklyn 5, NY Cat. No. 1051/1-12". NRFB: **$25.00 – 30.00.** Courtesy Gloria Telep.

❀ ADVERTISING DOLLS ❀

Since these dolls were made by various manufacturers, it is sometimes difficult to determine the company who made many of the characters collectors have dubbed as "advertising" dolls. Many of these dolls were obtained by mailing in cash and/or proofs of purchase for a product in order to receive the promotional doll, but occasionally advertising dolls were available in stores as well.

Burger King: This 16" soft-stuffed doll has "©1973 BURGER KING CORPORATION" printed on the back of his left foot. **$15.00 – 20.00.**

Burger King: A 14" soft-stuffed doll which was available around 1977. This doll was designed in the image of the mascot king that Burger King was using at the time. The doll was produced by the Chase Bag Company. "Burger King" is printed on his necklace and belt. "T.M." is printed on front of his left foot and "MADE IN U.S.A." is printed on the back of his right foot. **$15.00 – 20.00.**

Campbell Kids: These 10" vinyl dolls were a premium for sending in Campbell Soup labels and $2.00 for each doll. Circa 1972. The dolls are unmarked. **$20.00 – 25.00** each.

Dunkin' Munchkins: A Dunkin' Donuts character, this 15" soft-stuffed doll has "Dunkin' Munchkins" printed on her back. **$15.00 – 20.00.**

Eskimo Pie Boy: 15" plush doll which was available from around 1964 – 1974. The Eskimo Pie boy was produced by the Chase Bag Company. The doll is unmarked. **$15.00 – 20.00.**

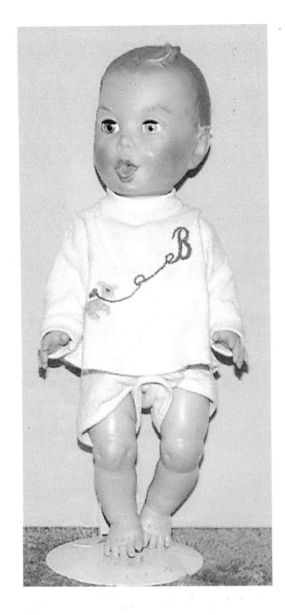

Gerber Baby: This doll was available as a premium sometime around 1966 – 1967. Because the doll's look wasn't too appealing, the doll was discontinued after a brief time. This 14" Gerber Baby is marked, "©Gerber Products Co./1966" on head. **$40.00 – 75.00.** Courtesy Debi Toussaint-Edgar/Photo by Steve Edgar.

Gerber Baby: 1978 Golden Anniversary edition of the Gerber Baby by the Atlanta Novelty Company. The 18" doll has flirty eyes that move side-to-side. MIB: **$60.00 – 75.00.** Courtesy Gayle Davisson.

Jolly Green Giant and Little Sprout: 15½" Jolly Green Giant and 10" Sprout mascots of Green Giant vegetables. Both dolls are unmarked. **$10.00 – 15.00.**

Gilbert Giddy-Up: Mascot from Hardee's, this doll was produced by the Chase Bag Company in 1971. **$15.00 – 20.00.**

Jack Frost: 19½" plush doll from the Jack Frost Sugar Company. The doll was produced by the Chase Bag Company. The doll's name is printed on the front of his outfit. **$15.00 – 20.00.**

Little Hans, The Chocolate Maker: Mascot from the Nestle Company, this 13" doll is circa 1970. It was produced by the Chase Bag Company. **$20.00 – 25.00.**

Tony the Tiger: This tiger was the mascot for Frosted Flakes breakfast cereal. Tony is a 14" soft-stuffed doll. On the front of his scarf is printed, "TONY©" with a backwards "N," and on the back of his right foot is printed, "©1973 Kellogg Co." **$20.00 – 25.00.**

❀ ALEXANDER ❀

Madame Alexander and the Alexander Doll Company have always been associated with high quality dolls, from the charming cloth dolls they made in the 1920s and 1930s to the exquisite hard plastic dolls of the 1950s. During the 1960s and 1970s the company continued production of many high quality vinyl dolls, both for play and display. Dolls that are all original with their boxes and tags or booklets still attached are the ones most sought after by collectors. Values for Madame Alexander dolls that are played with or missing their original clothing can be one-third the value of mint dolls.

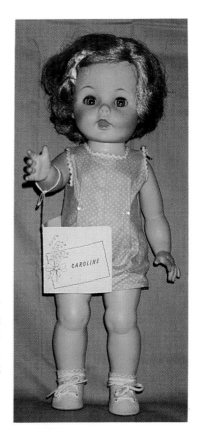

Caroline: Although the Kennedy name was not actually used, this doll represented young Caroline Kennedy. The doll was sold in various outfits and additional outfits could be purchased separately for her. This 15" doll is marked, "ALEXANDER/19©61" on her head. With original playsuit and tag: **$225.00 – 250.00.** Courtesy Elaine McGrath.

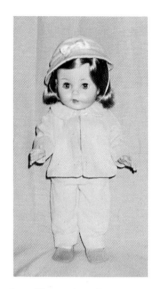

Caroline: Another example of Caroline wearing her pink three-piece playsuit. **$225.00 – 250.00.**
Courtesy Jeri E. Fowler.

Smarty: Madame Alexander's Smarty doll was sold in various outfits including the one shown here. The 12" doll is marked, "ALEXANDER/©/1962" on her head. **$65.00 – 85.00.** Courtesy Elaine McGrath.

Smarty and Caroline: Note the material used on both Smarty's and Caroline's outfits is the same. Courtesy Elaine McGrath.

Janie: 12" doll came with several hair colors and styles and was available in a variety of different outfits. The doll is marked, "ALEXANDER/19©64" on her head. MIB: **$150.00 – 185.00.** Courtesy Alice's Dolls.

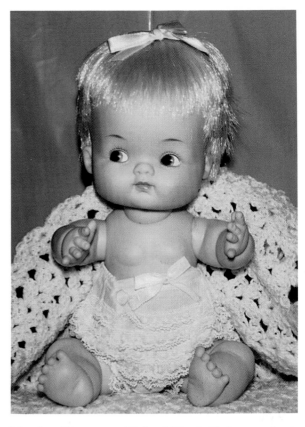

Little Shaver: This 12" doll is marked, "MME/ALEXANDER (in circle)" on her head. Her outfit is tagged "1963 Little Shaver." The blanket in the photo is not original. **$100.00 – 125.00.** Courtesy Marcia Fanta.

Pussy Cat: 20" Pussy Cat has a stuffed body with a crier inside and a vinyl head and limbs. The doll is marked, "ALEXANDER/19©65" on her head. MIB: **$150.00 – 175.00.** Courtesy Patty Massey.

Puddin: 19" doll has a stuffed body with a crier inside and a vinyl head and limbs. Puddin originally had a small ponytail on top of her head. The doll is marked, "ALEXANDER/19©65" on her head. Loose and redressed: **$35.00 – 50.00.**

Pussy Cat: These baby dolls were often well loved by young children so when played with and redressed as in the example here, they are only valued around **$25.00 – 40.00.** Same markings as the doll at bottom of page 16.

Gone with the Wind: This 14" vinyl doll represents the character of Scarlett O'Hara from the movie *Gone With the Wind*. Her original white gown is tagged, "Gone with the Wind/By MADAME ALEXANDER©/NEW YORK U.S.A." The doll is marked, "ALEXANDER, 19©65" on her head. Mint with tag: **$70.00 – 95.00.**

❀ ALLIED DOLL & TOY CORP. ❀

Because collectors aren't very familiar with dolls from this company, there isn't much demand for Allied dolls. Values on these dolls, even those mint-in-box, are relatively low at the time of publication.

Wee Bonnie Baby: 10" Wee Bonnie Baby is marked, "AE10/17" on her head and "AE/1" (the 1 is written backwards) on her back. Her box reads, "#401 ©1963." The doll was available as a brunette dressed in yellow, as well as a red head dressed in blue, and a platinum blond dressed in pink. She is similar to Effanbee's Fluffy doll. MIB: **$30.00 – 40.00.** Courtesy Gloria Telep.

Bonnie Dear: 17" doll marked, "©Allied Doll & Toy Corp. 1962 AE5/AE-478" on her head. MIB: **$25.00 – 30.00.** Courtesy Gloria Telep.

Bonnie Doll: This 13" doll has rooted brunette hair with molded hair underneath. She is marked "HD" on her head. MIB: **$20.00 – 25.00.** Courtesy Gloria Telep.

❀ AMERICAN CHARACTER ❀

This company did business under both the names American Character Doll Corporation and American Doll and Toy Corporation.

Tiny Tears

American Character's Tiny Tears doll was a popular seller throughout the 1950s and continued in various versions and sizes into the 1970s. The earlier dolls came with caracul wigs (curly poodle-like hair), and then later came with saran hair (coarse, wiry hair). Dolls with caracul wigs are more valuable than dolls with saran hair. Dolls also infrequently came with molded hair. Over the years, the materials used on the dolls changed from a rubber body with a hard plastic head, to a vinyl body with a hard plastic head, and finally to an all vinyl doll. The layette sets were varied, but almost always included a bubble pipe. In the 1960s the famous Tiny Tears name was expanded to include Teeny Tiny Tears, Teeny Weenie Tiny Tears, Baby Tiny Tears, and Lifesize Tiny Tears.

Tiny Tears: A variety of different Tiny Tears dolls from the 1950s and 1960s. Tiny Tears dolls are marked, "AMER. CHARACTER," or "PAT. NO. 2,675,644/AME.CHAR-ACTER" or AMERICAN CHARACTER DOLL/PAT. NO. 2,675,644" or "AMERICAN CHARACTER" on the backs of their heads. **$75.00 – 225.00** each. Courtesy Juliana Johnson.

Tiny Tears: Tiny Tears with rooted auburn hair, hard plastic head, and vinyl body. Tiny Tears is marked "AMERICAN CHARACTER" on the back of her head. **$75.00 – 100.00.** Courtesy Debi Toussaint-Edgar/Photo by Steve Edgar.

16 Inch
$10⁹⁸

TINY TEARS

· MY EYES CLOSE AS I'M ROCKED
· I DRINK, I WET, I CRY REAL TEARS

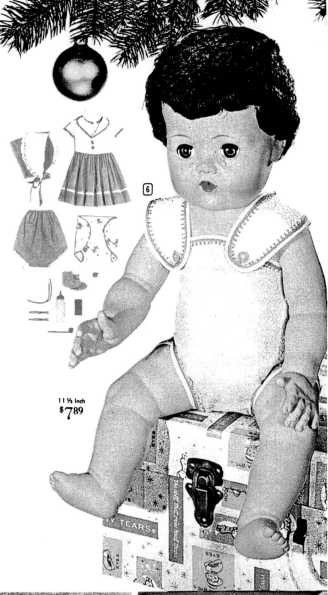

My Rock-A-Bye Eyes stay awake until I'm rocked, then they slowly close as I drift to dreamland. I drink, wet, really blow bubbles with my bubble pipe, and cry real tears. I'm fully jointed, too.

6 **Tiny Tears with Layette, Trunk.** She has curly rooted hair. She wears romper suit, her layette is packed in handy trunk— includes cotton dress, panties, bonnet, diaper, bottle, pins, sponge, bubble pipe, washcloth pacifier, bootees, pins.
48 T 3894—11½-In. Doll, Trunk, Layette. Wt. 3 lbs.......**$7.89**
48 T 3895—16-In. Doll, Trunk, Layette. Ship. wt. 5 lbs..... **9.98**
48 T 3897 M—20-In. Doll, Trunk, Layette. Wt. 6 lbs. 8 oz...**14.99**

7 **Tiny Tears, Playpen, Layette.** She can play in her very own 18-in. square collapsible playpen with comfy bottom pad. She has molded hair, wears romper suit, her layette includes dress, matching panties, diaper, bottle, pins, sponge, bubble pipe, washcloth, clothespins. Ship. wt. 5 lbs.
48 T 3898 M—16-In. Doll, Playpen, Layette............**$10.98**

8 **Tiny Tears, Spra-Bath, Layette.** Wash and shampoo Tiny Tears in her own polyethylene bath—real spray-action attachment operates on 3 "D" flashlight batteries (sold on P. 363), water recirculates. Bath has molded soap and accessory sections, rests securely on Brass-finished metal stand. About 27 in. high. Tiny Tears has rooted hair, wears romper suit; her layette includes dress, panties, diaper, bootees, pins, bottle, sponge, bubble pipe, washcloth, pacifier, clothespins.
48 T 3889 M—16-In. Doll, Bath, Layette. Wt. 5 lbs. 14 oz..**$15.95**

9 **Tiny Tears in Her Plastic Rocking Crib, Layette.** Has rooted hair, is dressed in romper suit. Her layette includes dress, matching panties, diaper, bootees, bottle, pins, sponge, bubble pipe and pacifier. Ship. wt. 5 lbs. 13 oz.
48 T 3899 M—16-In. Doll, Rocking Crib, Layette....... **$11.48**

10 **Tiny Tears and Layette.** Curly rooted hair, dressed in her comfy romper suit. Layette includes diaper, pins, bottle, sponge, bubble pipe, washcloth, pacifier and tissues.
48 T 3918—11½-In. Doll, Layette. Ship. wt. 2 lbs. 12 oz. ...**$5.49**
48 T 3920—13½-In. Doll, Layette. Also includes dress and panties. Ship. wt. 3 lbs. **$6.99**

11½ Inch
$7⁸⁹

$5⁴⁹

16 Inch
$11⁴⁸

16 Inch
$15⁹⁵

WARDS 287

Tiny Tears: 1961 Montgomery Ward Christmas catalog showing some of the Tiny Tears dolls and accessories available that year.

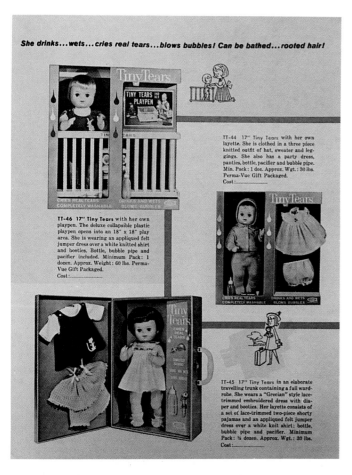

Tiny Tears: The updated version of Tiny Tears bears little resemblance to the earlier Tiny Tears dolls but was available in similar layette sets like the earlier dolls. These two photos show a variety of 17" vinyl Tiny Tears dolls available in 1963. Doll only: **$35.00 – 50.00.** MIB sets: **$125.00 – 175.00.** 1963 American Character catalog.

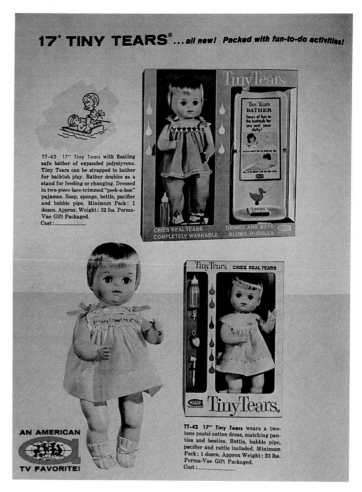

Tiny Tears: The American Character Company billed their 17" doll as Baby Tiny Tears but her original box as shown in the 1963 American Character catalog simply says Tiny Tears. The doll was available in a number of different outfits. All the 17" dolls came with Tiny Tears' famous bubble pipe. 1963 Doll only: **$35.00 – 45.00.** MIB sets: **$75.00 – 125.00.** 1963 American Character catalog.

Tiny Tears: The 21" Tiny Tears was considered "Lifesize" by the American Character Company, but again, the original box shown in their 1963 catalog only calls the doll "Tiny Tears." The 21" dolls were available in a number of different outfits. Doll only: **$40.00 – 50.00.** MIB set: **$80.00 – 130.00.** 1963 American Character catalog.

Teeny Tiny Tears: 12" vinyl doll marked, "Am. Char.©" on her head. Some versions of this doll have "rock-a-bye eyes" that slowly close as you rock the doll to sleep. Redressed: **$25.00 – 30.00.**

Teeny Tiny Tears: This 1963 catalog shows some of the clothing available for Teeny Tiny Tears, as well as a doll in her original box and a doll which came in a carrying case. Many of the same outfits were available for both the 12" and the 8½" dolls. 1963 American Character catalog.

Gently closes her eyes when you rock her to sleep

TEENY TINY TEARS
by American Character

Teeny with cradle
$7⁹⁹

It's a joy to care for this lovable 12-inch baby doll. She drinks, wets, cries real tears, blows bubbles. At bedtime, she slowly closes her rock-a-bye eyes as you rock her in her own cozy cradle. Of soft vinyl, she takes baths too. Rooted hair can be combed and brushed. Teeny wears a printed cotton flannel sleeper. Comes with 15-in. long plastic cradle with mattress cover; bottle, pacifier and bubble pipe.
49 N 3165—Shipping weight 2 lbs. 12 oz. $7.99

Teeny with trunk
$7⁹⁴

12-inch cry baby travels with trunk and layette, drinks, wets, cries real tears, blows bubbles. Soft vinyl with rooted hair. Wears lace-trimmed apron dress with applique, booties, panties. Lacy A-line dress, polka dot panties, pacifier, bubble pipe, bottle packed in trunk.
Shipping weight 2 lbs. 6 oz.
49 N 3167 . . . . $7.94

Teeny Doll only
$3⁹³

Like a real baby, 12-inch Teeny sheds big tears when she's sad. Slowly closes her rock-a-bye eyes when she's sleepy. Drinks, wets, blows bubbles too. Of soft vinyl with rooted hair. Wears cape dress. Bottle, bubble pipe, diaper and pacifier incl.
Shipping weight 1 lb. 5 oz.
49 N 3166 . . . . $3.93

Outfits for Teeny

1 **Travel-time Knit Set** . . sweater, leggings and bonnet keep 12 inch doll warm. Doll not included.
49 N 3077—Wt. 6 oz. $2.77

2 **Sheer Apron Dress** with leotards. For 12-inch baby doll (not included).
49 N 3041—Wt. 6 oz. $2.77

Teenie Weenie Tiny Tears with trunk $4⁹⁹

Only 9 inches tall, but what a charmer. She weeps real tears, closes her rock-a-bye eyes. Drinks, wets. Soft vinyl with rooted hair. Wears a dainty dress. Comes with trunk, clothes and accessories shown.
49 N 3168—Shpg. wt. 1 lb. 2 oz. . . $4.99

17-inch Tiny Tears . . almost life-size $9⁹⁷

Feels like a real baby cuddled in your arms. She drinks, wets, blows bubbles, cries real tears. Chubby, soft vinyl body. Rooted hair. Dress in cotton flannel sleeper. Layette includes blue dress and diaper, plus red pique dress with giraffe applique, and diaper. Instruction book, bubble pipe, bottle, pacifier.
49 N 3169C—Shipping weight 4 lbs. $9.97

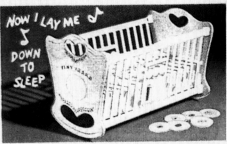

Tiny Tears Talking Cradle with 6 records $9⁷⁷ without battery

Insert record in side of cradle press lever . . and listen to the sound of nursery rhymes, prayers, lullabys. Dolly falls asleep as you rock her. Built-in phonograph has automatic shut-off. Plastic cradle, 18x12x11 in. With mattress cover. Sweet dreams for dolls up to 17 in. tall. Uses one "D" battery, order below.
79 N 9224C—Shipping weight 5 lbs. $9.77
79 N 4660 "D" Battery. Wt. ea. 4 oz. Each 16c, 4 for 60c

Teeny Tiny Tears: 1965 Sears Christmas catalog showing some of the Teeny Tiny Tears sets available.

24

Outfits, Accessories
May Vary Slightly

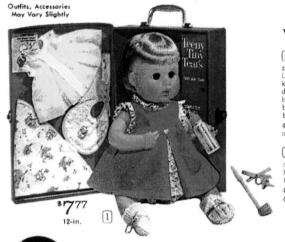

Teeny Tiny Tears with Layette, Trunk

Teeny Tiny Tears $3.99 12-in.

[1] POPULAR PLAYMATE TEENY TINY TEARS WITH LAYETTE AND TRUNK—wears pretty A-line dress, panties, booties. Layette includes dress, diaper, bib, blanket, bottle, bubble pipe, pacifier. She drinks, wets, cries tears and blows bubbles. Rock-a-bye eyes, washable vinyl body, rooted hair can be shampooed, brushed. About 12 in. tall.
48 T 8449—Teeny Tiny Tears, Layette and Trunk. Ship. wt. 2 lbs. 5 oz. . . . **$7.77**

[2] TEENY TINY TEARS in her lovely lace-trimmed dress, she can blow bubbles, drink, wet, cry tears, too. Rock her gently, her eyes will close. Included are pacifier, bottle and bubble pipe.
48 T 8450—12-IN. Ship. wt. 2 lbs. . . . **$3.99**
48 T 8451—17-IN. Ship. wt. 4 lbs. . . . **7.99**

$7.77 12-in. [1]

All Tiny Tears doll favorites now have rock-a-bye eyes that gently close and they fall asleep. They drink, wet and cry real tears

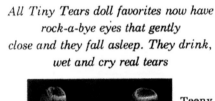

Teeny Weeny Tiny Tears with 2 new outfits

$4.99

SHE'S SO DAINTY AND PETITE—only 9 in. tall. She will drink from her bottle, cry real tears, and wet. Rock-a-bye eyes, soft tubbable vinyl body, rooted hair that can be washed, brushed. She wears romper suit—2 extra outfits include dress, diaper and play dress. Pacifier incl.
48 T 8447—DOLL AND OUTFITS. Ship. wt. 12 oz. . . . **$4.99**
48 T 8448—DOLL ONLY. Ship. wt. 8 oz. . . . **2.94**

218 WARDS BAOC

Teeny Tiny Tears: 1965 Montgomery Ward Christmas catalog showing additional Teeny Tiny Tears sets.

Teenie Weenie Tiny Tears: This is a smaller version of Teeny Tiny Tears. She is 8½". There is some discrepancy with the proper spelling of the doll's name. Although American Character spelled the doll's name "Teenie Weenie Tiny Tears" in their catalog, most store catalogs spelled it "Teeny Weeny Tiny Tears." The doll is marked, "19©64/AMER.CHAR.DOLL" on her head. She is wearing her original outfit. **$25.00 – 30.00.**

Betsy McCall: Although several different companies made Betsy McCall dolls in various sizes, the most popular one was American Character's delicate 8" hard plastic Betsy. 8" Betsy McCall is marked, "McCALL©CORP." in a circle on her back. The dolls in the photo are shown wearing outfits for her sold separately. Dolls with Betsy McCall outfits: **$85.00 – 225.00 each.**

Betsy McCall: This page from the 1963 American Character catalog shows the Betsy McCall "Starter Set" as well as many of the outfits available for the 8" doll.

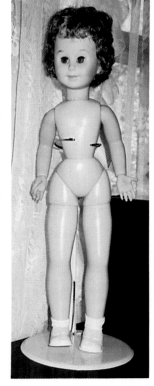

Betsy McCall: A 22" Betsy McCall doll with jointed neck, shoulders, wrists, waist, hips, thighs, and ankles. The doll is unmarked. Different sources have credited it to either American Character, Horsman, or the Uneeda Doll Company, but it is an American Character doll. Nude: **$50.00 – 80.00.** Courtesy Carla Marie Cross.

nyl head;
. Dressed
suit with
tie, shoes.
cluded.
lbs.. .$5.88

(Knucklehead)

erry's side-
vinyl head;
ly. Mouth
nipulation.
ton jacket
ront, pants,

lbs.. .$5.88

Speak to Little Miss Echo $19⁸⁸
..repeats everything you say
_{without batteries}

Teach her songs, rhymes, prayers or converse with her. Electronic voice uses 2 "D" batteries and one 9-volt transistor battery (order below). She listens, plays back at the turn of doll's knob. 3-transistor circuit with continuous magnetic tape. Tape erased automatically as you record again. 30 in. tall. Wears cotton dress, undies, has go-to-sleep eyes. Sturdy plastic with jointed arms and legs, turning head. Rooted Saran hair.

79 N 3682LM—Doll only. Shpg. wt. 8 lbs.......$19.88
79 N 4660—"D" battery. Wt. 4 oz. Each 16c; 4 for 60c
79 N 6417M—9-volt transistor battery. Wt. 4 oz. Ea. 45c

22-inch
Betsy McCall

ully jointed arms,
legs and turning
head—her wrist,
waist and feet
are also jointed
to enable you to
ose her 1001 ways

he delightful little
iss featured monthly
McCall's Magazine.
xpertly made of dur-
ble, lightweight
olded plastic with
lamorous, rooted
aran hair. Bright go-
-sleep eyes.

] In Ballerina Outfit . . stunning
rayon satin bodice, bouffant
lle tutu. Cotton leotard, slippers.
P N 3681C—Wt. 3 lbs.......$9.98

] In Plaid Dress . . charming
cotton flannel with linen-
rimmed yoke and matching cuffs.
lack cotton knit leotards, shoes.
9 N 3680C—Wt. 3 lbs.......$8.98

⑥ $9⁹⁸

⑦ $8⁹⁸

SAEG SEARS 403

Betsy McCall: 1962 Sears Christmas catalog shows 22" Betsy McCall in two different outfits.

VERYONE'S TALKING ABOUT AMERICAN'S LI

New Hi-Fi talking mechanisms*. Just press the magic button. No strings to pull! Eleven new child's phrases at random. One "D" cell battery produces loud and clear life-like voices. (Battery not included).

SALLY SAYS
Hi... I'm Sally Says push my MAGIC BUTTON...and I'll talk to YOU! "D" CELL BATTERY REQUIRED

SALLY SAYS
Hi... I'm Sally Says push my MAGIC BUTTON...and I'll talk to YOU! "D" CELL BATTERY REQUIRED

Presenting a talking toddler by

11 DIFFERENT PHRASES

11 DIFFE EN PHRA ES

Sally Says: This 19" battery-operated talking doll was available in two different outfits. Loose and original doll: **$30.00 – 45.00** MIB: **$75.00 – 80.00.** 1963 American Character catalog.

#911 19" SALLY SAYS 11 new fun and activity phrases. She comes in a luxurious sheer nylon "Grecian" style dress, set off by satin bows at shoulders, embroidered bodice, and lace insert with rows of tucks at bottom of skirt over pink taffeta slip. Matching taffeta lace-trimmed panties, shoes and socks. Minimum Pack: 1 dozen. Approx. Weight: 32 lbs.

#912 19" SALLY SAYS plays "Simon Says." The wonderful game, "Simon Says," that is enjoyed by all school children can now be played with a Sally Says doll! Press the button and Sally Says will play the girl's version of "Simon Says" with her favorite playmate, using 11 random new phrases. Sally Says wears a two-tone polka dot cotton dress with attached

Babie Says: A younger version of the Sally Says doll. This doll is 17" and came in a variety of outfits. Loose and original doll: **$30.00 – 45.00.** MIB: **$75.00 – 80.00.**1963 American Character catalog.

Baby Sue: This vinyl baby doll came in either 17" or 21" and was available in the outfits shown in the photo. Loose and originally dressed doll: **$40.00 – 50.00.** 1963 American Character catalog.

Whimsie

When it comes to American Character's Whimsie dolls, collectors either find them homely and awkward or adorable. First appearing in 1961, the Whimsies had molded heads and bodies that were one-piece stuffed vinyl. Their 19" to 21" size makes collecting the whole set difficult for those with limited space. Whimsie dolls include Annie the Astronaut, Betty the Beauty (wears banner reading "Miss Take"), Bessie the Bashful Bride, Dixie the Pixie, Fanny the Flapper, Fanny the Fallen Angel, Lena the Cleaner, Hedda Get Bedda (three-faced doll with knob on top of head), Hilda the Hillbilly (called Raggie in a 1961 American Character brochure), Monk or Friar (name unknown), Polly the Lolly, Simon the Degree (graduate), Samson the Strongman, Suzie the Snoozie, Trixie the Pixie (dressed like devil), Tillie the Talker, Wheeler the Dealer, Zack the Sack, and Zero the Hero (football player). Whimsies' marks vary slightly, but some dolls are marked, "Whimsies/19©60/AMER.DOLL.& TOY (all in circle)" on their heads and "AMER DOLL & TOY CORP./19©60" on their backs.

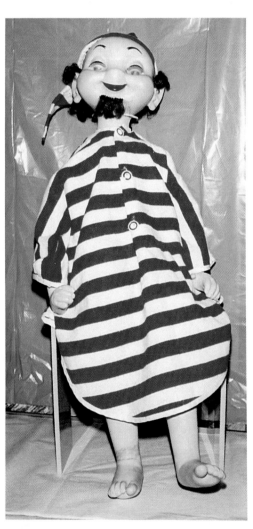

Whimsie: 21" Zack the Sack. **$75.00 – 95.00.** Courtesy Marcia Fanta.

Whimsie: Suzie the Snoozie. **$75.00 – 95.00.** Courtesy Marcia Fanta.

29

Chuckles: 23" Chuckles came with blond, brunette or red hair. She is marked, "AMER.DOLL & TOY CO./1961/©" on her head. **$100.00 – 125.00.** Courtesy Pat Solzak/Golden Apple.

Whimsies: Zero the Hero and Polly the Lolly in her original box. Zero with tag: **$85.00-100.00.** Polly MIB: **$175.00 – 200.00.** Courtesy Robin Randall.

Toodles: Toodles came in either 25" or 30" and was issued in several different outfits. It is unknown by the author if the outfit shown here is original. This 30" doll is marked, "AMERICAN DOLL & TOY CORP./19©60" on her head. **$200.00 – 300.00.**

Toodles: 1962 Sears Christmas catalog shows Toodles wearing a two-piece Capri pajama set. An additional dress outfit came with the set.

Toodles: 1961 Montgomery Ward Christmas catalog shows both 25" Toodles and 25" Baby Toodles.

Little Miss Echo: With the help of a continuous magnetic tape inside her, Little Miss Echo repeats whatever is said to her when the knob on her chest is turned. She came in different sizes, different hair colors and styles, and was issued in several different dresses including the one this 30" doll is shown wearing. The shoes she is wearing are replaced. The doll is marked: "PAT. PEND" on the battery compartment cover on her stomach. MIB: **$225.00 – 275.00.** Courtesy Patty Massey.

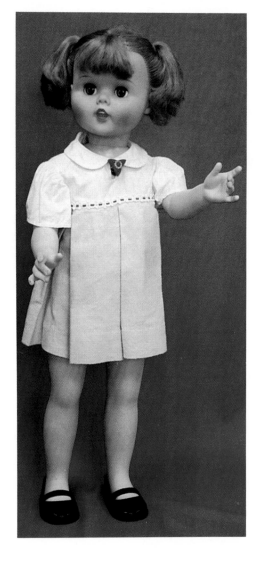

Little Miss Echo: 30" Little Miss Echo in another original outfit with a different hairstyle from the doll above. The skirt of this dress was made of flannel or corduroy. The doll in the photo is missing her original socks and hair ribbons. In original outfit: **$125.00 – 150.00.**

American Character's Miss Echo and Toodles are very similar in appearance.

Tressy

11½" Tressy with her "magic" growing hair strand was a novelty in the teenage fashion doll world. When the button on her stomach is pushed and her growing hair strand is pulled, Tressy's hair grows. When a "T" shaped key is inserted in a slot in her back, her hair goes short again. Although Tressy was only available in the U.S. from 1963 through 1967, she was very popular in other countries throughout the '70s and '80s. She was manufactured by Bella in France, Palitoy in England, and Regal in Canada. In Germany Tressy was called Kessy.

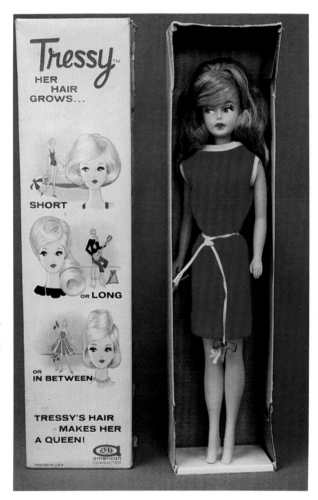

Tressy: 11½" Tressy in her original outfit with the key to shorten her hair. She is marked, "AMERICAN DOLL & TOY CORP./19©63" in a circle on her head. Sometimes markings are hidden underneath her hairline. MIB: **$75.00 – 100.00.**

33

Mary Makeup and Tressy: Tressy's one and only American friend was 11½" Mary Makeup. In European countries she was called Marilyn. Mary Makeup has a waxy coating on her face to allow makeup to be applied and washed off without bleeding into the vinyl. Tressy with the magic makeup face also has this waxy coating. From left to right, Mary Makeup, Tressy with the Magic Makeup Face, and Posing Tressy. Mary Makeup is unmarked. Tressy with the Magic Makeup Face appears to have no markings but when you look underneath her hair, high on her scalp you can find "T/3" or some other digit. Posing Tressy has the same round circle mark on her head as the previous Tressy dolls, but often the markings are so faint and hidden under her hairline that it sometimes appears she is unmarked. Mary Makeup, **$20.00 – 25.00**, Tressy with the Magic Makeup Face, **$25.00 – 35.00**, Posing Tressy, **$30.00 – 45.00**.

Tressy: A straight leg black version of Tressy. Another black version of Tressy came with bendable legs and a different looking face that sported a line of light blue, almost white, eyeliner. Both black versions are rare. Same markings as white Tressy. **$300.00+**.
Courtesy Cathy Kidney-Bremner

Close-up of the black straight leg Tressy.

Pre-Teen Tressy: This younger version of Tressy is not as common as the 11½" teenage version of Tressy. Like the 11½" Tressy, the 15" Pre-Teen Tressy has a grow-hair feature but her hair shortens with a knob on her back rather than with a key. She came in either dark blond or brunette hair. The more common outfit that Pre-Teen Tressy originally came wearing was a teal colored jumper with matching panties and hair ribbon, and a white three-quarter sleeve blouse. Some Pre-Teen Tressy dolls just say "Tressy" on the original box, while others have a sticker underneath the name that says "pre-teen." Pre-Teen Tressy is marked, "AM.CHAR. 63 ©" on her head. **$30.00 – 65.00.** Courtesy Janet and Mike Lawrence.

Pre-teen Tressy: Close-up of a brunette 15" Tressy. She is missing her original blouse and hair ribbon. **$30.00 – 65.00**.

Pre-teen Tressy: This cotton dress with a two-layered lace collar shown on this 15" doll was available on some dolls but is not as common as the teal colored jumper shown in the previous photos. The cotton dress has been seen in both yellow and blue, but was probably issued in other pastel colors as well. 1963 American Character catalog.

Tressy HER HAIR GROWS!

SHORT HAIR

MEDIUM HAIR

LONG HAIR

MAKE A POM-PON

MAKE A PONYTAIL

MAKE A PAGEBOY

TURN THE MAGIC KNOB   CHANGE HER HAIR LENGTH

Cricket

Tressy's 9" little sister wasn't on the market as long as her sister. It is believed that the earliest Cricket dolls are the ones with waist-long straight hair with bangs, but no documentation could be found to support this belief. The first Cricket dolls appearing in major department store catalogs in 1965 as well as dolls shown in Tressy's and Cricket's fashion booklets all show Cricket with shoulder-length hair and a long growing hair strand coming from the top of the doll's head. Cricket started off as Tressy's Little Cousin but was later changed to Tressy's Little Sister, but whether or not all the straight hair dolls were Tressy's Little Cousin, and only the dolls with the growing hair strand are Tressy's sister has not yet been confirmed. Like Tressy, Cricket enjoyed a long life in Europe. In France Tressy's little sister was called Toots and in England she was called Snouky.

Cricket: Three different Cricket dolls with long straight hair. The blond Cricket on the left has turquoise eyes, and the brunette in the center has blue eyes. The boxed Cricket has uncommon brown eyes looking off to her left side. All other examples of the straight hair doll the author has seen have sported blue or turquoise eyes looking to the right. All three dolls are marked, "AMER. CHAR. INC/19©64" on the back of their heads. Loose with blue/turquoise eyes: **$25.00 – 45.00** MIB: brown eyes: **$125.00 – 200.00**.

Cricket giftset: Collectors love to find gift sets like this one untouched in their original box. Although the set features Cricket, the accessories are marked, "Tressy." NRFB: **$200.00 – 250.00**.

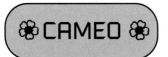

Popi: A plastic 12" doll that comes apart at the bust and waist for ease in dressing her with pre-printed vinyl clothing that was cut out by the owners. Plastic pegs connect the doll pieces. The doll is unmarked. MIB: **$75.00 – 100.00**. 1963 American Character catalog.

Miss Peep: 18" Miss Peep is vinyl with molded hair and beautiful inset eyes. Her unique shoulder pin-joints allows her arms to rotate completely around as well as move back and forth. Her leg joints allow a back-and-forth movement. This doll was also available in a smaller size. **$85.00 – 125.00**. 1969 Sears Christmas catalog.

Miss Peep: Photo showing Miss Peep's shoulder pin joints. She is marked "CAMEO©" on her head and back and has letters and digits on the under portion of her torso. In 1973 Miss Peep was sold through the Montgomery Ward catalog under the name Baby Wendy. Nude: **$50.00 – 75.00**.

Kewpie and Miss Peep: The 18" Kewpie doll on the left uses the same pin-jointed body as Miss Peep. Like Miss Peep, the doll is marked "CAMEO©" on the head and back and has letters and digits on the under portion of the torso. Nude Kewpie: **$50.00 – 75.00**.

Kewpie: 18" and 13" Kewpie dolls. The 13" doll is marked "©/CAMEO" on the back and "©CAMEO" on the head. Nude 13" Kewpie: **$25.00 – 30.00**.

❀ DELUXE READING ❀

The name of this company sometimes causes confusion because it did business under several different names including Deluxe Topper, Topper Corporation, and Topper Toys, among others. See Topper Toys for other dolls by this company.

Penny Brite

This 8" doll was popular for a short time with youngsters in the early 1960s. Clothing and carrying cases in various colors were issued for Penny Brite along with several playsets. Her playsets included a beauty parlor, a kitchen/dining room set, a bedroom set, a car, and a schoolroom. All the playsets, except the schoolroom, were reissued in the early 1970s for Topper Toys' Dawn line.

Penny Brite: Four dolls wearing various Penny Brite outfits. The markings on Penny Brite vary. Some Penny Brite dolls are marked, "A-9/68/DELUXE READING CORP/©1963" on their heads and "DELUXE READING CORP./ELIZABETH, N.J./PAT.PENDING" on their backs. **$15.00 – 20.00** each, outfits **$15.00 – 25.00** mint and complete.

1965 Montgomery Ward Christmas catalog showing the fashions available for Penny Brite.

1965 Montgomery Ward Christmas catalog showing Penny Brite and her accessories.

Suzy Cute: A 7" doll that drinks and wets. She originally came packaged strapped and sealed inside a plastic crib. Suzy Cute is marked, "DELUXE READING CORP./©1964/268/GX" on her head and "PAT.PEND./1" on her back. Her crib has brief instructions on the bottom on how to remove the doll and "CAT.NO.1309/MADE BY/DELUXE READING CORPORATION/ELIZA-BETHPORT, NEW JERSEY/U.S.OF AMERICA PAT.APPLIED FOR." Doll with crib: **$25.00 – 40.00.** Doll alone: **$15.00 – 20.00.**

Suzy Cute: Suzy shown with an outfit sold separately.

The 1965 Montgomery Ward Christmas catalog shows Suzy Cute and some of her clothing.

Everything mommy needs to make **Suzy Cute** *happy*

① $344

① SUZY CUTE CAN HAVE HER VERY OWN PLAYGROUND—outdoor swing set is scaled to her dainty size —yet looks like the real thing.
Mommy can help her up the steps and catch her at the bottom of the slide. Suzy also loves to be swung in her tot-sized swing complete with safety handle.
Or she can teeter-totter in her "bucket seat" seesaw.
Swing set is made of durable plastic in gay summertime colors— comes complete with sand pail and shovel and plastic ball. (Doll not included.) About 14x7¼x12 in. Ship. wt. 2 lbs. 8 oz.
48 T 4486 . . . . $3.44

② $349

③ $279

② KEEP SUZY CUTE'S WARDROBE NEATLY PUT AWAY in her gaily colored plastic dresser. 3 drawers and cabinet open—comes complete with simulated duck lamp, accessory tray, hangers and clothes tree. Abt. 10x4x8½ in.
48 T 4489—Ship. wt. 1 lb. 8 oz $3.49

Colors, Accessories May Vary

③ PLEASE MOMMY, SUZY CUTE WOULD LIKE TO Go for a ride in her plastic carriage—has wheels that actually roll and a movable canopy. Comes with extra feeding bottle. About 5x 11x9 in. (Doll not included.)
48 T 4481—Ship. wt. 1 lb. 6 oz $2.79

④ SUZY CUTE CAN GO WHERE MOMMY GOES—she enjoys riding in her plastic stroller. Sunshade keeps the sun off, keeps her comfortable. Has tray, footrest, also includes her favorite toys—plastic dog, rattle. (Doll not included.) About 4½x10½x 8½ in.
48 T 4483—Ship. wt. 1 lb. $2.99

⑤ MOMMY CAN KEEP SUZY CUTE FRESH AND CLEAN— just pop her into her plastic bathinette—bath really holds water. She can have lots of fun—float her duck and fish water toys and pretend bottles—then rub her dry with her own terry cloth towel. Abt. 9x 5x9 in. (Doll not included.)
48 T 4487—Ship. wt. 1 lb. 4 oz. $2.99

⑥ SUZY CUTE MINDS HER MANNERS when she sits in her plastic feeding chair—makes mealtime fun for her and mommy. Feed her with her plastic dish, spoon and cup while she wears her bib—also included are handy hassock and plastic toy. About 7x7x6 in. (Doll not included.)
48 T 4482—Ship. wt. 1 lb. $1.99

Suzy Cute Knows It's So Easy To Shop By Phone . . See Page 392

The 1965 Montgomery Ward Christmas catalog shows some of Suzy Cute's accessories.

Go-Go's: These 6½" dolls came packaged in clear plastic domes with cardboard backgrounds behind the doll. The dome lifted off a plastic base that doubled as a stand. There were 8 different Go-Go's including Brenda Brush (an artist), Cool Cat (a guitar player), Hot Canary (a nightclub singer), Private Ida (a spy/investigator), Slick Chick (a Hollywood star), Swinger (a dancer), Tomboy (a baseball player), and Yeah, Yeah (a modern woman). The vinyl dolls have wires inside their arms and legs allowing them to be posed. Although the name "Topper" appears on their dome cases, the Go-Go's are marked, "Deluxe Reading Corp/©1965" on their heads. Shown is Brenda Brush. Mint in original case: **$25.00 – 30.00**.

Go-Go's: This photo shows Private Ida (missing her original hat) and Cool Cat (missing her guitar). Loose: **$10.00 – 15.00** each.

Go-Go's: This catalog page shows the eight different Go-Go dolls available. 1966 Montgomery Ward Christmas catalog.

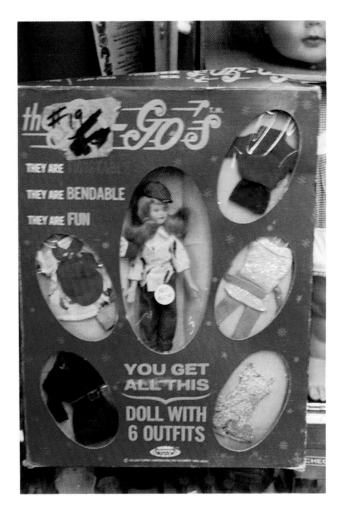

Go-Go's: This 1967 Go-Go's gift set includes Tomboy and the original outfits from Cool Cat, Slick Chic, Swinger, Private Ida, and Brenda Brush. The dolls and clothing included in these gift sets vary. It's possible these sets made use of whatever inventory remained with little consistency from set to set. MIB: **$50.00 – 65.00**. Courtesy Robin Randall.

Baby Magic: 18" doll that drinks, cries "real tears," and pouts with the aid of a magnetic "magic thimble." Although this doll is relatively easy to locate, it's hard to find a loose doll that still has her magnetic thimble. When thimble is included, value of the doll can increase $10.00 – 15.00. Baby Magic is marked, "EK 17/DELUXE READING CORP./©1966" on her head. Wearing all original clothing with thimble present: **$40.00 – 55.00**.

Baby Magic: The doll as she appeared in the 1967 Montgomery Ward Christmas catalog. A less common 10½" Tiny Baby Magic doll was also made and available around 1968.

❀ EEGEE ❀

This company also did business as The Goldberger Doll Manufacturing Company. The more familiar name of "Eegee" came from founder E.G. Goldberger's initials.

Puppetrina: Billed as half doll, half puppet, this 22" doll has a vinyl head and limbs, plastic legs and lower torso, and a foam upper torso. On her back stitched into the red and white striped fabric is a slot where you can insert your hand and fingers into the arms of the doll to move her like a puppet. Puppetrina came with either blond or red hair. The doll is marked, "©1963/EEGEE CO/PAT.PEND./1" on her head. A 16" younger version of this doll called Baby Puppetrina was also produced. **$30.00 – 50.00.**

Sandi: 14" doll circa 1964. NRFB: **$35.00 –
40.00**. Courtesy Pamela Grimes.

Stoneage Baby: This 14" doll was made in
the Pebbles Flintstone image without actually using the name. She is marked,
"EEGEE/150-7"on her head. MIB: **$150.00
– 175.00**. Courtesy Marcia Fanta.

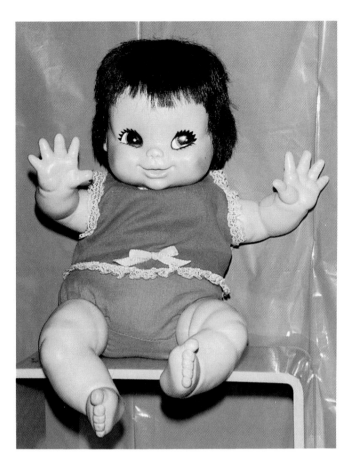

Baby Luv: This 14" doll has a vinyl head and limbs and a cloth body. Baby Luv is marked, "14 B.T/©EEGEE. CO." **$25.00 – 30.00**. Courtesy Marcia Fanta.

❀ EFFANBEE ❀

Sweetie Pie: The name Sweetie Pie was used for many years by Effanbee so there are numerous versions of dolls by this name. This version of Sweetie Pie used Effanbee's Twinkie's head mold. The 15" vinyl doll has a "squeaker" inside so when her tummy is squeezed she cries. She originally came with a pink suede pillow with white eyelet trim that matched her dress and wearing a beaded bracelet that said "Sweetie Pie." Sweetie Pie is marked, "EFFANBEE/©1959" on her head and "EFFANBEE/19©64" on her back. Pillow is tagged, "All new material/Felted acetate fibers/EFFANBEE DOLL CORP./262 TAAFFE PL. BKLYN." With original clothes and pillow: **$35.00 – 50.00**.

Fluffy: 10½" doll originally sold wearing only panties, socks, and shoes. Additional clothing was sold separately. The doll in the photo is redressed in a dress of the era. Fluffy is marked, "Fluffy/EFFANBEE" on her head and "EFFAN-BEE" on her back. **$30.00 – 40.00**.

Junior Girl Scout: These 8" dolls used the Fluffy face, a common mold for many different Effanbee dolls. Effanbee also made Scouting dolls in 11½" and 15" sizes. Dolls are marked, "EFFANBEE/19©65" on their heads. MIB white doll: **$75.00 – 95.00**. MIB black doll: **$85.00 – 110.00**. Courtesy Elaine McGrath.

Scouting Dolls: This photo shows two of the three sizes of scouting dolls made by Effanbee. Left to right, first row: 8" black version of Blue Bird; second row: 8" white version of Junior Girl Scout, 8" black version of Junior Girl Scout; third row: 8" Brownie Girl Scout, 8" Blue Bird; 8" Brownie; fourth row: 11" Camp Fire Girl, 11" Cadette Girl Scout. Loose dolls with their complete uniforms: 8" white Brownie or Junior Girl Scout: **$50.00 – 75.00**, 8" black Brownie or Junior Girl Scout: **$75.00 – 100.00**. 8" Blue Bird: **$70.00 – 90.00**. 11" Camp Fire Girl or Cadette: **$75.00 – 125.00**. Courtesy Elaine McGrath.

My Fair Baby: 18" vinyl doll comes with identification bracelet. Circa 1960. **$45.00 – 65.00**. Courtesy Dawn Thomas.

Mickey: 11" vinyl doll came dressed in over 20 different outfits. He was available from around 1960 and was still being shown in Effanbee catalogs as late as 1972. Front row, left to right: boxer, baseball player, sailor. Back row: football player, Cub Scout, soccer player. Black versions are harder-to-find than white versions. In full uniform: **$20.00 – 45.00**. Courtesy Elaine McGrath.

Gum Drop: Available in many styles, Gum Drop dolls are listed by most references as either 14" or 16", yet these two dolls measure 15". Gum Drop was available starting in 1963 and still being shown in Effanbee catalogs in 1972. Gum Drop is marked, "©1962/EFFANBEE" on her head. Redressed: **$20.00 – 35.00**.

Monique: 16" doll from Effanbee's 1978 Petite Fille series. MIB: **$50.00 – 60.00**.
Courtesy Marcia Fanta.

✿ ELLANEE ✿

Miss Toyland: This pretty 18" red-haired doll is simply marked "U" on her head. Tag on her dress reads, "Hold my left hand up and I will walk with you." MIB: **$50.00 – 75.00**. Courtesy Gloria Telep.

✿ FISHER-PRICE ✿

Fisher-Price Dolls: These 14" plush dolls have stuffed limbs and vinyl head and hands. From left to right are Jenny, Joey, and Natalie. They are circa 1973 – 1974. Other dolls in the line include Elizabeth, Mary, Audrey, and Baby Beth. Each doll, in addition to being marked on his/her head, has a Fisher Price body tag on his/her body that gives information about the company, where the doll was assembled, material content, and a number which is probably the catalog or style number that identifies the doll. Jenny is marked, "©1973/FISHER PRICE TOYS" on her head. Another number is printed above her hairline, but it is illegible because the hair is rooted right into it. In addition to the company and material information listed above, the tag on her body has the number "201" on it. Natalie is marked, "©1973/FISHER PRICE TOYS/A/6" on her head. Her tag has the number "202." Joey, who came out later than the female dolls, is marked, "90/179490/FISHER PRICE TOYS/19©74" on his head. His tag has the number "206". Although these dolls are common and easily found, it is difficult to find them in mint condition. Played with: **$10.00 – 15.00** Mint/complete with original clothing: **$40.00 – 55.00**.

7 Dollhouse with Dolls. Two 4-in. poseable dolls live in this big modern dollhouse. It has 3 stories and 5 beautiful rooms for children to arrange. Inside, there's a spiral staircase, sliding French doors, bay window, picture window, attic, "slate" patio, and realistic "wood and stone" floors. The outside is printed clapboard and hardboard. Easy to assemble. Instructions included. 15⅝x13¾x23⅜ in. high. Furniture not included—see [8] to [15], below. For ages 5 and up.
X 922-6770 A—Mailable: wt. 9 lbs 19.99

TOYS AREN'T JUST FOR CHRISTMAS. Save this catalog. Order anything on these two pages—at these low prices— until August 11, 1979.

5 My Friend Mandy 12⁹⁹

6 My Baby Beth 11⁹⁵

Sets. Furniture and appliances above.
nal dresser with 3 drawers 2.88
astic chairs. 2.44

[12] Bathroom. Sink and toilet. Special stall shower with realistic shower spray, faucets, and soap dish.
X 922-6636 A—Mailable: wt. 3 lbs 2.44
[13] Baby's Room. Spacious crib, dresser, and a rocking horse for baby to ride.
X 922-6612 A—Mailable: wt. 4 lbs 2.88
[14] Music Room. Grand piano and a stereo music center for

My Friend Mandy/My Baby Beth: In 1978 Fisher Price introduced the My Friend line that looked like older versions of the dolls at the bottom of page 53. Although catalogs list the dolls as being 16", they measure closer to 15½". My Friend Mandy was the first doll in the line followed by My Friend Jenny. In 1981 My Friend Becky and My Friend Mikey joined the other My Friend dolls. This 1978 J.C. Penney's Christmas catalog shows My Friend Mandy as well as a 17" My Baby Beth, another popular but larger-size Fisher Price baby doll. Mandy or Beth loose and original: **$25.00 – 40.00**.
©1978, JCPenney Catalog, J.C. Penney Company, Inc. Used by permission.

My Friend Mandy/My Friend Jenny: My Friend Mandy and My Friend Jenny are shown with some of the outfits sold separately for them. Mandy is marked, "20141/©1976/FISHER PRICE" on her head and tagged, "Fisher-Price Toys/East Aurora, N.Y./210/ASSEMBLED IN MEXICO" on her body. Jenny is marked, "23088/FISHER-PRICE-TOYS/ ©1976" on her head. Markings may vary on dolls. Mandy or Jenny loose and original: **$25.00 – 40.00**.
©1979 JCPenney Christmas Catalog, J.C. Penney Company, Inc. Used by permission.

12 My Friend Jenny 13⁴⁷

13 My Friend Mandy 13⁴⁷

14 Rain Slicker

18 Book

17 Jumper Outfit

16 Jogging Suit

15 Sweater Set

Fashion Book for My Friends
y. 12-page book contains stylish
ed to fit Mandy and Jenny. Pat-

19 My Sleepy Baby is so cuddly. She wears a one-piece attached stretch suit of soft nylon, and a removable hat. 18 in.-tall polyurethane foam-filled

❀ FUN WORLD ❀

Finger Ella: By placing two fingers inside the legs of these 5½" dolls, a child could make them walk. Dolls are marked, "Hong Kong" on both their heads and bodies. MIP: **$10.00 – 15.00** each. Courtesy Robin Englehart/Photo by Nancy Jean Mong.

Julie: 14" doll with orange rooted hair. Box says, "Another/Huggles/by Fun World." Julie is marked, "Made in/Hong Kong" on her back. MIB: **$20.00 – 25.00**.

❀ FURGA ❀

An Italian company bearing the name of the family that began it, Furga created many beautiful and lavishly dressed dolls throughout the 1960s and 1970s. Values for these dolls are often based on the size of the dolls and the elaborateness of their costumes. Larger dolls are often valued higher than smaller ones, but of course, there are exceptions to this. If a smaller doll is more elaborately dressed, her value could be higher than some larger Furga dolls.

Damina: This 13" doll is marked, "FURGA ITALY" on her head. MIB: **$50.00 – 60.00**. Courtesy Jeri E. Fowler.

Beautiful Belinda and Crown Princess: Two elaborately dressed Furga dolls complete with parasols. Belinda is 18½" and Princess is 14½". Belinda MIB: **$75.00 – 100.00**. Princess MIB: **$65.00 – 80.00**. 1968 Montgomery Ward Christmas catalog.

Furga Dolls: This 1968 catalog page shows some of the lavishly dressed Furga dolls available that year. Top to bottom, left to right: 18" Beautiful Bride, 15" Elegant Tonia, 17" Bewitching Paola, and 21½" Breathtaking Marion. MIB: **$75.00 – 100.00** each. 1968 Sears Christmas catalog.

❀ GABRIEL ❀

Lone Ranger/Tonto: An unmasked Lone Ranger doll with his horse Silver. He is missing his original hat, mask, neckerchief, and holster. He also came wearing a black belt, which cannot be seen in the photo. In the front is his friend, Tonto. Both dolls are 9½" and marked, "©1973 LONE RANGER/TEL INC./MADE IN TAIWAN/FOR GABRIEL IND. INC." on their backs. Without horse: **$30.00 – 45.00** each.

❀ GILBERT ❀

Honey West: Honey West was billed as a "T.V. Private Eye-Full." This 11½" doll was based on ABC's television character Honey West played by Anne Francis. Her original outfit included a black judo leotard, gold belt, holster, gun, and boots. Additional outfits and accessory packs were sold for this doll. The doll is marked, "R 67" on her head. This doll is popular with collectors of television memorabilia as well as doll collectors. MIB: **$200.00 – 265.00**. Courtesy Gloria Telep.

❀HASBRO❀

Hassenfeld Brothers, more commonly known as Hasbro, was and still is a maker of toys of all kinds. One of their biggest successes was G.I. Joe. Although some collectors refuse to think of G.I. Joe as a doll ("he's an action figure"), he still has gained the interest of numerous doll collectors. Representing all the various branches of service, G. I. Joe dolls' values can vary by hundreds of dollars depending on the particular doll and the outfit the doll is wearing. As these dolls often encountered rough play, only mint examples command book value.

G.I. Joe Action Sailor: An unplayed with example of G.I. Joe with all his accessories still in the original box. MIB: **$250.00 – 300.00**.

G.I. Joe Action Marine: MIB: **$250.00 – 300.00**.

G.I. Joe: This is a 1970s G.I. Joe called Mike Power, Atomic Man. He has an "atomic flashing eye" on his head. Here he is redressed in G.I. Joe tagged clothing. **$25.00 – 40.00**.

Little Miss No Name: 15" doll originally came dressed in a burlap dress and had a teardrop falling from her eye. It is common to find the teardrop missing from these dolls, so when present it adds about **$20.00** to the value. The doll is marked on her head, "©1965 HASBRO©". With teardrop and original dress: **$90.00 – 125.00**. ©1967, JCPenney Christmas Catalog, J.C. Penney Company, Inc. Used by permission.

Dolly Darlings: 4" Dolly Darling dolls either had molded hair or rooted hair. The molded hair dolls shown here came packaged inside round plastic hatbox cases and had a number of small accessories mounted on a cardboard backing in their hatbox. Dolls are marked, "©1965/HAS-BRO©/JAPAN" on their backs. From left to right are Cathy (from Cathy Goes to a Party), John (from John and His Pets), and Karen (from Karen Has a Slumber Party). Molded hair Dolly Darlings/no accessories: **$7.00 – 12.00.**

Peteena: 9" doll with head of a poodle and body of a doll. She is shown wearing her "Twinkle Toes" ballerina outfit which was sold separately. The outfit came with pink tights, not the tights in the photo. Peteena is marked, "©1966/HASBRO©/JAPAN/PATENT PENDING" on her back. The tail of the doll often comes off so if it is missing, value is on the lower end of listed value. **$25.00 – 35.00.**

Dolly Darlings: Two of the molded hair Dolly Darling dolls, Cathy Goes to a Party and Susie Goes to School, are shown in their original cases. Cathy's accessories were resewn onto a replaced cardboard backing the way they originally came. She is missing one spoon from her accessories. In case with all accessories: **$35.00 – 55.00.** Courtesy Karen Hickey.

Dolly Darlings: John and His Pets shown in their original case. The accessories were resewn onto the cardboard backing the way they originally came. In case with all accessories: **$35.00 – 55.00**. Courtesy Karen Hickey.

Dolly Darlings: 4" Dolly Darlings with rooted hair came packaged in rectangular cardboard boxes with cellophane fronts or inside a plastic bubble mounted on a cardboard backing. From left to right are Powder Puff, Go-Team-Go (missing original white blouse under jumper), and Boy Trap. This version of Boy Trap with orange hair is difficult to find. Values for rooted hair Dolly Darlings run a wide spectrum from one source to the next. Some dealers find common Dolly Darlings will sell at shows only if they are priced in the **$10.00 – 15.00** range for loose dolls, while other rare dolls have sold for as much as $100.00 to collectors searching for a particular doll to add to their collection. Dolly Darlings are marked, "©1967/HASBRO©/HONG KONG" on their backs. Rooted hair Dolly Darlings/no accessories: **$15.00 – 45.00.** Boy Trap with orange hair: **$45.00 – 55.00**.

Dolly Darlings: Rooted hair Dolly Darlings from left to right: Tea Time, Go Team Go (missing pom-poms), Slumber Party, Hipster, Slick Set (missing hat), Teeny Bikini, Boy Trap, Technicolor (missing hair band). **$15.00 – 45.00**. Courtesy Karen Hickey.

Dolly Darlings: Rooted hair Dolly Darlings from left to right: Casual (missing hair band), School Days, First Aid (missing hat), Sweetheart, Powder Puff, Honey, Sugar N Spice, and Dreamy. Powder Puff dolls do not normally have the molded gloves on the hands, so it is unknown whether the one shown here is an unusual variation or at some point the arms on the doll were switched. **$15.00 – 45.00.** Courtesy Karen Hickey.

Dolly Darlings: Rooted hair Dolly Darlings from left to right: Sunny Day, Fancy Pants, Lemon Drop, and Flying Nun. Sunny Day and Lemon Drop are harder to find than some of the other Dolly Darlings dolls. **$20.00 – 50.00.** Courtesy Karen Hickey.

Flying Nun Dolly Darling: Popular not only with Dolly Darling collectors but celebrity collectors as well, this 4" doll represented Sister Bertrille, the character played by actress Sally Fields on the television show *The Flying Nun.* She has painted-on black stockings and black shoes. She is marked the same as the other rooted hair Dolly Darlings, "©1967/ HASBRO©/HONG KONG" on her back. Loose: **$30.00 – 50.00.** MIB: **$75.00 – 120.00.** Courtesy Robin Randall.

Dolly Darlings: Play Rooms: Four different play rooms were issued for Dolly Darlings. They included a living room, bedroom, bathroom, and kitchen. The rooms came with a doll and had a removable plastic cover. **$50.00 – 85.00**.
Courtesy Karen Hickey.

Flower Darlings: 3½" dolls which stand inside plastic flower pins. On the left is Lily Darling and on the right is Daisy Darling. Other members of the Flower Darlings include Violet, Rose, Dahlia, and Daphne. The dolls are marked, "©1968 /HASBRO©/HONG KONG" on their backs. With flower pins: **$20.00 – 25.00** each.

Flower Darlings: 3½" dolls without their plastic flower pins. From left to right are Dahlia, Lily, Violet, and Daisy. Without flower pins: **$7.00 – 12.00** each.

Flower Darlings: Violet, Lily, and Rose inside their original package. Part of the cardboard was cut off these packages. MIB without card cut: **$55.00 – 75.00**.

Storykins: In 1969, Hasbro created these little dolls in response to the growing demand for smaller dolls. 2"– 3½" tall, there were 9 different Storykins sets. The dolls and their accessories originally came packaged inside a plastic bubble mounted on a cardboard backing. A small-sized 33⅓ rpm LP record was included with each set. Shown in photo are Mother Hubbard, Goldilocks, Cinderella, Prince Charming, and Sleeping Beauty. Other Storykin sets include Snow White, The Jungle Book, Rumpelstiltskin, and Pinocchio. The dolls are marked, "©1967/HASBRO/HONG KONG" on their backs. Dolls alone range in value from **$3.00 – 15.00** but when their accessories are included, loose sets range from **$15.00 – 45.00**.

Goldilocks Storykins: Storykins' Goldilocks doll shown in her original package with the 33⅓ rpm LP record. Goldilocks is marked, "©1967/HASBRO/HONG KONG" on her back. MIP: **$85.00 – 100.00.** Courtesy Robin Englehart/Photo by Nancy Jean Mong.

Snow White and the Seven Dwarfs Storykins: It is difficult to find this Storykins set complete with all the dwarfs and the cottage. In addition to this set, Snow White was also sold in another set with just Doc who had molded glasses, unlike any of the dwarfs that came in the complete set. Snow White is 3½" tall and is marked, "©1967/HASBRO/HONG KONG" on her back. The dwarfs are slightly under 2" tall and have no markings. Loose and complete Snow White, dwarfs, and cottage: **$80.00 – 110.00.**

World of Love Dolls: In 1971 Hasbro issued their World of Love line of dolls. Sporting mod names like Love, Peace, Soul, and Flower, the dolls in this line were probably about as hip as dolls get. Here the doll named Love is shown in her original box. Like all the female dolls in the line she has long rooted eyelashes and bendable legs. She is missing her original boots and has a replaced headband. The 9" doll is marked, "MADE IN/HONG KONG" on her back and "©HASBRO/U.S.PAT PEND" on her lower body. MIB: **$35.00 – 40.00**.

World of Love Dolls: The first issue World of Love dolls came in cardboard boxes with lids. All the dolls have the same markings as the doll above. MIB: **$35.00 – 50.00** each. Courtesy Joedi Johnson.

World of Love Dolls: Second issue World of Love dolls came in wider cardboard boxes with cellophane around them. Same markings as previous dolls. MIB: **$35.00 – 50.00 each**.
Courtesy Joedi Johnson.

Miss Breck: This promotional doll for Breck shampoo was made from the same mold as the female members of the World of Love dolls. Her dress is from the same material as Flower's but in a different style. The doll is marked "2/HONGKONG" on her back and "©HASBRO/U.S.PAT PEND" on her lower body: **$20.00 – 25.00**.

Leggy: This long legged vinyl doll is Kate from Hasbro's Leggy line of dolls. The Leggy outfit she is wearing is not her original outfit. Other Leggy dolls were Nan with brunette hair, Sue an Afro-American, and Jill with blond hair. Kate is 10" long and is marked, "©1972©/HASBRO/HONG KONG" on her lower body. **$20.00 – 25.00**. Courtesy Robin Englehart/Photo by Nancy Jean Mong.

Aimee: 18" Aimee wearing her original full-length "maxi" dress. Unfortunately the dyes used on Aimee's dress often reacted to the vinyl underneath so it's common to find these dolls have turned green or white on the arms, neck, and sometimes under the chin. Because most Aimee dolls have this flaw, when one turns up without any discoloration in the vinyl, the value would be slightly higher than those with discoloration. Aimee is marked, "HASBRO INC./©1972" on her head. All original/no discoloration: **$25.00 – 40.00**. Courtesy Pamela Grimes.

Sweet Cookie: This 18" doll originally came with several kitchen accessories. With the help of her owner, Sweet Cookie could "prepare" food. The doll in the photo has been redressed. She is marked, "©HASBRO IND./PAT.PEND.1972" on her head and "Hasbro©/MADE IN U.S.A." on her back. Redressed doll: **$15.00 – 20.00**.

Sweet Cookie: This 1972 catalog page shows both the white and black versions of Sweet Cookie along with the accessories she came with. Doll with accessories: **$45.00 – 75.00**. 1972 Montgomery Ward Christmas catalog.

Charlie's Angels: 8½" dolls represented the three main characters from the television show *Charlie's Angels*. From left to right are Kelly, Jill, and Sabrina, played by actresses Jaclyn Smith, Farrah Fawcett, and Kate Jackson. All three dolls are marked, "©1977/SPELLING-GOLDBERG PRODUCTIONS/ALL RIGHTS RESERVED/MADE IN/HONG KONG"on their backs and "HASBRO/U.S. PAT. 3740894"on their lower bodies. In addition, Kelly is marked "4862," Jill is marked "4860," and Sabrina is marked "4861" on their heads. Dolls could be purchased individually or in a set. A Kris doll representing Cheryl Ladd who later replaced Farrah Fawcett on the show was also produced in this size. The dolls originally came dressed in different colored jumpsuits like the one worn by the doll in the center, along with boots and neck scarves. The dolls on the left and right are wearing Charlie's Angels fashions, which were sold separately. In original clothing or wearing Charlie's Angels fashions: **$25.00 – 35.00** each.

❀ HORSMAN ❀

Like many doll companies, Horsman often reused the name of a doll. The company issued numerous dolls named Peggy Ann, Princess Peggy, Ruthie, and Gloria Jean, to name a few. These dolls were issued over many years and in many different outfits. Even in spite of their quality and beauty, surprisingly Horsman dolls from the 1960s and 1970s have yet to gain widespread interest with collectors. Many dolls from this company can still be found at bargain prices since interest is still low, especially with Horsman's baby dolls.

Credit for many of the dolls that came from Horsman goes to designer Irene Szor. Her name is found on the boxes of most if not all the dolls shown here.

Peggy Ann: This 17" tall doll from 1961 is made of heavy vinyl. She is marked, "HORSMAN" on her head and "17/HORSMAN" on her back. MIB: **$50.00 – 75.00.**
Courtesy Gloria Telep.

Ruthie: This 19" doll is just one of many different Ruthie dolls issued by Horsman. This one is Style No.5501. She is marked "HORSMAN/T.21" on her head. MIB: **$65.00 – 85.00.** Courtesy Gloria Telep.

70

Ruthie: This 14" Ruthie doll came in a plain cardboard box. MIB: **$65.00 – 85.00**. Courtesy Gloria Telep.

Ruthie: A 16" version of Ruthie with a more elaborate costume than previous dolls. With original tag: **$40.00 – 55.00**. Courtesy Marcia Fanta.

Mary Poppins

Beginning in 1963 Horsman's popular 11½" Mary Poppins doll delighted youngsters for many years. The doll was still available into the early 1970s. Since the doll was issued for so long, today it is relatively easy to find. A Mary Poppins doll in played-with condition without the original box and without her complete outfit is only worth about $15.00 – 20.00. Mint in box values vary depending on the set. The doll came packaged in a number of different ways and in different size boxes. Some sets came only with a dressed doll, others came with a dressed doll plus additional outfits. Mary Poppins' outfits included a purple and white dress with either a flower or bow at the collar, a blue overcoat, a blue hat with flowers, an umbrella, a carpet bag, a blue and white striped dress with separate white apron that said "Mary Poppins" on the front, a white and fuchsia dress, a white hat, vinyl gloves, shoes, black fishnet stockings, boots, and a measuring tape (for seeing how children measure up). Not all these items were included with each set. There were numerous variations in the clothing and accessories over the years including different material used, different trimming, different buttons, etc., but in general the style of the outfits stayed the same. In addition to the various Mary Poppins sets available, a Mary Poppins doll came in a gift set with two smaller dolls, Jane and Michael. The two children were also available together in a set without the Mary Poppins doll. Horsman produced Mary Poppins in other sizes as well, but at the time they weren't as popular as the 11" doll. Today these other sizes are hard-to-find.

Mary Poppins: Three different 11½" Horsman Mary Poppins dolls. The doll on the left has no bangs, the doll in the center has bangs, and the doll on the right has pink lip color instead of red. All three dolls are marked, "H" on their heads. The doll in the center is missing her original white hat. In original clothing: **$30.00 – 45.00** each.

Mary Poppins: This Mary Poppins set included an 11½" doll and three complete outfits. Circa 1965 – 1966. NRFB: **$150.00 – 200.00**. Courtesy Kathleen Tornikoski/Romancing the Doll.

Mary Poppins: One version of the 11½" doll without extra outfits. Circa 1967 – 1969. NRFB: **$85.00 – 125.00**.
Courtesy Gloria Telep.

Mary Poppins, Jane, and Michael: These dolls representing the characters from the Walt Disney movie *Mary Poppins* were available in a set with all three dolls, or Jane and Michael could be purchased in a set without the Mary Poppins doll. 8" Michael is marked, "©3(digit varies)/HORSMAN DOLLS INC./6682" on his head. 8" Jane is marked, "©7(digit varies)/HORSMAN DOLLS INC./6681" on her head. Loose dolls in original clothing: **$40.00 – 50.00** each. 1966 Sears Christmas catalog.

The adventurous three!

Set **$8⁹⁹**

Mary Poppins only **$4.66**

Jane, Michael and Mary Poppins

. . plus her extra Nanny uniform

Ready for more jolly tea parties. Vinyl . . fully-jointed arms and legs. Attractively dressed. Lovely rooted hair. Mary Poppins has an extra dress, apron and measuring tape for "measuring up." Jane, Michael 8 in., Mary Poppins 12 in. tall.
49 N 3822—Shipping weight 1 pound 2 ounces. . . . . Set $8.99

Mary Poppins only . . with umbrella and carpet-bag.

Cinderella

Horsman's 11½" Cinderella doll was issued in various sets starting in 1965. One set featured a doll with an upswept hairstyle, dressed in a ball gown. The set also came with a work dress and an extra head with long straight hair that could be swapped with the head with the more elaborate hairdo.

Cinderella: This particular doll was issued for Horsman's 100th anniversary in 1965. NRFB: **$175.00 – 200.00.** Courtesy Gloria Telep.

Patty Duke: This doll represents teenage actress Patty Duke when she was starring in *The Patty Duke Show* on television. The 11" tall doll is marked, "H" on her head. Her box reads, "Star of the Patty Duke Show/©1965, United Artists Television, Inc." The photo in the background is signed, "Thanks for watching! Patty Duke." The box originally came with a cardboard piece in back. This Patty Duke doll was available in 1965. In 1966 a "Go-Go with Patty Duke" doll was issued and included a 45rpm record in the box. The doll was dressed differently than the one shown here and sported a different hairstyle as well. Both versions of this doll are very hard to find. NRFB: **$300.00 – 375.00.**

Peggy: This 9½" doll could easily be mistaken for Ideal's Pepper doll. They are both the same size and are very similar in appearance. Peggy has three freckles under each eye. She came dressed in a number of different outfits including the one shown here and was also sold in sets with wardrobes. Hair color and style varied. Circa 1964 – 1965. Peggy is marked Horsman dolls/©64/900 on her neck. MIB: **$30.00 – 50.00**. Courtesy Sally Seikel.

Poor Pitiful Pearl: Poor Pitiful Pearl, despite her homely appearance, was a very popular doll with children and is popular today with collectors. Several different companies made Poor Pitiful Pearl dolls based on the cartoon character Brave Irene originated by William Steig. The first Poor Pitiful Pearl dolls were rag dolls but little information could be found about them including the company who made them. The Brookglad Company also known as Glad Toy made a stuffed vinyl Poor Pitiful Pearl doll as well as a vinyl version. Horsman followed with a vinyl and plastic version and then finally Tristar (see Tristar for additional photo). Horsman created their Pearl dolls in various sizes and sets including the 10½" doll shown here. NRFB: **$150.00 – 200.00**. Courtesy Alice's Dolls.

Teenie Bopper: Numerous dolls were issued under this name in both black and white versions wearing various outfits. The 12" doll is marked, "1/HORSMAN DOLLS INC./19©69" on her head and "HORSMAN DOLLS INC./T 11" on her back. MIB: **$40.00 – 45.00**.

Peggy Pen Pal: This 18" doll came with a writing desk. When a child drew or wrote on the opposite side of the desk, Peggy would draw or write too. Doll with desk: **$55.00 – 75.00**. Doll alone: **$25.00 – 30.00**. 1970 Sears Christmas catalog.

Peggy Pen Pal: Black version of Horsman's Peggy Pen Pal shown with Hasbro's 18" Sweet Cookie. It appears the two dolls' torsos and limbs were made from the same mold. Peggy Pen Pal is marked, "HORSMAN DOLLS. INC./19©70" on her head and "HORSMAN DOLLS INC./ © "on her back. Black doll with original clothing: **$30.00 – 40.00**.

Little Debbie: 1972 doll made for Little Debbie Snack Cakes' 25th Anniversary. The 11" doll is marked, "HORSMAN DOLLS, INC./19©72" on her head. This same face was used for many other dolls during the 1960s, 1970s, and 1980s. **$35.00 – 50.00**. Courtesy Patty Massey.

Pippi Longstocking: This 11" freckled doll uses the Little Debbie face mold. Her head and arms are vinyl, and her body and legs are plastic. Her orange hair came in two braids. In addition to the dress she is shown wearing, she came wearing pantaloons, thigh-high mismatched hose, and ankle-high black shoes. The 11" Pippi is marked, "12/ HORSMAN DOLLS INC./19©72" on her head. **$25.00 – 35.00**.

Pippi Longstocking: This 17½" Pippi was a 1973 Montgomery Ward Exclusive doll. She has the same face as the previous Pippi doll, but has a foam-filled body and vinyl limbs. The 17½" Pippi is marked, "3508" under her hair, "(illegible digits)/ (HORSMAN DOLLS INC./1972" on her head. Body is tagged with material contents and address of company. MIB: **$95.00 – 125.00**.

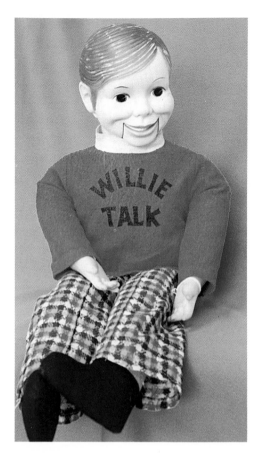

Elizabeth Taylor: Doll with three outfits from the 1976 movie *The Blue Bird*. Without the box, few people could tell this 12" doll was meant to represent Elizabeth Taylor. MIB: **$75.00 – 85.00**. Courtesy Marcia Fanta.

Willie Talk: This 22" ventriloquist doll has a string in the back to make his mouth move. The doll is marked, "HORSMAN DOLLS, INC. 10" on his head. **$25.00 – 35.00**.

Police Woman, Angie Dickinson: 9" doll representing the lead character from the 1970s television series *Police Woman* starring Angie Dickinson as Sergeant Suzanne "Pepper" Martin. The doll is marked, "HORSMAN DOLLS INC.//U//L CPT//19©76" on her head. NRFB: **$30.00 – 45.00**. Courtesy Sharon Wendrow/Memory Lane.

Patchwork Kids: 13" soft-bodied doll from 1976. MIB: **$25.00 – 35.00**. Courtesy Marcia Fanta.

❀IDEAL❀

Shirley Temple: Starting in 1934, Ideal made numerous versions of Shirley Temple dolls. The vinyl Shirley Temple dolls that they produced beginning in 1958 continued to be made and sold into the early 1960s. Values for Shirley Temple dolls can vary greatly depending on condition, size of the doll, and what outfit she is wearing. If the hair has been played with in any way, value is much lower than those dolls that still have tight curls. Of course, Shirley Temple dolls that are wearing original "Shirley Temple" tagged clothing are much more desirable than those dolls that are nude or have been redressed. Inclusion of the Shirley Temple script pin that came on many of the dolls will also raise the value of a doll. Photo shows one version of Ideal's 12" vinyl doll in her original box. The doll is marked, "IDEAL DOLL/ST-12" on her head and "ST-12-N" on her back. MIB: **$250.00 – 300.00**. Courtesy Gloria Telep.

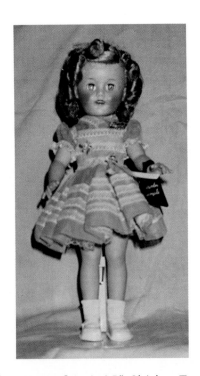

Shirley Temple: A 15" Shirley Temple wearing her original dress. The doll is marked, "IDEAL DOLL/ST-15-N" on her head and "IDEAL DOLL/ST-15" on her back. **$200.00 – 250.00.** Courtesy Jeri E. Fowler.

Shirley Temple: A 12" Shirley Temple doll. The doll is marked, "IDEAL DOLL/ST-12" on her head and "ST-12-N" on her back. **$175.00 – 225.00.**

TEMPLE DOLLS

15-in. dolls in beloved story book costumes

Dimple-cheeked Shirley is fashioned of unbreakable vinyl. Has jointed arms and legs. Curly, rooted Saran hair to wash, comb and brush. Closing eyes with long lashes.

[1] **Pretty as a picture** in her red cotton party dress. Gaily strung in rows of ric-rac. Attached lacy petticoat. Lace-edged panties. Socks, vinyl shoes, hat.
49 N 3312—Doll and outfit. Shpg. wt. 2 lbs..........$6.33

[2] **Shirley in her Swiss Mountain Outfit** styled after her movie hit "Heidi." Colorful cotton dress trimmed in lace and embroidery. Lacy undies. Socks, vinyl slippers.
49 N 3628—15-in. doll, outfit. Wt. 2 lbs. *Was $6.77...* **$5.97**
49 N 3629—17-in. doll, outfit. Wt. 2 lbs. 8 oz. *Was $8.88.* **7.99**

[3] **Shirley plays Cinderella** in beautiful nylon dress. With shiny speckled top and has beaded tiara on her head. Attached rayon taffeta petticoat. Lacy panties. White socks, vinyl slippers.
49 N 3317—Doll and outfit. Shpg. wt. 2 lbs..........$8.99

[4] **Shirley in blue and white cotton Bo Peep costume.** Printed panniers at sides. Bright red apron. Attached slip has lace and net ruffle. Pantaloons ruffled at ankles. Red straw hat ties becomingly. White socks and shoes.
49 N 3314—Doll and outfit. Shpg. wt. 2 lbs..........$7.99

[1] 6³³   [2] 5⁹⁷ 15-in.   [3] 8⁹⁹   [4] $7⁹⁹   PCB2 SEARS 323

A page from the 1961 Sears Christmas catalog showing 15" Shirley Temple dolls dressed in storybook costumes.

15 In.
6.99

12 In.
2.98

SHIRLEY TEMPLE

① **Shirley Temple and Fashion Wardrobe.** Curly rooted tresses, sleeping eyes, fully jointed, dimpled cheeks. She wears Bo Peep shepherdess dress with hat, panties, shoes, socks. New wardrobe includes party dress with attached slip, coat with pique trim, 3-pc. play outfit.
48 T 4006—15-In. Doll, with Wardrobe. Ship. wt. 2 lbs. 3 oz. **$9.99**
48 T 4382—Doll Only. Ship. wt. 2 lbs. **6.99**

② **Shirley Temple,** ready to dress in her outfits. Sleeping eyes, dimpled cheeks, rooted curls. Wears saucy play outfit, shoes. Ship. wt. 1 lb. 3 oz.
48 T 3866—About 12 in. tall. **$2.98**

③-⑦ **Outfits for Shirley Temple (2)**

(3) **Pedal Pushers,** print shirt, straw hat.
48 T 4198—Outfit only. Ship. wt. 4 oz. **$1.49**

(4) **Felt Coat,** beret with tassel, purse.
48 T 4199—Outfit only. Ship. wt. 4 oz. **$1.95**

(5) **Party Dress,** velveteen top. Straw hat, purse, panties, shoes, socks.
48 T 4200—Outfit only. Ship. wt. 4 oz. **$2.69**

(6) **Flannelette Pajamas,** night cap.
48 T 4188—Outfit only. Ship. wt. 4 oz. **$1.19**

(7) **Dainty Cotton School Dress,** purse.
48 T 4189—Outfit only. Ship. wt. 4 oz. **$1.19**

⑧ **Shirley Temple with Wardrobe.** Long a doll favorite, rooted hair in curly ringlets, dimpled cheeks—looks just like Shirley when she was little. Fully jointed, sleeping eyes. Wears play outfit, shoes. Wardrobe includes pajamas with night cap, school dress, pedal pusher and shirt with hat, coat, beret, purse. Ship. wt. 2 lbs. 3 oz.
48 T 4005—12-in. Doll and Clothes. **$7.97**

⑨ **Pollyanna and Her Wardrobe Trunk**—storybook and movie heroine wears gingham dress, petticoat, pantalettes, straw hat, vinyl shoes. Fully jointed, sleeping eyes, rooted hair. Wardrobe includes taffeta and velvet evening gown with bolero, cotton dress, pinafore, camisole, striped skirt, middy blouse, nylon net head scarf, 4 hangers.
48 T 4319—10½-In. Doll, Wardrobe, Trunk. Ship. wt. 3 lbs. 4 oz. **$6.99**
48 T 4347—17-In. Doll only. Wears dress, hat, spats, shoes. Ship. wt. 2 lbs. 10 oz. **$7.44**

⑩ **Glowing Bride, Trousseau, Trunk.** Rooted hair, sleeping eyes, fully jointed. Wears lovely lace gown, tulle, lace headpiece. In trunk—nightie, sundress, lounging pajamas, house coat, 2 dresses, "watch," shoes, comb, brush, mirror, curlers, tissues, hangers.
48 T 4218—15-In. Doll, Trousseau, Trunk. Ship. wt. 5 lbs. **$7.98**
48 T 4219—18-In. Doll, Trousseau, Trunk. Ship. wt. 5 lbs. 6 oz. **$9.99**

12 In.
7.97

278 WARDS CBASK²

10½ In.
6.99

15 In.
7.98

A page from the 1961 Montgomery Ward Christmas catalog showing a 15" Shirley Temple doll and some clothing available for the 12" dolls.

81

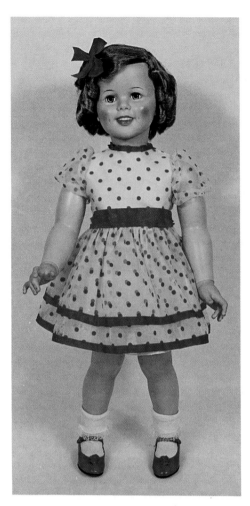

Shirley Temple: 16½" Shirley Temple from 1973. The doll is marked, "1972/IDEAL TOY CORP./S.T.-14-H-213/HONG KONG" on her head and "IDEAL/1972/2M-5634" on her back. **$60.00 – 75.00**. Courtesy Patty Massey.

Shirley Temple: 36" child-size doll featuring swivel wrists. She is marked, "IDEAL DOLL/ST-35-38-2" on her head and "IDEAL (circled)" on her back. This doll has been redressed in a copy of an original Shirley Temple outfit. Mint/redressed as in photo: **$750.00 – 900.00**. Courtesy Patty Massey.

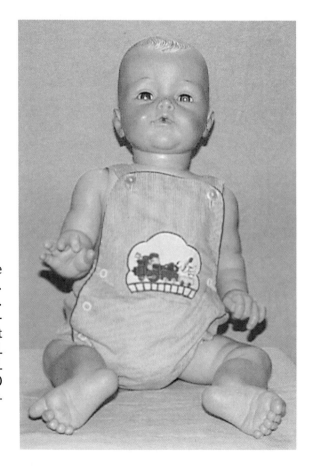

Bye-Bye Baby: Life-like 25" vinyl doll. Note the realistic details of the fingers and toes. The doll in the photo has been redressed. The doll originally came dressed in a snow-suit or kimono and came with a car seat with tray. Bye-Bye Baby is marked, "IDEAL TOY CORP./L25NB" on the head and "IDEAL TOY CORP./NB25" on the back. Circa 1960 – 1961. Redressed: **$250.00 – 300.00**. Courtesy Debi Toussaint-Edgar/Photo by Steve Edgar.

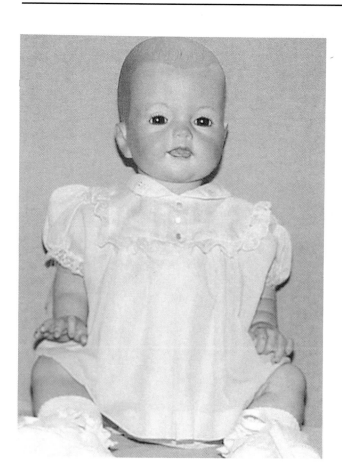

Bye-Bye Baby: This is an unusual porcelain version of Bye-Bye Baby. No information pertaining to when it was made or who made it could be found at the time of publication. The doll is marked, "8416" on the back. Not enough examples to determine a value. Courtesy Debi Toussaint-Edgar/Photo by Steve Edgar.

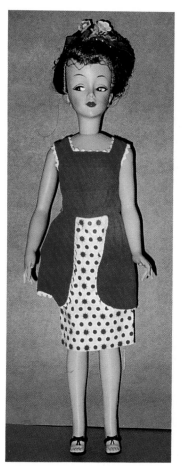

Carol Brent: 15" Carol Brent wearing her original Smart Print Sheath dress and flowered veil hat. **$65.00 – 85.00**. Courtesy Dawn Thomas.

Carol Brent: This 15" doll with her daintily positioned fingers was available in 1961 through Montgomery Ward. In 1962 the same doll was sold under the new name of Liz. She is marked "©IDEAL TOY CORP./M-15-L" on her head and "©IDEAL TOY CORP./M-15" on her back. **$65.00 – 85.00**. Courtesy Janet and Mike Lawrence.

Our Own Wishmaker Doll

CAROL BRENT

(11) (17) **Carol Brent**, Glamorous Fashion Doll, goes to Hollywood. Her wardrobe is designer-inspired to take this young starlet through her star-studded round of activities. Elegantly styled for her career, too—choose the part you want her to play and select the outfit for the part—from fringed Bikini to taffeta cocktail sheath. Doll, outfits below.

(11) **Carol Brent Doll**, fresh from her beauty sleep in fluffy 3-piece baby-doll pajamas, trimmed with lace panties, bra, sleep coat, dainty plastic slippers. Carol can be posed prettily—jointed at shoulder, neck, legs. Rooted hair is dressed in fluttering chignon. Her lovely, finely molded features are delicately made up. 48 T 4377—About 15 in. tall, Doll, 3 Pc. Sleeping Outfit. Wt. 1 lb. $3.99

Outfits for Carol Brent (11)

(12) (17) **(12) Sundress** with dainty flower appliqués, matching stole. Necklace, purse. Ship. wt. 4 oz. 48 T 4069—Outfit only $2.49

(13) Smart Print Sheath, solid over dress. Delicate, flowered veil hat. Necklace, purse. Ship. wt. 4 oz. 48 T 4068   Outfit only $2.29

(14) Leopard Print Slacks, jersey overblouse. Straw hat, smart leisure-time style. Wt. 4 oz. 48 T 4067—Outfit only $2.27

(15) Shimmering Taffeta Sheath, with luxurious fur-like stole. Necklace, purse. Ship. wt. 4 oz. 48 T 4071   Outfit only $2.88

(16) Swim Fun—Bikini Bathing Suit, straw beach hat. Ship. wt. 4 oz. 48 T 4066   Outfit only $1.77

(17) Skirt, Blouse, chic coat, hat, necklace, purse. Ship. wt. 4 oz. 48 T 4070   Outfit only $2.87

1961 Montgomery Ward Christmas catalog showing Carol Brent and the clothing available for her.

Patti Playpal: Patti Playpal was a doll the size of a three-year-old. The 35" doll came in a number of different hair colors, hairstyles, eye colors, and outfits. She was available starting in 1959 and continuing through 1961. This brunette with curly hair is harder to find than dolls with long straight hair. The doll in the photo has replaced socks otherwise she is all original. Patti Playpal is marked, "G-35/IDEAL DOLL" on her head and "IDEAL" on her back. Many other companies put out similar 35" dolls that looked like Patti, but only those with the Ideal markings are genuine Patti Playpal dolls. MIB: **$400.00 – 500.00**. Courtesy Patty Massey.

Patti Playpal: A page from the 1961 Montgomery Ward Christmas catalog showing Patti Playpal wearing a red and green plaid dress.

I Walk
With You
$19⁹⁹
36 Inch
12

Patti Playpal: Patti with curly blond hair and green eyes. This doll has been redressed. She is marked, "IDEAL TOY/35" on her head and "IDEAL" on her back. Redressed: **$275.00 – 325.00**. Courtesy Debi Toussaint-Edgar/Photo by Steve Edgar.

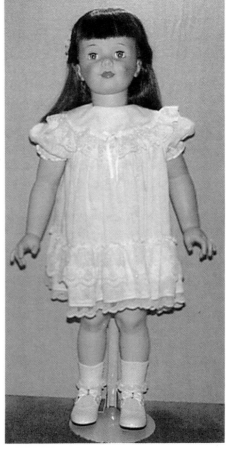

Patti Playpal: Brunette Patti with straight hair and blue eyes. This doll has been redressed. She is marked, "IDEAL/G-35" on her head and "IDEAL" on her back. Redressed: **$250.00 – 300.00**. Courtesy Debi Toussaint-Edgar/Photo by Steve Edgar.

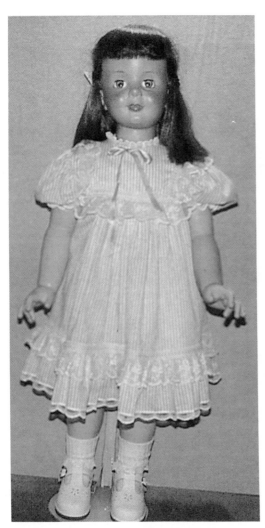

Patti Playpal: Patti with straight auburn hair and green eyes. This doll has been redressed. She is marked, "IDEAL/G-35" on her head and "IDEAL" on her back. Redressed: **$250.00 – 300.00**. Courtesy Debi Toussaint-Edgar/Photo by Steve Edgar.

Patti PlayPal: In 1981 Ideal reissued Patti Playpal again, only now the second "P" in the PlayPal name was capitalized. To the unsuspecting eye, the reissued doll looks very much like the original Patti, but values for the two are very different so buyers and sellers need to determine if their doll is the original or the reissued Patti PlayPal. A loose redressed 1960 Patti is valued about **$275.00 – 325.00** but a loose 1981 Patti PlayPal even in original clothing is only worth about **$100.00 – 150.00**. The 1981 white version of Patti was issued in only one hair color and style, straight blond hair with a shiny almost frosted look to it. She was also issued in a black version with black hair. The vinyl on the arms of the doll is pliable, so if you squeeze it, it gives very easily. Her eyes do not open and close like on the earlier dolls but are stationary. The doll shown here is the reissued 1981 Patti PlayPal in her original box. MIB: **$200.00 – 250.00**. Courtesy Marcia Fanta.

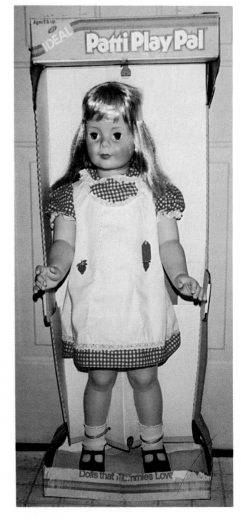

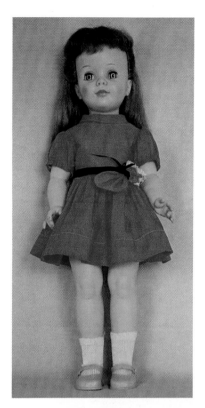

Patite: 18" doll looks like a miniature version of Patti Playpal. Patite is marked, "©/IDEAL TOY CORP/G18" on head and back. This doll is popular with collectors because of her similarity to Patti Playpal. The doll in the photo has been redressed. **$250.00 – 350.00**. Courtesy Janet & Mike Lawrence.

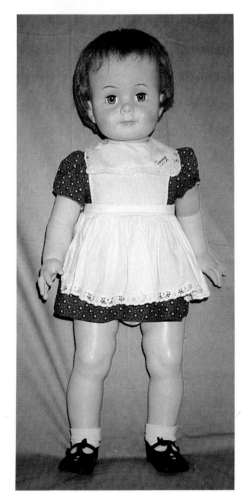

Saucy Walker: 32" doll from the Playpal family. The doll is marked, "©IDEAL TOY CO/BYE S285" on her head and "IDEAL TOY CORP./T-32/PAT.PEND." on her body. The doll in the photo is missing her original shoes and socks. **$150.00 – 225.00**.

Saucy Walker: 28" Saucy wearing a different original outfit than the larger doll above. **$150.00 – 225.00**. Courtesy Elaine McGrath.

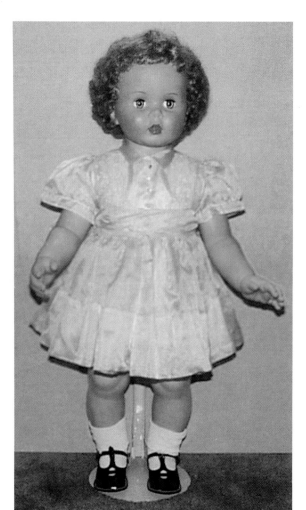

Penny Playpal: This 32" doll is Patti Playpal's two-year-old sister. Although she was available only in 1959, she couldn't be left out of this book simply because she doesn't quite fall under the realm of a 1960s doll. Penny came with curly hair in varying lengths and was issued in both blond and brunette. The blond doll shown in this photo has been redressed. She is marked, "IDEAL TOY CO./32-E-L" on her head and "IDEAL" on her back. Redressed: **$300.00 – 350.00**. *Courtesy Debi Toussaint-Edgar/Photo by Steve Edgar.*

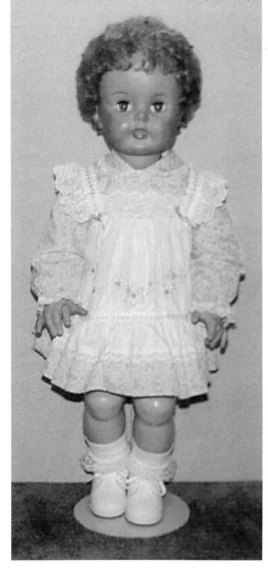

Susy Playpal: This 28" doll is Patti Playpal's one-year-old sister. She came with curly or straight hair in varying lengths and was issued in both blond and brunette. The blond doll shown in this photo has been redressed. She is marked, "IDEAL DOLL/06 28-5" on her head and "IDEAL" on her back. Redressed: **$150.00 – 225.00**. *Courtesy Debi Toussaint-Edgar/Photo by Steve Edgar.*

Bonnie Playpal: This 24" doll is Patti Playpal's three-month-old sister. She has a twin brother name Johnny who is the same size and has molded hair. Bonnie in this photo has been redressed. She is marked, "OEB 24-3" on her head and "IDEAL" on her back. Redressed: **$300.00 – 375.00**. Courtesy Debi Toussaint-Edgar/Photo by Steve Edgar.

Peter Playpal: 38" freckled face Peter Playpal came in blond or brunette. The doll in the photo is missing his original hat. His brunette hair has oxidized to a reddish color. Peter is marked, "©IDEAL TOY CORP./BE-35-38" on his head and "©IDEAL TOY CORP. W-38/PAT.PEND" on his back. **$700.00 – 750.00**. Courtesy Patty Massey.

Lori Martin: Lori Martin was a young actress who played Velvet Brown on the television series *National Velvet* which aired from 1960 – 1962. Dolls of Lori Martin as Velvet Brown came in sizes ranging from 29" to 42". The 38" doll shown in the photo is marked, "METRO GOLDWYN MAYER INC./MFG. BY/IDEAL TOY CORP./38" on her head and "©IDEAL TOY CORP./G-38" on her back. **$800.00 – 950.00**. Courtesy Patty Massey.

Daddy's Girl: This 42" doll came with blond or brunette hair. The doll shown is wearing replaced shoes. She is marked, "IDEAL TOY CORP./G-42" on her head and "©IDEAL TOY CORP./G-42" on her back. **$1,000.00 – 1,600.00.** Courtesy Patty Massey.

Miss Ideal/Terry Twist: This 1961 doll came in a 25" size, like the one shown here, as well as in a 30" size. Miss Ideal was issued in 1961 and came in various hair colors and styles. She was available in many different outfits including the Capri-styled outfit she is wearing in the photo. She has a swivel waist and jointed ankles and wrists. In 1962 Miss Ideal was called Terry Twist. The doll is marked, "©IDEAL TOY CORP./SP-S" on her head and "©IDEAL TOY CORP./P-25" on her back. **$275.00 – 325.00.** Courtesy Patty Massey.

1961 Montgomery Ward Christmas catalog shows Miss Ideal wearing three different outfits.

Play "beauty shop"..

MISS IDEAL

has rooted nylon hair that's so
real you can shampoo it, set it,
in many different styles

Upswept hairdo   Popular pony tail

Beauty kit with
comb, curlers,
waving lotion

25-in. doll
in Capri Outfit

Fully jointed .. she can even balance on one foot

Doll of molded plastic and shaped like a grammar school girl. So delicately tinted and precisely defined, she almost comes alive. Her large, smiling eyes are twinkled with thick lashes, open and close. Jointed arms, hips, ankles. Has moving waist. Takes lots of lifelike poses. Carries beauty kit fitted with comb, curlers and waving lotion.

Miss Ideal in Town and Country Outfit. Long, curly bob with French bangs for versatile styling. Yellow and white checked sleeveless cotton dress teamed with black velvet. Floaty skirt with tiny bows. Velvet and lace trim top, velvet belt. Rayon velvet jacket. "Straw" hat. Sewn in petticoat, has net ruffle. Lace trim panties. Vinyl shoes.
79 N 3669C 25-in. doll, Wt. 5 lbs. $17.99
79 N 3671C 30-in. doll, Wt. 7 lbs. 19.99

Miss Ideal in Campus Outfit. Long flowing hair easily pulled back into a long pony tail. Pink dress has puff sleeves. Red trim and bouquet set-off deep midriff. Top overlaid with sheer embroidery has squared neckline. Attached petticoat circles in gathers, net ruffle over hem. Lace-edged panties, vinyl slippers.
79 N 3667C 25-in. doll, Wt. 5 lbs. $16.99
79 N 3668C 30-in. doll, Wt. 7 lbs. 17.88

Miss Ideal in Capri-styled Outfit (at right). Wears hair braided in long pig-tails with wispy curls fringing her pretty face. Gold-colored cotton smock top is gathered in billowy folds from rounded neckline yoke, snaps in back for easy dressing. Capri pants have flirty slash at side of leg. Carries sunglasses. Wears vinyl shoes.
79 N 3663C 25-in. doll, Wt. 5 lbs. $15.88
79 N 3666C 30-in. doll, Wt. 7 lbs. 16.99

A page from the 1961 Sears Christmas catalog showing Miss Ideal in various outfits.

Terry Twist Dolls

Pose us in any position ..
we even stand on one foot

$11⁹⁹
25-inch

$17⁹⁹
30-inch

$13⁹⁸
25-inch

We all have lovely
rooted nylon hair
to shampoo and set

Famous Miss Ideal "Terry Twist" now at savings from $2.00 to $4.00. Doll of molded plastic, shaped like a grammar school girl. Delicately tinted, precisely defined she almost comes alive. Her large eyes have thick lashes, open and close. Jointed arms, hips, ankles. Dresses may vary. Has Beauty Kit with comb, curlers, lotion.

In Town-and-Country outfit. Curly   In Campus Outfit. Long flowing

1962 Sears Christmas catalog showing the doll now called Terry Twist wearing the
same three outfits as the previous year.

Kissy: Kissy puckers up her lips and blows a kiss when her arms are pulled together. She came in several different sizes and was issued in various outfits. The 22" Kissy doll in the photo is shown in her original box. She is marked, "©IDEAL TOY CORP./K-21-L" on her head and "©IDEAL TOY CORP./K-22 /PAT.PEND" on her back. MIB: **$100.00 – 125.00**. Courtesy Pamela Grimes.

Kissy: Another 22" Kissy in a different original outfit than the previous dolls. She is marked, "©IDEAL TOY CORP./K-21-L" on her head and "©IDEAL TOY CORP./K-22 /PAT.PEND" on her back. MIB with tag: **$115.00 – 150.00**. Courtesy Marcia Fanta.

Kissy: 22" Kissy wearing replaced shoes. Same markings as doll above. Loose/original dress/replaced shoes: **$55.00 – 75.00**. Courtesy Patty Massey.

Kissy: 22" Kissy with blond and auburn hair. The blond doll has been redressed. Loose and original: **$55.00 – 75.00**. Redressed: **$30.00 – 45.00**.

Tiny Kissy: 22" Kissy shown with 16" Tiny Kissy. Tiny Kissy has a longer section of hair on the top of her head for a ponytail. She is marked, "©IDEAL TOY CORP./K-13-1" on her head and "©IDEAL TOY CORP./K-16" on her body. The Tiny Kissy in the photo has been redressed. Redressed Tiny Kissy: **$25.00 – 40.00**.

KISSY DOLLS

Clap our hands, play pat-a-cake..
we'll pucker up and give you
a real big kiss

IDEAL

Tiny Kissy .. 16-inch toddler
in your choice of 4 perky outfits

Doll
with outfit **$7⁷⁷** each

She gives you a real kiss with a resounding smack. She
loves to have you comb her hair, even goes to sleep.
Her jointed plastic body lets her sit or stand. Moving vinyl
head and arms.

1 So much fun to take on an
outing in her crisp red-and-
white check dress with matching
panties. White shoes and socks
match white trim on her dress.
49N3009—Wt. 2 lbs. 8 oz..$7.77

2 Tiny Kissy loves to have lunch
and play with you in 2-in-1
aqua gingham check play outfit
with matching appliqued dress.
49N3070—Wt. 2 lbs. 8 oz..$7.77

3 Take Tiny Kissy to park or
playground . . she's in a playful mood in her pert and pretty
pink-and-white cotton playsuit
and dress combination.
49N3071—Wt. 2 lbs. 8 oz..$7.77

4 She's wearing her Sunday
best to meet all your friends.
A one-piece red cotton outfit
with starchy white pinafore.
49N3072—Wt. 2 lbs. 8 oz..$7.77

De luxe Kissy
22 inches tall **$12⁴⁹**

5 More grown-up, but
just as sweet and
affectionate as her
smaller sisters. She's
dressed for a party in a
pink dress with match-
ing slip, lace-trimmed
panties. Jointed plas-
tic body. Vinyl head,
arms. Rooted Saran
hair. Shpg. wt. 5 lbs.
79 N 3073C . . $12.49

Kissy Baby
22 inches long **$12⁴⁹**

6 Just the size of a
real baby. She's
cute and dimpled; even
her legs are curved
into baby sitting posi-
tion. Kisses like her
older sisters, goes to
sleep, has fully jointed
plastic body, vinyl
head, arms. Rooted
Saran hair. Wt. 5 lbs.
79 N 3010C . . $12.49

Smoochie .. hugs, kisses. 3 extra outfits

7 Press her tummy. She hugs, kisses with real kissing
sound. 16 in. long. Soft cloth body, vinyl head, legs,
arms. Rooted Saran hair to comb, style. Goes to sleep.
49 N 3059—Shipping weight 1 lb. 10 oz. $5.99

Bibsy .. feed her and she really drools

8 Let her drink, squeeze her gently . . bubbles like real
baby. Makes baby noises too. Vinyl body. Plastic bib
keeps dress dry. Bottle, formula, spoon included. 23 in.
79 N 3019C — Shipping weight 4 lbs. $12.89

16-inch Baby Doll with fuzzy kitten

9 She's just come in from playing in the snow and is still
wearing her soft, warm snowsuit. All vinyl jointed
body, she drinks from a bottle and wets. Platinum
rooted hair in pixie-cut. Go-to-sleep eyes. Kitten included.
49 N 3012 —Shipping weight 1 lb. 8 oz. $4.92

12 SEARS 2PCBDL

1963 Sears Christmas catalog showing Tiny Kissy, 22" Kissy, and Kissy Baby.

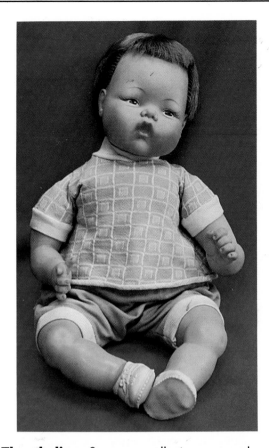

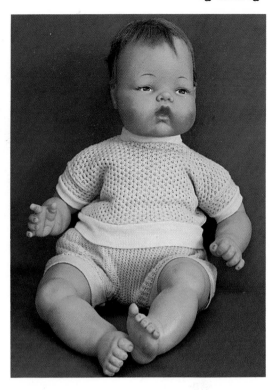

Tiny Thumbelina: This 21" Tiny Thumbelina has a plastic wind-up knob and a crier in the plush body. Unlike the doll at left, she has holes in the middle of her ears and about a dozen holes on the back of her head hidden underneath her hair. The doll in the photo has been redressed. **$100.00 – 150.00**.

Tiny Thumbelina: So many collectors remember the doll Thumbelina from their childhood. There were a whole variety of Thumbelina dolls produced in the 1960s and 1970s, but the most popular one with collectors today is Tiny Thumbelina with the wind-up knob on her back. Available in several different sizes, Tiny Thumbelina looks like a newborn baby, and when her wind-up knob is turned, she squirms and wiggles like a newborn. She has a plush body and vinyl head and limbs. The hair on Tiny Thumbelina often didn't hold up well over the years so finding a doll with a full head of hair that didn't fall out from repeated brushings is a big challenge for collectors. The 20" Tiny Thumbelina shown here has a wooden wind-up knob and is marked, "©IDEAL TOY CORP./OTT-19" on her head. **$125.00 – 200.00**.

Tiny Thumbelina: Two Tiny Thumbelina dolls showing the difference between the plastic and wooden wind-up knobs.

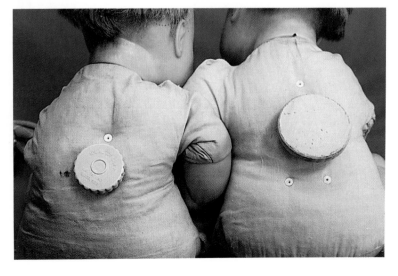

The THUMBELiNA

Dolls by **IDEAL**

③ $1⁶⁶

② $1⁹⁴

⑤ $3²⁶

④ $1

⑥ $2⁶⁴

$3³⁷ ⑦

Busy Tiny Thumbelina needs several Outfits

① **$5⁹⁹**

Tiny Thumbelina wiggles 'n stretches

1 She's 14 inches long. Just wind disc in back and she makes lifelike movements. Vinyl head, arms, legs. Cotton body. Rooted Saran hair. Wears lace-trimmed cotton organdy dress, cotton slip, diaper, and booties.
49 N 3211—Shipping weight 1 lb. 8 oz....$5.99

2 Pajama Set. Pretty pajamas for sleepy-time hours, hot water bottle to keep feet warm, cotton terrycloth animal for a bedtime companion. No doll.
49 N 3046—Wt. 6 oz....$1.94

5 Pram Suit. "And this keeps me warm on chilly days." 2-pc. suit with attached hood, bootees, 2 hangers. No doll.
49 N 3244—Wt. 7 oz....$3.26

3 Sleeper Set. "This is what I wear when I sleep in my buggy." Sleeping gown, matching cap, a rattle to sound a gay rat-a-tat-tat. No doll.
49 N 3047—Wt. 6 oz....$1.66

6 Knit Suit. Take Tiny for a walk in this cotton knitted suit, matching beret, bootees, rattle. Doll not included.
49 N 3049—Wt. 6 oz....$2.64

4 Creeper Set. Now what little mother could resist Tiny in this cunning cover-all set, bootees. Three clothespins for wash-day use. No doll.
49 N 3242—Wt. 6 oz....$1.99

7 Christening Dress made of cotton organdy, trimmed with lace, plus petticoat, bonnet, and bootees. No doll.
49 N 3048—Wt. 6 oz....$3.37

Here's everything needed to keep Tiny Thumbelina happy and healthy

8 Rocking Crib. Nestle Tiny into this crib and rock her to sleep. Dainty heart decorations, soft pad. Plastic. 19x10x14 in. high overall. Shpg. wt. 3 lbs.
79 N 9209C....$2.89

9 Carrying Case in imitation calf finish. Inside has heart-print lining. Includes clothes rack and 5 plastic hangers; roomy accessory drawer. 14x4x14 in. high. Doll not included. Shpg. wt. 2 lbs. 11 oz.
49 N 9208......$2.97

10 Primp and Bath Set to keep little Tiny looking her prettiest. Contains oil and Q-Tip jars with covers, talc, sponge, soap, towel, comb and brush, nail scissors. Shipping weight 5 ounces.
49 N 9218.......77c

11 Feed and Formula Set. 3-sectioned heart-shaped feeding dish, orange squeezer, feeding spoon, 2 milk bottles, sterilizer rack and handle, measuring cup and spoon. Plastic. Shpg. wt. 7 oz.
49 N 9226....$1.47

12 Check-up Table has quilted-look top. 7 pockets store hypo, scissors, thermometer, tongue depressor, tweezers, comb, brush. Plastic. 19x10x 11 in. high. Shipping weight 3 pounds.
79 N 9217C. ..$2.89

13 Play Pen keeps Tiny Thumbelina from getting into mischief. Steel frame with nylon net. Hardboard floor in colorful Thumbelina pattern. 18x18x12½ in. high. Shpg. wt. 4 lbs.
79 N 9214C.....$2.99

6 SEARS 2PCBOL

This 1963 Sears Christmas catalog shows the 14" Tiny Thumbelina and some of her accessories.

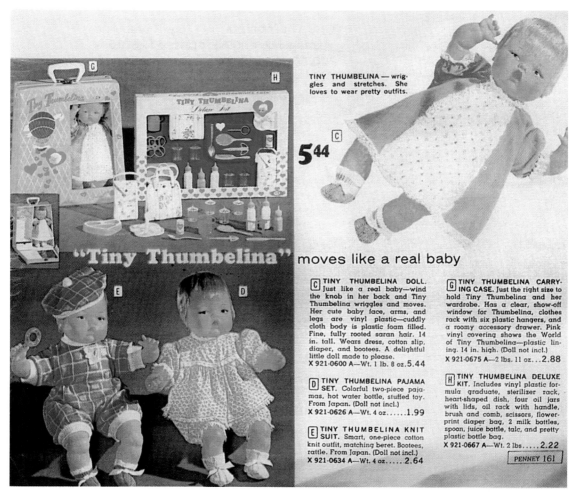

TINY THUMBELINA — wriggles and stretches. She loves to wear pretty outfits.

5^{44}

"Tiny Thumbelina" moves like a real baby

C **TINY THUMBELINA DOLL.** Just like a real baby—wind the knob in her back and Tiny Thumbelina wriggles and moves. Her cute baby face, arms, and legs are vinyl plastic—cuddly cloth body is plastic foam filled. Fine, fully rooted saran hair. 14 in. tall. Wears dress, cotton slip, diaper, and bootees. A delightful little doll made to please.
X 921-0600 A—Wt. 1 lb. 8 oz..5.44

D **TINY THUMBELINA PAJAMA SET.** Colorful two-piece pajamas, hot water bottle, stuffed toy. From Japan. (Doll not incl.)
X 921-0626 A—Wt. 4 oz......1.99

E **TINY THUMBELINA KNIT SUIT.** Smart, one-piece cotton knit outfit, matching beret. Bootees, rattle. From Japan. (Doll not incl.)
X 921-0634 A—Wt. 4 oz.....2.64

G **TINY THUMBELINA CARRYING CASE.** Just the right size to hold Tiny Thumbelina and her wardrobe. Has a clear, show-off window for Thumbelina, clothes rack with six plastic hangers, and a roomy accessory drawer. Pink vinyl covering shows the World of Tiny Thumbelina—plastic lining. 14 in. high. (Doll not incl.)
X 921-0675 A—2 lbs. 11 oz...2.88

H **TINY THUMBELINA DELUXE KIT.** Includes vinyl plastic formula graduate, sterilizer rack, heart-shaped dish, four oil jars with lids, oil rack with handle, brush and comb, scissors, flower-print diaper bag, 2 milk bottles, spoon, juice bottle, talc, and pretty plastic bottle bag.
X 921-0667 A—Wt. 2 lbs.....2.22

PENNEY 161

1964 J.C. Penney Christmas catalog showing Tiny Thumbelina and some of her accessories. © JCPenney Catalog, J.C. Penney Company, Inc. Used by permission.

TINY THUMBELINA Moves Like a Real Baby

6 2^{97}
Travel Case Only

5

5 WIND HER, SHE MOVES LIKE A REAL BABY. S soft and limber so lifelike has cotton stuffed body, vinyl arms, legs, rooted hair in pixie painted eyes. Wears dress, pants, booties. About 14 in. tall.
48 F 4261 Ship. wt. 1 lb. 8 oz.

5^{66}
Doll Only

180 WARDS

6 TRAVEL CASE hangers, drawer, clothes r
48 T 4490 (N Ship. wt 2 lbs. 10 oz. 5

1964 Montgomery Ward Christmas catalog showing a 14" Tiny Thumbelina doll and her carrying case.

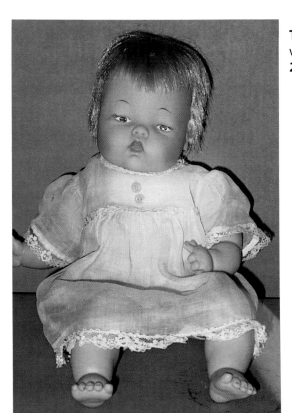

Tiny Thumbelina: 14" Tiny Thumbelina wearing her original dress. **$125.00 – 200.00**. Courtesy Dawn Thomas.

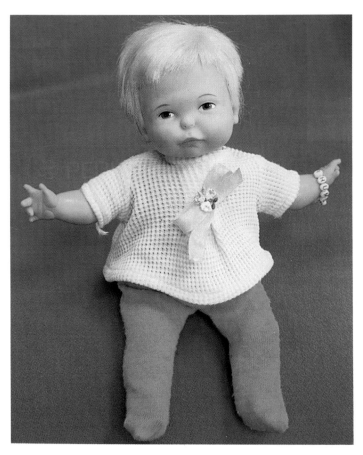

Thumbelina: This 1967 version of Thumbelina used a different head mold than the earlier dolls. She has a plastic wind-up knob on her back. The 14" doll is marked, "©1966/IDEAL TOY CORP/TAT-14-H-62". Redressed: **$65.00 – 85.00**. Courtesy Dawn Thomas.

Newborn Thumbelina: This 9½" version of Thumbelina has a pull-string that makes her wiggle and squirm. She is marked, "©1967/IDEAL/TT-9-H106/JAPAN" on her head and tagged, "IDEAL TOY CORP./HOLLIS, NEW YORK, NY/ALL NEW MATERIAL/POLY-URETANE-FOAM/MADE IN JAPAN" on her plush body. **$55.00 – 75.00**.

Newborn Thumbelina: More than likely, this 9½" doll was manufactured later than the previous Newborn Thumbelina. Her hair coloring is a more golden blond than the platinum doll above. She is marked, "©1967/IDEAL/TT-9-H106" on her head and tagged on her body, "NEWBORN /THUMBELINA©/IDEAL ALL NEW MATERIAL/POLYURETANE-FOAM./MADE IN HONG KONG." The doll in the photo has been redressed. Redressed: **$25.00 – 30.00**.

Toddler Thumbelina: One version of Toddler Thumbelina came with a walker. The doll is 10½" with a pull-string on her back to make her wiggle her head and move her legs, and when she does, she pushes her walker. NRFB: **$75.00 – 110.00**.

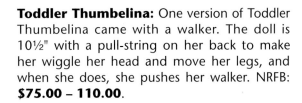

328

1970 N
able th

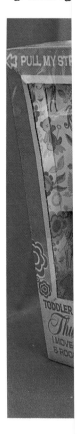

Baby Snoozie: This doll came with a wind-up knob on her back to make her squirm and close her eyes. She is often mistakenly called Thumbelina with open and shut eyes, since her wind-up mechanism is similar to Thumbelina's. The 14" Baby Snoozie also came in a 20" size called Snoozie. This doll is marked, "©1965/IDEAL TOY CORP./YTT 14-5" on her head and "IDEAL TOY CORP. U.S. PAT. NO. 3,029,552" on her wind-up knob. The doll in the photo has been redressed. **$50.00 – 75.00.**

Tammy: Beginning in 1962 Ideal issued a teenage fashion doll called Tammy. Following Tammy's success, Ideal issued a family for her including a mother, a father, a brother, and a little sister. Several other friends in the line followed them. Numerous versions and variations of the dolls were issued, so only a few examples are shown here. This photo shows a straight-legged Tammy in her original box. She is marked, "©IDEAL TOY CORP. BS-12" on her head and "©IDEAL TOY CORP. BS-12/1" (last digit varies on Tammy dolls) on her back. MIB: **$65.00 – 85.00.**

Toddler Th
they were s
with a car a
her car." Ho
referred to
Whether or
confirmed. A
walker show
left is tagge
KONG." The
Thumbelina.
dler Thumb
– **45.00.** Re

Tammy: The straight leg version of Tammy was available in various hair colors in varying lengths as illustrated in this photo. Loose dolls: **$25.00 – 45.00.**

Newborn Thumbelina: More than likely, this 9½" doll was manufactured later than the previous Newborn Thumbelina. Her hair coloring is a more golden blond than the platinum doll above. She is marked, "©1967/IDEAL/TT-9-H106" on her head and tagged on her body, "NEWBORN /THUMBELINA©/IDEAL ALL NEW MATERIAL/POLYURETANE-FOAM./MADE IN HONG KONG." The doll in the photo has been redressed. Redressed: **$25.00 – 30.00**.

Toddler Thumbelina: One version of Toddler Thumbelina came with a walker. The doll is 10½" with a pull-string on her back to make her wiggle her head and move her legs, and when she does, she pushes her walker. NRFB: **$75.00 – 110.00**.

Toddler Thumbelina: This version of Toddler Thumbelina came with a rocking horse and when the pull-string on her back is pulled, she rocks her horse. NRFB: **$75.00 – 110.00**.

Toddler Thumbelina and Sister Thumbelina: These two dolls are obviously made from the same mold, but they were sold as both Toddler Thumbelina and Sister Thumbelina. One version of Toddler Thumbelina was sold with a car and on her original box it said, "Toddler Thumbelina" and underneath the doll's name it reads, "with her car." However, in one store catalog a doll was called Car Toddler Thumbelina while another store catalog referred to her as Speedy Thumbelina, and still another called a slightly different version ByeBye Thumbelina. Whether or not Ideal actually sold the Toddler Thumbelina with her car under each of these names hasn't been confirmed. Another Toddler Thumbelina called Jingles Thumbelina was sold both with the rocking horse and the walker shown above wearing a green two-piece play outfit and bells on her shoes. In the photo, the doll on the left is tagged, "Toddler Thumbelina©/IDEAL ALL NEW MATERIAL/POLYURETANE-FOAM./MADE IN HONG KONG." The doll on the right is tagged the same except her tag says "Sister Thumbelina©" instead of "Toddler Thumbelina." Both dolls are 10½" and have pull strings on their backs to make their heads and legs move. Toddler Thumbelina is wearing her original outfit. Sister Thumbelina has been redressed. Loose and original: **$25.00 – 45.00**. Redressed: **$20.00 – 25.00**.

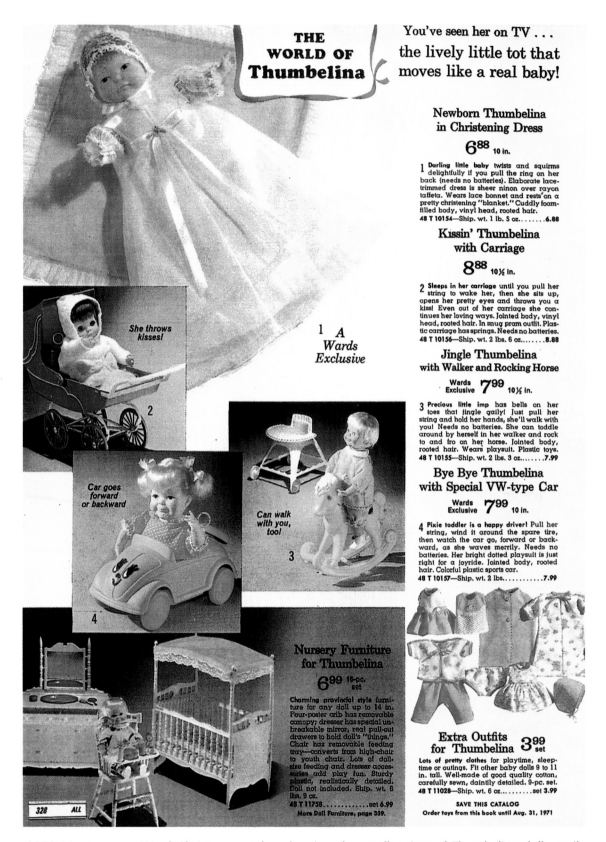

THE WORLD OF Thumbelina

You've seen her on TV . . . the lively little tot that moves like a real baby!

She throws kisses!

2

Car goes forward or backward

Can walk with you, too!

3

4

1 *A Wards Exclusive*

Newborn Thumbelina in Christening Dress

6^{88} 10 in.

1 **Darling little baby** twists and squirms delightfully if you pull the ring on her back (needs no batteries). Elaborate lace-trimmed dress is sheer ninon over rayon taffeta. Wears lace bonnet and rests on a pretty christening "blanket." Cuddly foam-filled body, vinyl head, rooted hair.
48 T 10154—Ship. wt. 1 lb. 5 oz. 6.88

Kissin' Thumbelina with Carriage

8^{88} 10½ in.

2 **Sleeps in her carriage** until you pull her string to wake her, then she sits up, opens her pretty eyes and throws you a kiss! Even out of her carriage she continues her loving ways. Jointed body, vinyl head, rooted hair. In snug pram outfit. Plastic carriage has springs. Needs no batteries.
48 T 10156—Ship. wt. 2 lbs. 6 oz. 8.88

Jingle Thumbelina with Walker and Rocking Horse

Wards Exclusive 7^{99} 10½ in.

3 **Precious little imp** has bells on her toes that jingle gaily! Just pull her string and hold her hands, she'll walk with you! Needs no batteries. She can toddle around by herself in her walker and rock to and fro on her horse. Jointed body, rooted hair. Wears playsuit. Plastic toys.
48 T 10155—Ship. wt. 2 lbs. 3 oz. 7.99

Bye Bye Thumbelina with Special VW-type Car

Wards Exclusive 7^{99} 10 in.

4 **Pixie toddler** is a happy driver! Pull her string, wind it around the spare tire, then watch the car go, forward or backward, as she waves merrily. Needs no batteries. Her bright dotted playsuit is just right for a joyride. Jointed body, rooted hair. Colorful plastic sports car.
48 T 10157—Ship. wt. 2 lbs. 7.99

Nursery Furniture for Thumbelina

6^{99} 15-pc. set

Charming provincial style furniture for any doll up to 14 in. Four-poster crib has removable canopy; dresser has special unbreakable mirror, real pull-out drawers to hold doll's "things." Chair has removable feeding tray—converts from high-chair to youth chair. Lots of doll-size feeding and dresser accessories add play fun. Sturdy plastic, realistically detailed. Doll not included. Ship. wt. 6 lbs. 9 oz.
48 T 11758 . . . . set 6.99
More Doll Furniture, page 339.

328   ALL

Extra Outfits for Thumbelina 3^{99} set

Lots of pretty clothes for playtime, sleeptime or outings. Fit other baby dolls 9 to 11 in. tall. Well-made of good quality cotton, carefully sewn, daintily detailed. 9-pc. set.
48 T 11028—Ship. wt. 6 oz. . . . . set 3.99

SAVE THIS CATALOG
Order toys from this book until Aug. 31, 1971

1970 Montgomery Ward Christmas catalog showing the smaller sizes of Thumbelina dolls available that year.

Baby Snoozie: This doll came with a wind-up knob on her back to make her squirm and close her eyes. She is often mistakenly called Thumbelina with open and shut eyes, since her wind-up mechanism is similar to Thumbelina's. The 14" Baby Snoozie also came in a 20" size called Snoozie. This doll is marked, "©1965/IDEAL TOY CORP./YTT 14-5" on her head and "IDEAL TOY CORP. U.S. PAT. NO. 3,029,552" on her wind-up knob. The doll in the photo has been redressed. **$50.00 – 75.00**.

Tammy: Beginning in 1962 Ideal issued a teenage fashion doll called Tammy. Following Tammy's success, Ideal issued a family for her including a mother, a father, a brother, and a little sister. Several other friends in the line followed them. Numerous versions and variations of the dolls were issued, so only a few examples are shown here. This photo shows a straight-legged Tammy in her original box. She is marked, "©IDEAL TOY CORP. BS-12" on her head and "©IDEAL TOY CORP. BS-12/1" (last digit varies on Tammy dolls) on her back. MIB: **$65.00 – 85.00**.

Tammy: The straight leg version of Tammy was available in various hair colors in varying lengths as illustrated in this photo. Loose dolls: **$25.00 – 45.00**.

Tammy: Grown Up Tammy was a more sophisticated version of Tammy than the earlier dolls. Here she is wearing a hard-to-find Tammy fashion called On the Avenue. Grown Up Tammy is marked, "©IDEAL TOY CORP./T-12-E" on her head and "©IDEAL/T-12" on her right hip. Doll without outfit: **$30.00 – 40.00**.

Pepper: Tammy's freckled face little sister Pepper is 9½" tall. Like Tammy, she came in several hair colors and styles. The orange hair doll is in her original playsuit. The other dolls are wearing outfits sold separately for Pepper. Pepper is marked, "©IDEAL TOY CORP. G9-E" on her head and "©IDEAL TOY CORP. G-9-W/1" (last digit varies on Pepper dolls) on her back. Loose/no box: **$20.00 – 25.00.** Orange hair doll: **$30.00 – 45.00**.

1 to 6 OUTFITS THAT TAMMY WILL LOVE TO WEAR.
[1] Nurse's Aid. Striped jumper, blouse, cap, and shoes.
X 921-3356 A—Shipping weight 4 oz......Outfit only, 1.94
[2] Cheerleader. Bulky sweater, flared skirt. Cap, shoes.
X 921-3349 A—Shipping weight 6 oz.....Outfit only, 2.39
[3] Ring-a-Ding. Pants, overblouse, wedgies. Phone, fruit.
X 921-1442 A—Shipping weight 8 oz.....Outfit only, 2.64
[4] Model Miss. Felt coat, hat. Shoes, bag, bracelet, hatbox.
X 921-3323 A—Shipping weight 6 oz.....Outfit only, 3.43
[5] Fraternity Hop. Dress, stole. Flowers, bag, pumps.
X 921-3315 A—Shipping weight 4 oz.....Outfit only, 2.39
[6] Sleepytime. Brief pajamas. Slippers, comb, curlers.
X 921-1046 A—Shipping weight 3 oz.....Outfit only, 1.59

7 to 13 FASHION-RIGHT OUTFITS FOR PEPPER.
[7] Pajama Set. Cotton flannel pajamas, pompon trim.
X 921-0964 A—Shipping weight 2 oz......Outfit only, 97c
[8] Coat and Hat. Smart braid-trim coat, pile collar, hat.
X 921-0972 A—Shipping weight 2 oz.....Outfit only, 1.59
[9] Birthday Party. Dress, headband. Phonograph, records.
X 921-3364 A—Shipping weight 4 oz.....Outfit only, 1.94
[10] Snowflake. Ski pants, hooded parka, plus pile mittens.
X 921-3372 A—Shipping weight 4 oz.....Outfit only, 2.84
[11] Flower Girl. Long gown, headpiece, gloves, basket.
X 921-3380 A—Shipping weight 4 oz.....Outfit only, 2.39
[12] Teacher's Pet. Dress, scarf. Bag, shoes, bulletin board.
X 921-3398 A—Shipping weight 4 oz.....Outfit only, 1.24
[13] Slack Set. Cotton flannel slacks, knit cardigan.
X 921-0980 A—Shipping weight 2 oz.....Outfit only, 1.24

teenage *Tammy*

and her sister *Pepper*

[A] TAMMY® DOLL. Typical teenager, from the top of her fluffy hair to her high-style wardrobe (order smart outfits at left). Jointed plastic body. 12 in. tall. Wears playsuit.
X 921-0915 A—11 oz.......1.92

[B] PEPPER DOLL. Rarin' to go anywhere in the cutest wardrobe a pre-teen ever owned (order outfits at left). Jointed plastic body, 9 in. tall. Wears playsuit.
X 921-1053 A—8 oz.......1.87

[C] POS'N TAMMY®. Similar to [A] but more fun—arms, legs bend; can be posed in lifelike positions. Wears leotard, tights.
X 921-3299 A—14 oz.......3.74

[D] POS'N PEPPER. Like [B], but arms, legs bend; doll can be posed in lifelike positions. Wears striped play dress.
X 921-3307 A—10 oz.......2.77

Where Tammy and Pepper entertain

TAMMY'S PLAY HOUSE. A little girl's dream—and no wonder. Has table tennis, shuffle-board court, soda fountain, TV set, juke box—even a patio with barbecue. Doll not included.
X 921-1418 A—Shipping weight 8 lbs. 11 oz...............4.79

Tote 'n' Store Cases for Tammy and Pepper on the move

TAMMY PHONE CASE. Space for 2 dolls and their clothes—2 phone booths, too. With "Princess" phones. Green plastic. *
X 921-3406 A—1 lb. 11 oz.......2.99

FASHION TRUNK. Room for a fashion doll up to 12½ in. tall, plus room for accessories, clothes. With hangers. *
X 921-0907 A—1 lb. 4 oz.......2.87

PENNEY 159

Outfits for Tammy and Pepper are imported from Japan.   * Dolls and costumes shown not included.

1964 J.C. Penney Christmas catalog shows some of the Tammy and Pepper dolls and outfits available that year. ©1978, JCPenney Catalog, J.C. Penney Company, Inc. Used by permission.

Glamour Misty, the Miss Clairol Doll: Tammy's best friend was Misty. The straight leg, platinum blond version like the one in the photo was called Glamour Misty, the Miss Clairol Doll, and she featured hair which could be colored with special hair color applicators. Other Misty dolls came with light brown hair in a shoulder-length style or a long flip curl and came with either straight or posing legs. 12" Misty is marked, "©1965 Ideal Toy Corp. W-12-3" on her head and "©1965 Ideal (in circle) M-12" with a single digit number on her lower body. The straight legged doll in the photo is wearing one of the outfits she was issued in. **$25.00 – 45.00**.

Tammy's Family: The other members of Tammy's family included Tammy's Mom, Tammy's Dad, and her brother Ted. Tammy's 12½" Mom is marked, "©Ideal Toy Corp.W-13-L" on her head and "©Ideal Toy Corp w-13" on her back. **$30.00 – 45.00**. Tammy's 13" Dad is marked, "©Ideal Toy Corp. M-13-2" on his head and "©Ideal Toy Corp B-12½" on his back. **$25.00 – 30.00.** 12½" Ted is marked, "©Ideal Toy Corp./B-12½-W-2" on his head and "©Ideal Toy Corp./B-12½ (sometimes with a digit underneath) on his back. **$20.00 – 25.00**.

Misty: Misty in various hair colors and styles. The two blond dolls have straight legs and the two brunettes have posing legs. The dolls shown are wearing four different Tammy and Misty fashions. Dolls without fashions: **$25.00 – 45.00** each.

Samantha: Shown here is a loose 12" Samantha doll. She is marked, "©1965/IDEAL TOY CORP./M12-E-2" on her head and "©1965/IDEAL/M-12" on her hip with a single digit on her lower body. With original dress, hat, shoes, and broom: **$300.00 – 400.00.**

Samantha: This 11" doll represented Elizabeth Montgomery in the role of Samantha on the television show, *Bewitched*. The doll used the same body as Ideal's Pos'n Misty doll. Rarely found MIB, this doll appeals not only to doll collectors but collectors of television and/or *Bewitched* memorabilia. MIB: **$1,000.00 – 1,500.00.** Courtesy Elaine McGrath.

Samantha/Misty: Close-up of Ideal's Samantha and Misty dolls showing the difference between the two dolls. Samantha's head is smaller, her lips are not as full, and she has olive eyes and eyeshadow. Misty has turquoise eyes with turquoise eyeshadow.

Betsy Wetsy: Betsy Wetsy is a name many people recognize due to the fact that the name Betsy Wetsy was used on Ideal dolls from 1937 through the 1980s. Over the years the doll went through so many transformations she often didn't look like the same doll from one version to the next. Some of the dolls were called Betsy Wetsy while others were given variations of Betsy's name like Little Betsy Wetsy, Betsy Baby, Big Baby Betsy Wetsy, Tiny Betsy Wetsy, and Tearie Betsy Wetsy. Betsy Wetsy dolls ranged in sizes from 8" to 25". The toddler version of Betsy Wetsy shown here is from 1962. She is 18½" with a vinyl head and arms, and a plastic torso and legs. She is marked, "©IDEAL TOY CORP./GN-18-M" on her head and "©IDEAL TOY CORP./GN-18" on her back. **$75.00 – 100.00**.

Betsy Baby: This smaller version of Betsy Wetsy was called Betsy Baby in 1965 catalogs. She was available in 11½" or 13". **$30.00 – 45.00**. Courtesy Elaine McGrath.

Betsy Wetsy and Betsy Baby: Three different versions of Betsy Wetsy dolls. The doll in the front was the same doll as Ideal's Tearie Dearie. **$25.00 – 45.00** each. Courtesy Elaine McGrath.

Tearie Dearie: 9" Tearie Dearie cried "real" tears, drank from a bottle, and wet. She came packaged in this plastic bed-case that could also be used as a crib, a cradle, or a bath. Tearie Dearie dolls were available in a variety of hair colors. Tearie is marked, "©IDEAL TOY CORP./BW9-4" on her head and "©IDEAL TOY CORP/1964/BW9" on her back. In original case: **$35.00 – 45.00**.

Tearie Dearie: This blond doll came packaged inside a plastic carrying case along with a high chair. When turned upside-down, the case could double as a diaper pail for Tearie Dearie. In original case: **$35.00 – 45.00**. Courtesy Mala Drzewicki.

ing Time

h Betsy has receiving
nd feeding accessories

$**4**^{99}$

al baby, Betsy is hungry and
Feed her, then press her stom-
contentedly. Soft vinyl body
eyes and rooted saran hair
mbed or brushed. Dressed in
, she comes with 4 bottles and
lder, measuring cup, spoon,
th flower applique, and flannel
sket.
Shpg. wt. 1 lb. 9 oz....$4.99

yette for $**2**^{99}$
-inch Betsy

Feeding, Bathing, Sleeping Time

9 ½-inch Betsy Wetsy with high chair,
crib-tub and accessories $**3**^{99}$

So tiny, so adorable, yet she acts just like a real baby. She has a
washable body. Her rooted saran hair can be washed, combed and
brushed to keep it shiny and soft. She's dressed in a lovely lace-
trimmed sleeping sack and diaper. Her nursery furniture consists
of a cute plastic crib that converts easily to a bathtub, a plastic

Betsy Wetsy: The 1967 Sears catalog shows the doll that used to be sold as Tearie Dearie being sold under the Betsy Wetsy name. Even the accessories are the same as those that came with the earlier Tearie Dearie dolls, only the name on the bed-case has been changed to Betsy's. 1967 Sears Christmas catalog.

Tearie Dearie/Betsy Wetsy: It is undetermined if these 9" dolls are actually Tearie Dearie or Betsy Wetsy since they are essentially the same doll. The doll on the right with the red hair is wearing a Betsy Wetsy original romper. She is marked, "©1964/IDEAL TOY CORP./1964/BW9-4" on her head and "3/©IDEAL TOY CORP./1964/BW9" on her back. The brunette doll has the same markings only the markings on her back also have "HONG KONG" underneath. Her dress is not original. **$20.00 – 25.00** each.

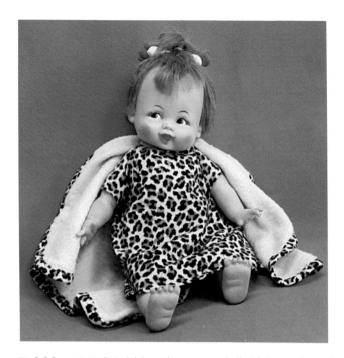

Pebbles: 14½" Pebbles Flintstone doll. This version of Pebbles has a stuffed cloth body and vinyl head and limbs. The doll is marked, "©HANNA BARBERA PRODS.INC/IDEAL TOY CORP./FS-14" on her head. With original clothing, blanket and bone in her hair: **$65.00 – 85.00**.

Pebbles: 12" Pebbles Flintstone doll with vinyl head and arms, plastic body and legs. The paper cup shown in front was found inside the box of this particular doll but does not go with the doll. The doll is marked, "©HANNA BARBERA PRODS.,INC./IDEAL TOY CORP./FS-11-2" on her head and "©HANNA-BARBERA- PRODS.,INC./IDEAL TOY CORP./F.S.11½" on her back. MIB: **$150.00 – 200.00**. Courtesy Marcia Fanta.

Pebbles: This 8" Pebbles comes packaged inside her Cave House. Rare when found still in her cave house. MIB: **$175.00 – 225.00**. Courtesy Marcia Fanta.

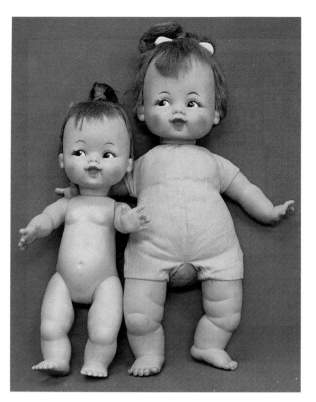

Pebbles: A 12" plastic body Pebbles shown with the 14½" cloth body Pebbles.

Bamm-Bamm: 16" doll with his original box. He has a vinyl head, vinyl arms, a plastic torso, and plastic legs. His right arm is jointed at the elbow, but his left arm is not. The doll is marked, "©HANNA-BARBERA PRODS., INC./ IDEAL TOY CORP./BB-17" both on his head and back. MIB: **$150.00 – 200.00.** Courtesy Dawn Thomas.

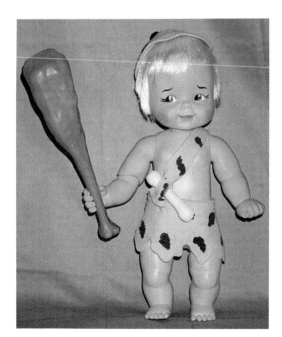

Bamm-Bamm: 12" doll wearing his original outfit. Bamm-Bamm is marked, "©HANNA BARBERA PRODS.,INC./IDEAL TOY CORP./BB-12" on his head and back. All original: **$50.00 – 80.00.** Courtesy Elaine McGrath.

PEBBLES
and
BAMM BAMM

Adorable Stone Age Sweetheart and
Her Caveman Protector . .
Based on TV Show
"The Flintstones"

① $3⁹⁶

② $3⁹⁶

③ $2²³
Cradle
only

Outfits
May
Vary

④ $7⁷⁷

① ② TINY PEBBLES AND HER CAVEMAN BOY FRIEND, TINY BAMM BAMM—fully jointed, rooted hair, painted eyes. Abt. 12 in.
(1) TINY BAMM BAMM is so shy, yet carries his club, ready to defend his sweetheart.
48 T 8364—Ship. wt. 1 lb. 2 oz. $3.96
(2) TINY PEBBLES dressed in her "prehistoric" outfit, realistic bone in her ponytail.
48 T 8363—Ship. wt. 1 lb. 2 oz. $3.96

③ PLASTIC ROCKING CRADLE looks like a hollowed-out log, Tiny Pebbles or Tiny Bamm Bamm can sleep so comfortably.
48 T 4492—(No doll). Ship. wt. 2 lbs. . .$2.23

④ BABY PEBBLES snuggly wrapped in her fleecy blanket, pretend "animal skin" nightie. Rooted hair with make-believe bone, soft body, painted eyes. About 14 in.
48 T 4059—Ship. wt. 2 lbs. $7.77

1964 Montgomery Ward Christmas catalog shows the 12" Pebbles and Bamm-Bamm dolls made of vinyl and plastic as well as the 14½" Pebbles with the stuffed cloth body.

Talk of the Town value

PEBBLES *and*
BAMM BAMM

The caveman kids
ride the Rockadile $5⁹⁹
All 3

⑨ TINY PEBBLES AND HER CAVEMAN BOY FRIEND, TINY BAMM BAMM—adorable stone age kids from comics and TV show "The Flintstones"—they are having a rollicking good time riding their plastic Rockadile—he looks so ferocious but he's really tame. Pebbles, Bamm Bamm are fully jointed, have rooted hair, painted eyes—dressed in "cavekid" outfits. About 8 in. tall.
48 T 8579—2 Dolls, Rockadile. Ship. wt. 1 lb. 4 oz. . . .$5.99

⑩ BAMM BAMM is so shy, yet carries his club ready to defend his sweetheart. Wears pretend "leopard skin." Has rooted hair, fully jointed body, painted features. Abt. 12 in. tall.
48 T 8364—Ship. wt. 1 lb. 2 oz. $3.95

⑪ PEBBLES in her prehistoric outfit, so realistic up to the bone in her ponytail. Rooted hair, painted features, jointed.
48 T 8363—About 12 in. tall. Ship. wt. 1 lb. 2 oz. $3.95

⑫ PEBBLES AND BAMM BAMM HAVE THEIR OWN "CAVE HOUSE"— looks so real—sturdy corrugated fiberboard colorfully printed; includes furniture. For 8-in. and 12-in. dolls—not incl.
48 T 4505—Easy to assemble. Ship. wt. 4 lbs. $1.99

⑪
Bamm Bamm
12 In.
$3⁹⁵

⑫ Pebbles
12 In.
$3⁹⁵

Colors, Outfits, Accessories May Vary Slightly

⑬ Pebbles and Bamm Bamm
Can Set Up Cavekeeping
Cavehouse $1⁹⁹

1965 Montgomery Ward Christmas catalog featured 12" Pebbles and Bamm-
Bamm dolls riding a "Rockadile" and playing in the Flintstone Cave House.

Honey Moon: 14" doll from the Dick Tracy comic strip representing the character who was the daughter of Junior Tracy and Moon Maid. The doll has a vinyl head and limbs and a plush body. Loose dolls usually are missing their helmets. Honey Moon is marked, "©1965 C.T.-N.Y.N.S./IDEAL TOY CORP./HM 14-2-2H" on her head. Doll without helmet: **$30.00 – 40.00**. With helmet: **$50.00 – 65.00**. Courtesy Dawn Thomas.

Goody Two Shoes: 19" battery-operated walking doll. The doll originally came dressed in a blue polka-dot dress and with two pairs of shoes. Goody Two Shoes is marked, "©1965/IDEAL TOY CORP./TW18-4-LH4" on her head and "©1965/IDEAL TOY CORP./WT 18/PAT.PENDING." on her back. Redressed: **$35.00 – 50.00**.

Giggles: 18" doll giggles and moves her eyes side-to-side when you pull her arms together. Her original mini dress came in various fabrics. The two dolls shown here are both wearing original dresses. The doll on the right has had a slight hair trim. Both dolls are marked, "©1966/IDEAL TOY CORP./GG-18-H-77" on their heads and "©1967/IDEAL TOY CORP./GG-18" on their lower bodies. **$35.00 – 50.00.**

Posie Doll: This 18" doll has a foam body and vinyl head and hands. Her arms and legs are made of foam with wires inside for posing. The Posie dolls included Rosie, Daisy, Petal, and Lillie, and they came in various outfits. It is believed this doll is Daisy, and her outfit may or may not be original. The doll is marked, "©1967 IDEAL TOY CORP./E-18-F M-8941" on her head. **$30.00 – 35.00.**

Giggles: 18" Giggles shown in her original box wearing a different version dress from the two previous dolls. MIB: **$125.00 – 200.00.** *Courtesy Robin Englehart/Photo by Nancy Jean Mong.*

Baby Giggles: 16" Baby Giggles moves her eyes side-to-side and laughs when her left arm is lifted and lowered. Baby Giggles came with brunette, blond, or red hair. Shown here with the 18" version of Giggles are two dolls wearing their original outfits. Both dolls are missing their original sandals. They are marked, "©1968/IDEAL TOY CORP./BG-16-H-118" on their heads and "©-1968/IDEAL TOY CORP./BG-16" on their lower bodies. **$30.00 – 45.00**.

Betty Big Girl: 32" Betty Big Girl is a battery-operated talking doll. Her original outfit consisted of brown culottes, a yellow blouse, a tan vest, a paisley-print scarf tied at the neck, and loafers. Betty is marked, "1968/IDEAL TOY CORP./HD-31-H-127" on her head and "1969/IDEAL TOY CORP./HB-32" on her back. Redressed: **$75.00 – 100.00**.

Crissy

A lot of youngsters growing up in the early 1970s played with Ideal's Beautiful Crissy with "growing" hair. Crissy had shoulder-length red hair with a section of hair that came from a hole in the top of her head that could go from shoulder length down to her knees. Her hair grew by pushing a button on her belly and pulling on the growing section of hair. Turning a knob on her back could make her hair shorter again. Crissy was available starting in 1969 and continued to be sold through 1974. She was available again as Magic Hair Crissy in 1977. During the years she was made, many different versions of Crissy were produced along with a whole host of growing hair friends to go with her. Crissy's cousin Velvet came after Crissy and today she is the second most common doll to find in the line next to Crissy. Velvet's little sister Cinnamon is also fairly common. Some of the more difficult members of the Crissy family to find are Tressy, Dina, Mia, Kerry, Brandy, Cricket, and any of the black versions of the dolls in the line. Overall, Crissy enjoyed a relatively long market life for a doll. Because of her popularity years ago, she is relatively easy to find today. Due to the large number of dolls sold in the 1970s, the standard Crissy doll is easily found as low as **$20.00 – 25.00** at many doll shows, and often times even lower at flea markets and yard sales.

Crissy: 18" standard Crissy and a black version of Movin' Groovin' Crissy. The difference between the standard Crissy doll and the Movin' Groovin' Crissy is that the latter had a jointed waist. Both the standard and Movin' Groovin' white version dolls have red hair, while the black versions of the dolls came with black hair. The dolls have eyes that open and close. Crissy is marked, "©1968/IDEAL TOY CORP/GH-17-H129" on her head and "1969/IDEAL-TOY-CORP./GH-18/US PAT. # 3.162.976" on her lower body. Movin' Groovin' Crissy is marked, "©1968/IDEAL TOY CORP/GH-17H-129" on her head, "©1971/IDEAL TOY CORP/MG-18/US. PAT. 3.162.976/OTHER.PAT.PEND." on her back and "©1971/IDEAL TOY CORP/MG-18/2M-53 18-02/2" on her lower body. Standard white Crissy: **$25.00 – 35.00**. Standard black Crissy: **$80.00 – 125.00**. Movin' Groovin' Crissy white version: **$35.00 – 40.00**. Movin' Groovin' Crissy black version: **$100.00 – 135.00**.

Velvet: Like Crissy, cousin Velvet came in a number of different versions. From left to right is the standard version of Velvet. She is wearing a dress made of velvet material which earlier version dolls wore. The center doll is wearing a dress made with corduroy material, which later Velvet dolls wore. The doll on the right is Movin' Groovin' Velvet. Standard Velvet: **$25.00 – 35.00**. Movin' Groovin' Velvet: **$35.00 – 40.00**.

Crissy and Friends: From left to right are Brandi, Kerry, a standard Crissy doll shown wearing her original turquoise satin mini dress that the later dolls came issued in, and Talky Crissy. 17½" Brandi has painted eyes and is marked, "©1972/IDEAL TOY CORP/GHB-18-H-185/HONG KONG" on her head and "©1971/IDEAL.TOY.CORP./MG-18/US.PAT.3.162.976/OTHER.PAT.PEND. HONG KONG.P" on her back. 18" Kerry is marked, "©1970/IDEAL TOY CORP/NGH-18-H-172/HONG KONG" on her head and "1969/IDEAL TOY CORP/GH-18/US PAT 3,162,976" on her hip. Talky Crissy is marked, "©1968/IDEAL TOY CORP./GH-17-H129" on her head and "©1972/IDEAL TOY CORP./U.S.PAT 3 162 976/OTHER PATENTS PENDING" on her hip. MIB Brandi: **$100.00 – 150.00.** MIB Kerry: **$100.00 – 150.00.** MIB Crissy: **$65.00 – 80.00.** MIB Talky Crissy: **$75.00 – 90.00.** Courtesy Janet & Mike Lawrence.

Crissy and Friends: Ideal's growing hair dolls model some of their fashions. From left to right: Velvet wearing Dandy Denims and Brandi in Funky Feathers. Back row: Velvet wearing Loverly, Tressy in Grape Drape, Crissy in The Peace Poncho, Brandi wearing The Burlap Bag, and Crissy wearing Turned On Mini. Old store stock of Crissy and Velvet outfits often turn up on the secondary market. It isn't unusual in some areas to still find MOC outfits available for as low as **$15.00 – 20.00** each and boxed outfits **$20.00 – 25.00**, while in other areas where they are not as readily available outfits run closer to **$25.00 – 45.00** each. Courtesy Janet & Mike Lawrence.

Cinnamon: 13½" Cinnamon from the Crissy line was originally just called Velvet's Little Sister but was later named Cinnamon. She is marked, "52/©1971/IDEAL TOY
CORP./6H-12-H-188/HONG KONG" on her head and
"©1972/ IDEAL TOY CORP./U.S.PAT 3.162.976/OTHER
PAT.PEND/HONG KONG P." on her back. Cinnamon's
orange polka-dot outfit also came in a variation of the one
shown in the photo. It did not have the white ribbon belt,
but had a white eyelet trimmed collar with a green bow
instead of the white eyelet trim around the neck and arms
like the one shown. MIB: **$50.00 – 75.00**. **Tara:** Although
nowhere on the box does it mention her being a friend of
Crissy or Velvet, most collectors lump this 15½" doll with the
Crissy growing hair family. Tara was issued in 1976 when
Baby Crissy was the only growing hair family member being
sold. Tara is marked, "IDEAL TOY CORP/H-250/HONG
KONG" on her head and "©1970 /IDEAL TOY CORP/GH-
15/2M 5169-01" on her lower body. MIB: **$100.00 –
150.00**. Courtesy Janet & Mike Lawrence.

Baby Crissy: Baby Crissy, a chubby 24" baby version of Crissy with red "growing" hair, was issued
starting in 1973 and continued through 1977. In
the 1980s and 1990s Baby Crissy was reincarnated
when Tyco, the company who obtained the rights
to Ideal dolls, issued a similar doll with a growing
hair feature using the Baby Crissy name. 24" Baby
Crissy is marked, "©1972/IDEAL TOY CORP./2M-
5511/B or GHB-H-225" on her back. The doll in
the photo has been redressed. Redressed: **$35.00
– 45.00**.

Magic Hair Crissy: In 1977 the 18" Crissy tried to make a comeback as Magic Hair Crissy. She no longer had the growing hair feature that was the signature item of the line, but instead came with five hairpieces to change her hairstyle. Her face took on a more sophisticated look than the earlier Crissy dolls. The 18" doll is marked, "©1977/IDEAL TOY CORP./M.H.C.-19-H-281/HONG KONG" on her head and "©1974/IDEAL/HOLLIS, N.Y.11423/2M-5854-01/1" on her lower body. MIB: **$65.00 – 90.00.** Courtesy Marcia Fanta.

Diana Ross: 18" doll of singer Diana Ross made with the Crissy mold. NRFB: **$350.00 – 500.00.** Courtesy Nancy Schwartz/Treasures.

Harmony: 21" tall "music-making" doll. "Harmony's battery-operated amplifier plugs into her back and when a record is placed inside the amplifier, Harmony's arms and head move. She is marked, "H-200/©1971 IDEAL" (Ideal is circled) on her head and "©1972 IDEAL TOY CORP." on her back. On the left Harmony wears Rehearsal Rags (missing neck scarf) and on the right she is wearing her original outfit. MIB: **$75.00 – 100.00.** Courtesy Janet & Mike Lawrence.

Flatsys

Flatsy dolls came in four sizes; 2½", 4¼", 4¾" and 8½". The 4¾" size Flatsys are the most common ones. Originally each poseable 4¾" vinyl Flatsy doll came packaged like a 3-D picture. The doll and his or her accessories were mounted on an illustrated cardboard backing, and the set was framed with a plastic picture frame. The frame was placed in a cardboard base with the Flatsy name on it, and both frame and base were sealed with cellophane. Some of the same Flatsy dolls that appeared in picture frames later were issued mounted on the cardboard background without the frame and packaged inside a white cardboard box instead of shrink-wrapped with the cardboard base. Some of the dolls that came in frames were also issued inside oval lockets without their accessories. Loose Flatsy dolls general run only about **$5.00 – 15.00** each. Dolls in frames with all the accessories values vary from **$35.00 – 95.00** depending on rarity of the set.

Judy Flatsy: Judy Flatsy shown in her original frame with the cardboard base. Judy is marked like all the 4¾" Flatsy dolls, "IDEAL/©1969/PAT.PEND./HONG KONG" on her back. NRFP: **$55.00 – 70.00**. Courtesy S. DeDivitis.

Dewie Flatsy: One of the more common 4¾" Flatsys is Dewie, shown here in her original frame. In frame/no cardboard base: **$30.00 – 40.00**.

Rally Flatsy: Rally is considered a common Flatsy and is usually not difficult to find. Without cardboard frame underneath and no cellophane: **$30.00 – 40.00**.
Courtesy S. DeDivitis.

Dewie Flatsy: Dewie packaged inside a locket instead of in a frame with her accessories. The doll's name does not appear anywhere on the packaging. It is believed that leftover stock may have been used in the Flatsy lockets, and Ideal randomly used whichever Flatsy doll happened to be left over. NRFP: **$25.00 – 35.00**. Courtesy S. DeDivitis.

Casey Flatsy: Ideal also packaged their Flatsy dolls in boxes rather than in a shrink-wrapped plastic frame with a cardboard base. These dolls have been dubbed as "white box Flatsys" by collectors. MIB: **$30.00 – 45.00**. Courtesy S. DeDivitis.

Funny Little Flatsy Dolls . . .
You Can Wash and Comb Their Hair

1 to **6** THE FLATSY DOLL. Comes mounted in picture frame suitable for wall or table-top display—when removed 4½ in. high plastic doll is poseable. Each has long, shiny rooted hair that can be combed. Outfits are interchangeable. A fun self-standing accessory is provided with each. Plastic adapter clips included so dolls may be worn anywhere.

[1] Rally Flatsy. In a driving ensemble. With car.
X 921-2887 A—Shipping weight 0.75 lb....... 2.44
[2] Filly Flatsy. In a riding outfit. With horse.
X 921-2895 A—Shipping weight 0.75 lb........ 2.44
[3] Dewie Flatsy. Pulls little wagon with kitten.
X 921-2945 A—Shipping weight 0.75 lb........ 2.44
[4] Nancy Flatsy. Wheels a carriage containing sister.
X 921-3067 A—Shipping weight 0.75 lb........ 2.44
[5] Candy Flatsy. Celebrates. With table, 2 chairs.
X 921-3273 A—Shipping weight 0.75 lb........ 2.44
[6] Cookie Flatsy. Chef's outfit. With stove.
X 921-3430 A—Shipping weight 0.75 lb........ 2.44

*Buy any 2 Flatsys for 4.50: Choose any 2 dolls. *State catalog number of each on same order blank.*

Flatsies Town House with pop-up floor and furnishings

7 TOWN HOUSE FOR FLATSY DOLLS. Oblong shape—perfect home setting for the little Flatsy People. Two floors, and two see-through windows with a Flatsy doll in each. Pop-up floors and furnishings. Sturdy vinyl construction in bright colors. Brass-plated steel turn lock. 18½ in. high.
X 921-5120 A—Shipping weight 2 lbs. 5.99

Kozmic Kiddles are out of this world

8 to **10** KOZMIC KIDDLES. 2-in. high. While riding in their own roll-along space ships, they jiggle and swivel—heads bob up and down and eyes jiggle. Kiddles can be removed from shape and played with. At night their heads glow in the dark. Sturdy plastic.
[8] Greenie-Meenie. Shipping weight 0.50 lb.
X 921-4610 A............. .... 1.77
[9] Bluey-Blooper. Shipping weight 0.50 lb
X 921-5062 A. 1.77
[10] Purple-Gurple. Shipping weight 0.50 lb.
X 921-5070 A........... . ... 1.77

Flavor-Scented Kiddle Kones

11 to **13** KIDDLE KONES. 2-in. high kiddles in a transparent plastic ice cream cone. Removable kiddles are vinyl, with rooted hair that may be combed. Costume colors correspond to flavor themes. From Hong Kong. Shipping weight 0.70 lb.
X 921-3976 A —[11]. Tutti-Frutti Kone........... 1.77
X 921-3463 A—[12]. Orange-Ice Kone. 1.77
X 921-3547 A —[13]. Frosty-Mint Kone 1.77

Flavor-Scented Lolli-Kiddles

14 to **16** LOLLI-KIDDLES. 2-in. high. Luscious-smelling, flavor-scented kiddles in a transparent plastic lollipop. Kiddles are vinyl with rooted hair that may be combed. Bright, cheerful costumes in colors to correspond to flavor themes. Kiddles can be removed from pop.
[14] Lolli-Grape. Shipping weight 0.70 lb.
X 921-4107 A. 1.77
[15] Lolli-Mint. Shipping weight 0.70 lb.
X 921-4511 A.................... ...... 1.77
[16] Lolli-Lemon. Shipping weight 0.70 lb.
X 921-4222 A................................ 1.77

**Buy any 3 kiddles for 5.00. Choose any 3 and *state catalog number of each on same order blank.*

2⁴⁴ each, any 2 for 4⁵⁰*

7 5⁹⁹

1⁷⁷ Each, any 3 for 5⁰⁰**

1969 J.C. Penney's Christmas catalog page shows six of the 4¾" Flatsy dolls available that year: Rally, Filly, Dewie, Nancy, Candy, and Cookie. ©1978, JCPenney Catalog, J.C. Penney Company, Inc. Used by permission.

122

Kookie Flatsy: Another hard-to-find Flatsy, especially in her original frame. In frame: **$85.00 – 100.00**. Courtesy S. DeDivitis

Grandma Baker: From the Flatsyville series of Flatsys, Grandma Baker came in a frame shaped like a Cape Cod house. The dolls from this series were not available as long as the ones in the standard picture frames, so consequently are much harder to find. In frame with cardboard base: **$80.00 – 95.00**. Courtesy S. DeDivitis.

Spinderella Flatsy: This doll, unlike other Flatsys, came in a clear plastic dome. A pull string started her base to spin so she could "dance." Spinderella Flatsys came in yellow, pink, and green versions as well as blue. Doll in photo is missing her tutu and hair ornaments. Doll with dome case: **$35.00 – 50.00**. Courtesy Robin Englehart.

Candy Mountain Flatsy: The doll in the photo is called Cornball from the Candy Mountain series of Flatsy dolls. At one time all the dolls from this series were hard to find, but in 1997/1998 a large amount of never-sold store stock of Cornball started appearing on the collectibles market, so the value of this doll has come down a little. Although the card mentions her car, the majority of the old store stock that has turned up does not include the car, nor are there any holes on the card where the car would have been mounted. Other examples of Cornball on her card with her orange car have been found as well but are less common. Even more examples of old stock have turned up with Cornball mounted on a smaller card minus the "and her car" printing on it. The three other Candy Mountain Flatsys include Scoop with pink hair, Fizzy with blue hair, and Creamy with purple hair. Unless a large amount of old stock of these three dolls has turned up since the printing of this book, they are considerably harder to find than Cornball. Cornball MOC without car: **$20.00 – 25.00**. MOC with car: **$25.00 – 35.00**.

Fashion Flatsy Gwen: Fashion Flatsys were the tallest of the Flatsy dolls. Each Fashion Flatsy came dressed in one of three different outfits. Here 8½" Gwen is shown wearing Blazer Suit. NRFP: **$45.00 – 65.00**. Courtesy Sharon Wendrow/Memory Lane.

Fashion Flatsy Ali: 12" Flatsy doll shown wearing Knit Mini. NRFP: **$45.00 – 65.00**.
Courtesy Sharon Wendrow/Memory Lane.

Fashion Flatsy: Four Fashion Flatsy dolls shown in the different outfits they came in. NRFP: **$45.00 – 65.00** each. 1970 Sears Christmas catalog.

2½-inch tall Mini-Flatsys **$3**⁸⁷ 2 dolls
live in plastic clock with clock

(9 thru 11) Lovable vinyl
Flatsys have clips on their
backs so you can wear them.
Clocks have movable hands.

10 Mini Play Time. 2 girls,
pony and cart with
wheels that move.
49N37052-Wt. 1 lb. 4 oz.. $3.87

9 Mini Slumber Time. 2
girls with double deck
beds and ladder.
49N37054-Wt. 1 lb. 4 oz.. $3.87

11 Mini Munch Time. Boy
and girl with roll-about
hot dog stand.
49N37053-Wt. 1 lb. 4 oz.. $3.87

Mini Flatsy: Three different sets of the 2½"
Mini Flatsy dolls: Slumber Time, Play Time
and Munch Time. NRFP: **$50.00 – 85.00**
each. *1970 Sears Christmas catalog.*

Flatsy: Four different sizes of Flatsy
dolls: Fashion Flatsy Cory, Candy, Baby
Flatsy, and Slumber Time Mini Flatsy.
The three smaller sized dolls are
marked, "IDEAL/©1969/PAT.PEND./
HONG KONG" on their backs and the
8½" doll is marked, "IDEAL/©1969/U.S.
PATENT/No. 3500578/HONG KONG"
on her back Loose dolls/no accessories:
$5.00 – 15.00 each.

Belly Button Baby: These 9" dolls have a push button on their stomachs that makes their arms, legs, and heads move. The black doll on the left is marked, "©1970/IDEAL TOY CORP./E9-2-H165/HONG KONG" on her neck. The white doll is marked, "©1970/IDEAL TOY CORP./E9-1-H164/HONG KONG" on her neck. Both are marked, "IDEAL TOY CORP/HONG KONG/2A-0156" on their backs. **$20.00 – 25.00** each.

Belly Button Baby: A Belly Button Baby is shown in the original box. Same markings as white doll above. MIB: **$30.00 – 45.00**.

Patti Playful: A soft bodied 16" doll that had a handle in the back that you squeezed to make her open and close her mouth to feed her. Patti Playful was available in 1973, but two years earlier the same doll was issued with short orange curly hair as Patti Partridge, a doll billed as Tracy Partridge's doll from the Partridge Family. Patti Playful is marked, "©1970/IDEAL TOY CORP./LL-16-H-162" on her head. **$25.00 – 35.00**.

Rub-A-Dub Dolly: 17" heavy vinyl doll originally came dressed in a diaper and terry cloth cover-up. She had a tugboat shaped "shower" that she could bathe in. Several outfits were sold separately for her. Rub-A-Dub Dolly is marked, "1973/IDEAL TOY CORP./RAD-16-H-233" on the head and "©1973/IDEAL TOY CORP./RAD-16-B-49" on the body. Loose and nude: **$15.00 – 20.00**.

Tiffany Taylor and Tuesday Taylor

These dolls both have scalps that rotate to change them from brunettes to blondes. 18" Tiffany Taylor was available in a black version as well as the white version. The black version of 11½" Tuesday Taylor was given the name Taylor Jones, even though the two dolls were essentially the same. Other versions of Tuesday Taylor included Suntan Tuesday Taylor, Tuesday Taylor Beauty Queen, and Tuesday Taylor Super Model.

Tiffany Taylor 18" and **Tuesday Taylor** 11½" as brunettes. Tuesday's clothing is not original. Tiffany is marked, "©1973 IDEAL/CG-19-H-230/HONG KONG" on her head and "©1974 IDEAL/ HOLLIS N.Y. 11423/2M-5854-01/1" on her lower body. Tuesday is marked, "©1975/IDEAL/H-248/HONG KONG" on her head and "©1975/Ideal/U.S. Pat No. 399903640/HOLLIS N.Y. 11423/HONG KONG P" on her lower body. Tiffany: **$20.00 – 45.00**. Tuesday with original clothing: **$10.00 – 25.00**.

Tiffany Taylor and Tuesday Taylor as blondes.

Tuesday Taylor Beauty Queen: 11½" Tuesday Taylor as a beauty queen. NRFB: **$45.00 – 50.00.** Courtesy Sharon Wendrow/Memory Lane.

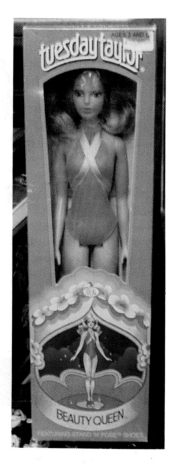

Suntan Dodi: 9" member from the Suntan line of dolls. Put her in the sun and she tanned within minutes; take her out of the sun and she returned to normal. For added effect, she came with "doodles" to give her a tattooed tan. Suntan Dodi is marked, "©1964/IDEAL TOY CORP./D0-9-E" on her head, "©1977 IDEAL ©circled)/HOLLIS N.Y. 11423" on one side of hip, and "HONG KONG P" on her other hip. NRFB: **$45.00 – 50.00.**

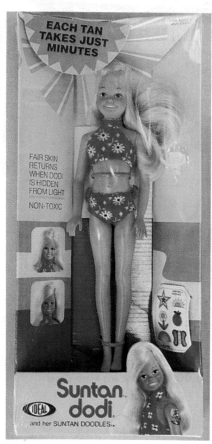

Jody, An Old Fashioned Girl: 9" doll with ankle-length red hair. From left to right, Jody is shown wearing Party Formal (missing hat), Country Calico, and Gibson Girl (missing hat and belt). Jody could be purchased in any of these three different outfits. Jody is marked, "©1974/IDEAL/9G-H-/241" on her head and "©1974/IDEAL/HONG KONG" with a backwards digit underneath on her back. **$20.00 – 25.00** each.

Jody, An Old Fashioned Girl: Shown with her general store playset. MIB Store: **$25.00 – 30.00.** Courtesy Carla Marie Cross.

Dorothy Hamill: The doll representing Olympic skater Dorothy Hamill used the same body as Tuesday Taylor. She came with a plastic "skating rink" that the doll could spin around on. Dorothy is marked, "©1977 D.H./Ideal/H-282/HONG KONG" on her head and "©1975/Ideal/U.S. Pat No. 399903640/HOLLIS N.Y. 11423/HONG KONG P" on her lower body. **$20.00 – 25.00** without rink.

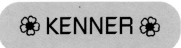

❀ KENNER ❀

Kenner was a division of General Mills Fun Group, Inc. Many Kenner dolls carry the General Mills markings.

Crumpet: 18" doll with jointed wrists and waist. She is battery-operated with a pull-string on her back. She is marked, "1970/KENNER PRODUCTS CO./235-225" on her head and "KENNER/PRODUCTS CO/CINCINNATI, OHIO/PATENT PENDING/MADE IN HONG KONG" on her back. 1971 J.C. Mint with accessories: **$40.00 – 45.00**. ©JCPenney Christmas Catalog, J.C. Penney Company, Inc. Used by permission..

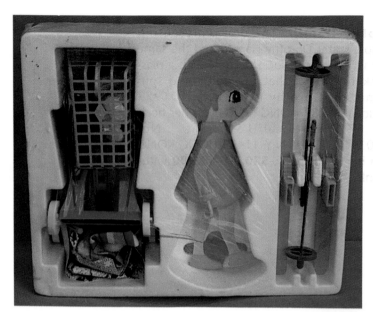

Madcap Molly: Madcap Molly, "the do-it-all-dolly." A plastic wind-up doll from 1971. The 12" pink doll with a hot pink dress and red hair comes with a shopping cart with groceries, a scooter, skis with boots and ski poles, and three different mod style hats. When she is wound, she pushes her cart, skis, walks, or scoots on her scooter. Marks unavailable. MIB: **$75.00 – 85.00.** Doll alone: **$15.00 – 25.00**.

Madcap Molly: Original box lid to Madcap Molly.

Madcap Molly: Photo on side of Madcap Molly's box shows all the accessories in her set.

Gabbigale: 18" doll that repeats what you say. The doll is marked, "©1972/KENNER PRODUCTS CO./16" on her head and "GABBIGALE/1972 KENNER PRODUCTS/GENERAL MILLS/FUN GROUP INC./PATENTS PENDING"on her back. MIB: **$35.00 – 55.00.**
Courtesy Marcia Fanta.

Blythe: An unusual 11" doll with an overly large plastic head on a petite vinyl body. There is an 8" long pull ring coming from her head that when pulled changes her eye color. Eyes can be changed to four different colors. In the photo the doll is shown with green eyes. Blythe is marked, "Blythe ©/KENNER PRODUCTS/CINCINNATI, OHIO/©1972 GENERAL MILLS/FUN GROUP INC./PATENT PENDING/MADE IN HONG KONG" on her back. **$400.00 – 700.00.**

Blythe: Same doll shown with blue, orange, and pink eyes.

Blythe: A blond Blythe shown in her original box. MIB: **$3,000.00 – 4,000.00.** Courtesy Robin Englehart/Photo by Nancy Jean Mong.

Blythe: Back of Blythe's box showing dolls with different hair colors, different original styles of dresses, and some of the fashions sold separately. Courtesy Robin Englehart/Photo by Nancy Jean Mong.

Blythe: Blythe with dark brunette hair. In the front are two wigs sold separately for her. MIB: **$1,200.00 – 1,500.00.** Courtesy Robin Englehart/Photo by Nancy Jean Mong.

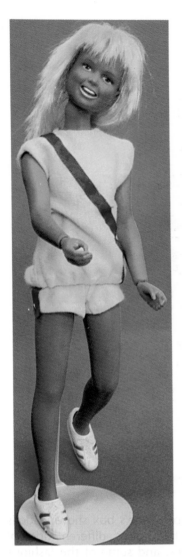

Dusty: An action-oriented fashion doll, Dusty was touted as a sports superstar. The 11½" doll has a jointed waist that when turned swivels quickly back, allowing her to swing a bat, a tennis racket, or other sporting equipment. Her jointed hands are cupped to grasp items, and she has bendable knees and elbows. Fashions for Dusty included outfits for tennis, golf, volleyball, softball, gymnastics, and skiing. Dusty was sold in either a swimsuit or a sporting outfit. She is marked, "185/©G.M.F.G.I." on her head and "©1974G.M.F.G.I. KENNER PROD./CINCINNATI, OHIO 45202/"DUSTY"/MADE IN HONG KONG" on her lower back. The doll in the photo has been redressed. Redressed: **$15.00 – 20.00.**

Dusty: Some of the outfits and accessories available for Dusty are shown in this 1975 Montgomery Ward Christmas catalog.

The Six Million Dollar Man/The Bionic Woman

The television show *The Six Million Dollar Man,* staring Lee Majors as Steve Austin, spawned a doll and a whole line of adventure play sets. Oscar Goldman, Steve Austin's boss on the show, and Maskatron, Steve Austin's robot enemy of many disguises, were two characters on the show also made into dolls. *The Bionic Woman* was a spin-off show from *The Six Million Dollar Man,* featuring Lindsay Wagner as Bionic Woman Jaime Sommers. Soon after the spin-off show hit television, Jaime Sommers dolls hit the toy shelves, followed by a host of playsets for the doll.

Six Million Dollar Man: A 13" doll made in the image of actor Lee Majors who played the character of Steve Austin on the television program *The Six Million Dollar Man.* The doll in the photo is wearing his Mission to Mars spacesuit. He is marked, "©1975 GENERAL MILLS FUN/ GROUP, INC. BY ITS DIVISION/ KENNER PRODUCTS, CINCINNATI/OHIO 45202 CAT. NO. 65000/MADE IN HONG KONG/ Character: /©Universal City Studios,/Inc. 1973/All rights reserved" on his back. **$20.00 – 30.00. Maskatron:** Steve Austin's enemy of many disguises is wearing a face mask to disguise himself as Steve's boss, Oscar Goldman. The 13" doll is marked, "B" on his head and, "©1976 G.M.F.G.I. KENNER PROD./CINCINNATI OHIO 45202/CAT.NO. 65600/MADE IN HONG KONG/ CHARACTER: /©UNIVERSAL CITY STUDIOS, INC. 1973/ALL RIGHTS RESERVED" on the inside of the compartment cover on his back. The doll came with three removable plastic face masks. The Maskatron in the photo has been redressed. **$45.00 – 65.00. Bionic Woman:** A 12½" doll made in the image of actress Lindsay Wagner. The doll is marked, "©GENERAL MILLS FUN GROUP INC. 1976 BY ITS DIV. KENNER PRODUCTS/CINCINNATI OHIO 45202/ NO. 65900/MADE IN HONG KONG/ Character: /©Universal City Studios,/Inc. 1974/All rights reserved" on her back. **$20.00 – 30.00.**

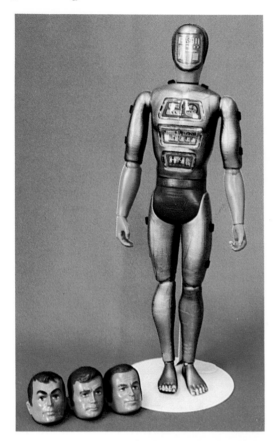

Maskatron: Shown with his three removable masks. The doll also features removable arms and legs. This doll is more difficult to find than the Six Million Dollar Man or Oscar Goldman dolls. Loose with three masks: **$45.00 – 65.00**.

Oscar Goldman: Oscar Goldman was the boss of Steve Austin, the Six Million Dollar Man. Doll is shown in his original box. MIB: **$45.00 – 65.00**.

Darci: In 1978 Kenner introduced their 12½" fashion model doll. She came in three hair colors: brunette, blond, and red. A host of outfits were available for Darci. Her friends included Dana (African-American) and Erica (red head). MIB: **$75.00 – 100.00** each.

Dana: Darci's 12½" friend Dana. Dana is marked, "HONG KONG/©G.M.F.G.I.1978" on her head and "©G.M.F.G.I.1978/ KENNER:CIN'TI.,O./ #47000:MADEINHONGKONG" on her back. MIB: **$100.00 – 125.00**.

Darci: Close-up of brunette Darci. She is marked, "115 (some dolls don't have this number)/HONG KONG/©G.M.F.G.I.1978" on her head and "©G.M.F.G.I.1978/ KENNER:CIN'TI.,O./#47000:MADEIN-HONGKONG" on her back. She is wearing a Darci fashion called Autumn Days. Loose and dressed in Darci fashion: **$25.00 – 40.00**.

Dana: Close-up of Darci's friend Dana.

❁ KNICKERBOCKER TOY COMPANY ❁

Holly Hobbie: Starting in 1974 Holly Hobbie captured the hearts of both children and adults. Everything from tote bags to bedspreads were made bearing the image of the popular Holly Hobbie. This 1977 J.C. Penney Christmas catalog shows four different sizes of Holly Hobbie rag dolls available that year along with a 16" Baby Holly Hobbie. The rag dolls are tagged on their dresses, "The Original/HOLLY HOBBIE(/copyright ©AMERICAN GREETINGS CORPORATION/ALL NEW MATERIALS/COTTON AND SYNTHETIC FIBERS" on one side and "KTE/KNICKERBOCKER/KNICKERBOCKER TOY COMPANY, INC./MIDDLESEX, NJ 08846 U.S.A./MADE IN TAIWAN, REPUBLIC OF CHINA." **$15.00 – 35.00** each. ©JCPenney Christmas Catalog, J.C. Penney Company, Inc. Used by permission.

Sunbonnet Babies: May, Molly, and Mandy were issued at a time when the television series *Little House on the Prairie* was airing on T.V. and the "prairie" look was in. The Sunbonnet Babies seemed to be a knockoff of Knickerbocker's own Holly Hobbie doll. The 6½" dolls are marked, "MADE IN TAIWAN/1975" on their heads and "K N I C K E R B O C K E R / T O Y CO.INC.1975/ MADE IN TAIWAN" on their backs. MIB: **$20.00 – 25.00** each.

Carrie: This doll is Carrie, Laura Ingalls' little sister from the television series *Little House on the Prairie*. The 12" doll is marked, "1978 ED FRIENDLY PRODUCTIONS, INC./LIC JLM/MADE IN TAIWAN T-2" on her head. The doll is missing her original apron. **$15.00 – 25.00**.

❀ LIBBY ❀

I Dream of Jeannie: 20" plastic and vinyl doll portraying actress Barbara Eden who played the part of Jeannie in the television series, *I Dream of Jeannie*. The doll in this photo is wearing a reproduction of the original outfit. The doll is marked, "4/1966/Libby" on her head. **$75.00 – 125.00**. Courtesy Elaine McGrath.

❀MANUFACTURER UNKNOWN❀

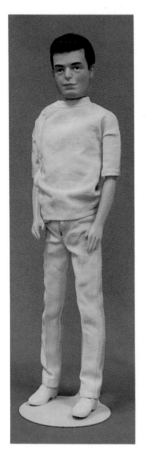

Ben Casey: This unmarked 12" doll represents the television character Dr. Ben Casey played by Vincent Edwards. He originally came wearing white scrub pants and white shoes similar to the ones shown. The mark on his original shirt has faded but should read "BEN CASEY" and underneath "M.D." on either side of a medical insignia. **$75.00 – 95.00**.

Bride, trunk, 3-pc. outfit

$4⁹⁹

11½-inch bride with embroidered bridal gown plus 3 complete changes: robe, party dress and sport outfit. Jointed plastic. Trunk has plastic handle.
Shpg. wt. 2 lbs. 8 oz.
49 N 3873.....$4.99

Teenage Doll, trunk, outfit

$4⁹⁹

12-in. doll with rooted hair. Plastic. Wears shoes, multicolor print dress. 4 extra outfits: sport outfit, street dress, afternoon dress, playsuit. With trunk. Wt. 2 lbs. 8 oz.
49 N 3874.....$4.99

Ben Casey and Nurse

$4³⁷

12-in. Ben has stethoscope, intern's outfit. 11½-in. nurse wears dress, cap, cape. Plastic. Movable arms, legs, head. Each can wear clothes of like-size dolls.
Shpg. wt. 1 lb. 4 oz.
49 N 3957.....$4.37

Debbie Drake does exercises

$2⁸⁴

11½-inch plastic doll assumes almost any pose. She's fully jointed, amazingly flexible. Has leotard, just like the real Debbie. Can wear clothes of like-size doll. Wt. 12 oz.
49 N3958.....$2.84

32 SEARS ᴾᶜᴮᴰᴸ

Ben Casey: The 1963 Sears Christmas catalog shows the Ben Casey doll available in a set with a nurse doll, but he may have been available separately as well.

Pollyana: This 28" doll represents the character Pollyana based on the Disney movie of the same name. The doll has a vinyl head and plastic torso and limbs. Markings on this particular doll are hard to read but are something like, "V <illegible> F/2 0" on her head. **$100.00 – 125.00**.

Susie Sad Eyes: Many people may recognize the face on this doll but do not know the name. A large number of these inexpensive dolls were sold in the 1960s/1970s. She was sold as Susie Sad Eyes and her original box says, "Made exclusively for S. Rosenberg Co. Inc." She came in a number of different outfits, but the most common ones seem to be dresses in various colors and fabrics similar in style to the dress the doll on the left in the photo is wearing. Susie was also sold wearing a rain coat, hat, and boots and was called Susie Slicker, and her box read, "Made by Fun-World, Inc." Another example of Susie Sad Eyes discovered was a doll wearing a banner that read, "Valentine Susie Sad Eyes by Whitman;" most likely the doll was sold with Whitman's Valentine candy. It is possible Susie Sad Eyes was produced by a company which sold the doll to other companies to dress and use as their own. A common problem with many of the Susie Sad Eye dolls is that the vinyl of their heads discolors to a white or greenish color. Other examples of the dolls seem to retain their coloring. Just a few years ago, these dolls had little value because they are of inferior quality, and they are easily found. However, a small following of collectors feel the dolls were modeled after or inspired by the work of artist Margret Keane, famous for her big-eyed children portraits which were especially popular in the 1960s. Because of recent interest by Keane collectors in these dolls, values are just starting to rise. 8" Susie Sad Eyes is marked, "L. (bell shaped design) B./915/66 A/MADE IN HONG KONG" on her head and "MADE IN HONG KONG" on her back. The doll on the right has been redressed. In original clothing: **$15.00 – 25.00**.

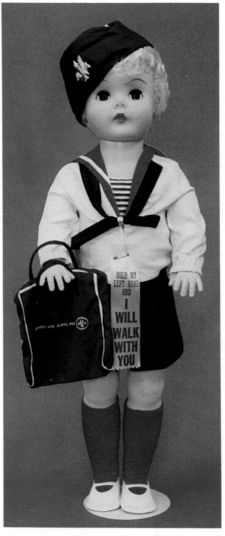

Unknown doll: This 35" walking doll could be the product of Uneeda or Natural Doll Company. She is marked, "U/14" on her head. Her banner reads, "I WALK WHEN YOU HOLD MY LEFT ARM/'IT'S A NATURAL'." Her hair is an unusual combination of white and purple. She originally came in an unmarked brown cardboard box. Although many of the large-sized dolls from well-known manufacturers like Ideal or Horsman are often valued in the **$200.00 – 400.00** price range, large-sized dolls from lesser-known companies or unknown manufacturers are easily found priced under $65.00. Dressed in original clothing: **$35.00 – 65.00.**

Unknown doll: This unmarked, all-original walking doll is a bit of a novelty. She is dressed in Mattel's Charmin' Chatty's original outfit (with the exception of her shoes) as well as an American Airlines bag and a hat which is stapled onto her head, both of which came in the highly valued Charmin' Chatty "Let's Talk 'N Travel in Foreign Lands" giftset. A "Hold My Left Hand and I Will Walk With You" tag has been added to the outfit. Mattel's Charmin' Chatty clothing tag has been cut out of the dress, with just the ends remaining, confirming that it was indeed Charmin' Chatty's outfit and not a reproduction. The 22" doll is marked, "4577/K9" on her neck. It is possible that this doll was sold by a company other than Mattel using remaining stock of their Charmin' Chatty clothing some time after Charmin' Chatty was no longer available on the market or it may have been a promotional doll sold or given away by American Airlines. In a case like this, the clothing is actually worth more than the doll. Normally an unknown plastic doll like this would be worth around **$10.00 – 15.00** but the clothing alone can be worth from **$30.00** to as much as **$100.00** depending on if it is sold as a set or individually piece-by-piece to Chatty collectors. Courtesy Gloria Telep.

Wee Three Yacht Club: More than likely these dolls were modeled after Mattel's popular Sunshine Family. The arms of the dolls and the jointed legs are similar to the Sunshine Family dolls. The father is 9", the mother is 8", and the baby is 2½". The father and mother are marked, "HONG KONG" on their backs. The baby is unmarked. The back of the vinyl case reads, "©/DESIGNED SPECIALLY FOR F.W. WOOLWORTH/ALL COPY RIGHTS RESERVED - "HUNTER/"DIST. BY F.W. WOOLWORTH CO., NEW YORK, N.Y. 10007/MADE IN HONG KONG". Mint in case: **$25.00 – 30.00**.

❀ MARX TOYS/LOUIS MARX & CO. ❀

Louis Marx founded his toy company in the 1920s. Under his direction the company prospered and became one of the largest toy companies in existence. In the 1960s, Louis Marx & Co., Inc. put out numerous playsets, mostly geared for young boys, but Marx also manufactured dolls during this time.

Miss Seventeen: This plastic doll came in 11", 15", and 18" sizes and was issued with black, brunette, blond, or red hair. Miss Seventeen has molded earrings, which are painted black. Shown here is the 18" size. She is marked, "U.S. PATENT 2925684/BRITISH PATENT 804566/MADE IN HONG KONG" on her back. She is missing the trophy she originally came with. **$85.00 – 135.00**.

Miss Seventeen: A 15" Miss Seventeen in her original box. She is wearing one of the outfits sold separately. MIB: **$175.00 – 220.00**. Courtesy Cathy Kidney-Bremner.

Miss Seventeen: A 15" Miss Seventeen beside the 18" size. The 15" doll is missing her robe, banner, crown, and shoes. Both dolls are marked, "U.S. PATENT 2925684/BRITISH PATENT 804566/MADE IN HONG KONG" on their backs. Loose and original either size: **$85.00 – 135.00**.

Jane West: The dolls in the Best of the West line were considered action figures since they were primarily geared for boys who liked to play cowboys and Indians. The female members of the line helped entice girls to play with the figures as well. The Best of the West line was sold from 1973 – 1975. The figures are molded heavy vinyl with pin-jointed limbs and molded-on Western clothing as well as one or two removable pieces of clothing and approximately 20-35 small plastic accessories like guns, campfire cooking equipment, and horse equipment. Some figures could be purchased with or without horses, and horses were available separately as well. Johnny West was the most popular member of the line and the one most collectors are familiar with. Other members include his wife Jane West, his daughter Josie West, his son Jamie West, villain Sam Cobra, Fighting Eagle, Chief Geronimo, Chief Cherokee, Princess Wildflower, Sheriff Garrett, Captain Maddox, scout Bill Buck, trooper Zeb Zachary, and General Custer. Values for any of the dolls increase with condition and the number of accessories included. In the photo is 11" Jane West. She is marked, "MARX TOY/©/MCMLXXIII/MADE IN/U.S.A." in a circle on her back. Her blue skirt is removable, but the rest of her clothing is molded-on. Without accessories: **$20.00 – 25.00**.

Sindy: Originally produced by Pedigree, Britain's top teenage fashion doll never achieved the success in America that she did in other countries. The U.S version of Sindy was manufactured by Marx Toys. Here are three versions of the Marx Sindy doll. All three dolls have both rooted and painted eyelashes. The doll on the right is not wearing an original Sindy skirt, but the other two dolls are in their original outfits. The dolls are marked, "2 GEN 1077//033055X" on their heads and "Made in Hong Kong" on their backs. See Pedigree for other Sindy dolls. **$25.00 – 30.00** each.

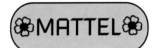

❀MATTEL❀

Barbie

No doll book from this era would be complete without including Barbie and her friends since these dolls were important in the lives of so many young children growing up in the 1960s and 1970s. Barbie was patented in 1958 and first came on the market in 1959. The number of different 11½" Barbie dolls manufactured throughout the 1960s and 1970s is very extensive as are the many different friends and family members created for her. People who don't know a lot about vintage Barbie dolls need to be aware that the dates marked on the dolls can be misleading. A large number of dolls have the years 1958 or 1966 on them. These are years that Mattel took out patents for the design of Barbie. Many dolls being made today still carry the 1966 date. Oftentimes people find "1966" Barbie dolls at yard sales for a dollar or less and mistakenly believe they have discovered old Barbie dolls that are worth lots of money. To figure out what year a Barbie doll was actually made requires research and knowledge that can be obtained from reading one or several of the many books on the market devoted solely to Barbie. Of all the dolls from the 1960s – 1970s era, Barbie dolls are the hardest to determine values for. The selling prices of similar dolls from source to source can vary hundreds of dollars. A little flaw such as a tiny lip rub can distract from value and a virtue such as an unusual hair color can increase value. For these reasons, two similar dolls in seemingly similar condition can be worth very different amounts. It is wise for buyers to shop around a little before purchasing vintage Barbie dolls so they can see the differences in prices and make comparisons.

For those looking to sell Barbie collections, it would be wise to contact several buyers to make offers on the collection. Different people will offer different amounts based on what a collection is worth to them. Keep in mind selling a collection as a whole rarely brings in the same amount you would get if you sold the collection piece-by-piece to individuals. If you are willing to put in the time to try to find the right buyer for each doll and each outfit in the collection, you can expect to get more for it. If you decide to break up the collection and sell it by the piece, it is better if you set prices for each item rather than take offers on them.

Figuring out what to set the prices at involves time and work. First, you need to read several reference books on Barbie dolls to learn as much about them as possible. Second, attend at least one local doll show to see what the asking prices are for some of your dolls or clothing or similar items like you have. Keep in mind what are marked on the items are "asking" prices and doesn't necessarily mean the dealer will get that much for the items. Also, keep in mind the dealer may have the items for years and will take them from show to show before he will sell them at the marked prices. If you don't want to wait that long or are not able to expose your dolls and clothing to that many collectors, you will probably need to price your pieces lower. Last, if possible, talk to several Barbie dealers or collectors to get advice and tips about pricing and/or selling your dolls and clothing.

While many dealers usually don't have the time to give free appraisals to everyone who asks or offer heaps of free advice about selling your Barbie collection (potentially to the same people they are trying to sell to), you will find many dealers are willing to answer a few questions if you approach them politely and don't take up too much of their time.

For those wanting to sell their Barbie dolls, values given here will serve only as a guideline. Again, the value can vary tremendously given every little detail about a particular doll including which version of a doll it is, the hair color, how good the facial makeup is, any flaws, and how the doll is dressed. It is hoped that the photos will help in identifying different Barbie dolls, but because of the large number of factors that come into play when pricing these dolls, the range of values provided is broad.

Barbie: This is the third issue of Barbie, commonly called a #3 Barbie by collectors. Her pale white skin color is common in the first three issues of the Barbie doll. She is shown wearing a Barbie fashion called, "After 5". Originally she came dressed in a black and white striped swimsuit. The doll is marked, "BARBIE™/PATS.PEND./©MC-MLVIII/BY/MATTEL/INC." on her lower body. Doll without outfit: **$500.00 – 800.00.**

Barbie: In 1961 the ponytail Barbie doll was joined by a Barbie with a new hairstyle called a bubble cut. Earlier bubble cut Barbie dolls are marked, "BARBIE®/PATS.PEND./©MCMLVIII/BY/MATTEL/INC." on their lower bodies. Later dolls are marked, "MIDGE™/©1962/BARBIE®/©1958/BY/MATTEL, INC." Available in various shades, loose and nude bubble cut Barbie dolls can range in value from **$75.00 – 250.00** depending on condition and rarity of hair color. Value also depends on what outfit they are wearing, if any. The outfits shown on the dolls here can range from **$25.00** for the Cruise Stripes dress on the right to as much as **$500.00** for the Gold 'n Glamour outfit in the center. Like the dolls themselves, these values for outfits can vary depending on condition and whether or not all the accessories are with the outfits.

Fashion Queen Barbie and Miss Barbie: Fashion Queen Barbie arrived in 1963. She had molded-on hair with a blue headband and was issued with three wigs. Miss Barbie came out in 1964 and was the first Barbie to feature bendable legs and open and shut eyes. She also had molded hair and an orange headband. Like the Fashion Queen Barbie, Miss Barbie came with three wigs. The straight-legged Fashion Queen Barbie is marked, "MIDGE™/"©1962/BARBIE®/©1958/BY/MATTEL, INC./PATENTED" on her lower body (earlier dolls didn't have the "PATENTED" marking). Extra Fashion Queen heads were sold in several accessory packs so children could interchange the heads of their dolls. It's not uncommon to find these extra heads placed on any of the early Barbie bodies, so markings may vary depending on what body the head ended up on. Miss Barbie is marked, "©M.I." on the back of her head and "©1958/MATTEL, INC./U.S. PATENTED/U.S.PAT.PEND." on her lower body. Values for both these dolls vary based on whether or not the dolls have any rubs to the paint on their hair, if their headbands are still attached to their heads, if they have their original swimsuits and wigs, and if Miss Barbie's eyes and bendable knees are in good working order. Wearing original swimsuit and caps (not including wigs or other accessories): Fashion Queen: **$65.00 – 95.00**. Miss Barbie: **$150.00 – 225.00**.

Midge: Beginning in 1963 Barbie's best friend was Midge. She had blue eyes and freckles and came in blond, brunette or red hair (also known as titian). She originally came dressed in a two-piece swimsuit. Midge dolls are marked, "MIDGE™/"©1962/BARBIE®/©1958/BY/MATTEL, INC./PATENTED" on their lower bodies. The dolls shown here are wearing various Barbie fashions. Dolls without fashions: **$45.00 – 75.00**.

Skipper: Barbie's little sister is 9" tall. The earliest straight-legged dolls are marked, "SKIPPER/©1963/MATTEL, INC." on their lower bodies. Later when Skipper's friends Skooter and Ricky used the same body as Skipper's, the "SKIPPER" name was dropped from the markings so later dolls are marked, "©1963/MATTEL, INC." on their lower bodies. Dolls without fashions: **$35.00 – 75.00**.

Francie: Barbie's "MODern" cousin Francie is 10½" and has a body which is shaped differently than Barbie's so that the two dolls couldn't share clothing. Naturally, a whole line of Francie clothing was produced by Mattel for the smaller-sized doll. Like many of the dolls in the Barbie line, Francie came in many different versions. The Francie dolls shown in the photo are a short-haired brunette, a short-haired blond, a straight waist non-bendable knee doll with long brunette hair and a long blond-haired doll with a twist-and-turn waist and bendable knees. The dolls are wearing various Francie fashions. Francie dolls are marked, "©1965/MATTEL, INC./U.S. PATENTED/U.S. PAT.PEND./MADE IN/JAPAN" or "©1965/MATTEL, INC./U.S. PATD./U.S. PAT.PEND./MADE IN JAPAN." Dolls without fashions: **$55.00 – 100.00**.

Barbie: After the "straight-legs/molded lashes" era of Barbie dolls, Barbie got an updated look in 1967 that included long straight hair, bendable legs, twist waist, and rooted eyelashes. This doll is called the Twist 'N Turn Barbie by collectors or referred to by the abbreviated name of TNT Barbie. When Mattel first introduced this new look to Barbie, they offered her for $1.50 with the trade-in of any old Barbie doll. The promotional Barbie with the Twist 'N Turn waist came in the box pictured in the photo, but this same doll was also sold in an open-front box sealed with cellophane. MIB Trade-In Barbie: **$325.00 – 375.00**.

Barbie Friends: Barbie had some famous fashion-doll-sized friends over the years. Her famous friends in the photo include model Twiggy who is the same size as the 10½" Francie doll; 11½" Truly Scrumptious, the character played by Sally Ann Howe from the movie *Chitty Chitty Bang Bang*; and 11½" Julia, representing the nurse played by Diahann Carroll in the television series *Julia*. While not exactly billed as friends of Barbie's at the time, they were sized to share clothing and accessories with the Barbie line of dolls. Values are for dolls with all original clothing: Twiggy: **$85.00 – 150.00**, Truly Scrumptious: **$125.00 – 200.00**, Julia: **$85.00 – 150.00**.

Busy Hands Barbie: Shown here are dolls from the Busy Hands and Talking Busy Hands line of Barbie dolls. Front row left to right: Busy Hands Francie, Busy Hands Barbie, Busy Hands Steffie. Back row: Talking Busy Hands Ken, Talking Busy Hands Barbie, Talking Busy Hands Steffie. When original clothing is missing, value diminishes about 50%. Loose and original: **$65.00 – 125.00** each.

Live Action P.J., Barbie, and Ken On Stage: These dolls were sold either alone or in a "Live Action On Stage" set that included the doll with his or her stage, microphone, and 45rpm record. Live Action Christie (shown here singing backup) was only sold alone, not in an "On Stage" set. The dolls date from 1971. Loose dolls fully dressed without their stages are valued from **$45.00 – 75.00**. Christie is less common than the other three and worth a bit more: **$75.00 – 100.00**. With stage, microphone and record as shown here, P.J.: **$75.00 – 125.00**, Barbie: **$85.00 – 150.00**, Ken: **$65.00 – 95.00**.

Tutti and Todd: These 6½" dolls were Barbie's little sister Tutti and her twin brother Todd. Standard Tutti dolls came in either blond or brunette hair. Dolls were also issued in red (called titian) or black hair but these hair colors were usually reserved for dolls that came in special giftsets and the hair was usually styled differently. Most Todd dolls have titian hair, but some Todd dolls can be found with brunette hair. Both Tutti and Todd were made with the same body mold and have wires inside their arms and legs allowing them to be posed. It's not uncommon to find these wires have broken from overuse or have chemically reacted over the years with the vinyl surrounding it, leaving green stains on the doll and devaluing it. Tutti is much easier to locate than her twin brother since she was available for a longer period of time. Tutti and Todd were reissued and sold in Europe for many years after they were discontinued in the United States. Tutti and Todd are marked, "©1965/MATTEL, INC./JAPAN" on their backs. Tutti: **$30.00 – 50.00.** Todd: **$45.00 – 75.00.**

Chris: One of Tutti's 6½" friends was Chris. She came in blond or brunette hair that sometimes oxidized to an auburn or red color. Her hair was held by a green barrette on one side, and two green hair ribbons tied in bows on both sides held small sections of her long hair. There is sometimes confusion between Chris and Tutti since they have the same bodies and similar hairstyles. The key to telling the two apart is that Chris has brown eyes, while her friend Tutti has blue. Markings are the same as Tutti and Todd's "©1965/MATTEL, INC./JAPAN" on her back. **$45.00 – 75.00.**

Carla: Available only in Europe, this 6½" friend of Tutti's and Todd's has a heavier vinyl body than the Tutti/Todd-type dolls made for the American market. Like all the European Tutti and Todd sized dolls, Carla's limbs don't pose as easily as the U.S. dolls and the vinyl has a shiny look to it. Carla is marked, "©1965/MATTEL, INC./HONG KONG" on her back. **$75.00 – 125.00.**

Nan 'N Fran: There are three different sets of Mattel's Pretty Pairs dolls. These sets consist of a 6½" doll, which used the same head and body molds as Tutti and Todd, and a smaller size doll made using Mattel's Liddle Kiddle head molds. The photo shows Pretty Pairs Nan and her doll Fran. Nan is marked "398" on her head and "©1965/MATTEL, INC./JAPAN" on her back. Her doll Fran is 3½" and is marked, "©M.I." on her head. NRFP: **$200.00 – 295.00**. Courtesy Robin Englehart.

Angie 'N Tangie: Another Pretty Pairs set of dolls. Angie has the same markings on her back as both Nan, Tutti, and Todd. Tangie is marked, "MATTEL, INC." on her head. NRFP: **$200.00 – 295.00**. Courtesy Robin Englehart/Photo by Nancy Jean Mong.

Lori 'N Rori: Pretty Pairs Lori in the photo is missing her original socks and shoes. She has a number or letter under her hairline but is difficult to see. She also has the same Tutti/Todd markings on her back. 3" Rori is marked, "C/103/©M.I." on the back of his head under hat. Loose and all original: **$100.00 – 135.00**. Courtesy Robin Englehart.

SuperSize Barbie: In 1977 an 18" size Barbie was produced called SuperSize Barbie (shown in center). Her original outfit consisted of a white satin and metallic silver swimsuit with a matching long skirt and a pair of white satin slacks with metallic silver trim. The same doll came dressed in a bridal outfit and was issued as a department store special as SuperSize Bridal Barbie. Barbie's black friend Christie was also produced in an 18" "SuperSize" and originally came dressed in a blue version of SuperSize Barbie's original outfit. Christie shown here is redressed in one of the SuperSize fashions, which was sold separately for the 18" dolls. In 1979 an 18" growing hair Barbie was issued called SuperSize Barbie with Super Hair. She came with "Quick Curl" hair that had thin wires throughout that allowed for ease in holding curls. In addition, a long section of hair came out from a hole in the center of her head. This section of hair could be lengthened or shortened with a pull string on the back of her neck. All three dolls are marked, "TAIWAN/©1976 MATTEL INC." on their heads and "©MATTEL INC. 1976/U.S.A." on their backs. SuperSize Barbie and SurperSize Barbie with Super Hair: **$65.00 – 85.00**. SuperSize Christy: **$85.00 – 135.00**.

Chatty Cathy

Chatty Cathy revolutionized the talking toy industry with her pull-string talking mechanism. Following her success, Mattel produced a large number of pull-string talking dolls and toys.

Chatty Cathy: The first Chatty Cathy doll on the market came dressed in this red and white voile sundress with a red sunsuit underneath. The outfit came only on the first issue doll and was never sold separately. While most Chatty Cathy dolls are marked, this first issue doll bears no markings. MIB: **$275.00 – 325.00**.

Chatty Cathy: There are many variations of Chatty Cathy dolls. Variations include the hair length and style, eye color, positioning of fingers, shape of the speaker grill on the stomach, hard or soft vinyl on the doll's head, and lots of other subtle characteristics resulting in a large variety of Chatty Cathy dolls for the collector. Original Chatty clothing adds quite a bit to the value, so when Chatty dolls are not wearing either their original clothes or any Chatty clothing sold separately, the value is approximately half of book value. Here are just four examples of different Chatty dolls and four outfits Chatty Cathy either came in or which were sold separately. From left to right: blond doll with straight fingers and hexagon voice box (missing white eyelet bolero like the one on doll to the right of her, shoes and socks), blond with pointed finger and round covered voice box, brunette with blue eyes and hexagon voice box (missing white eyelet apron like the one on the doll to the right of her), brunette with brown eyes and hexagon voice box (missing shoes and socks). The 20" dolls are marked, "CHATTY CATHY®/PATENTS PENDING/©MCMLX/BY MATTEL, INC./HAWTHORNE, CALIF." on their backs. With tagged Chatty clothing: **$85.00 – 200.00**, lower end if mute, higher end if talking.

Chatty Cathy: Chatty Cathy with pigtails. The two dolls here have hard vinyl heads, but some pigtailed Chatty Cathys have soft vinyl heads. The dolls are marked, "CHATTY CATHY®/©1960/CHATTY BABY™/©1961/ BY MATTEL, INC./U.S.PAT. 3,017,187/OTHER U.S. &/FOREIGN PATS. PEND./PAT'D IN CANADA 1962" on their backs. With original clothing: **$85.00 – 200.00**, lower end if mute, higher end if talking.

I'm Chatty Cathy

I can say 18 different phrases.

Just pull the "Chatty-Ring" and

I'll talk to you

MATTEL

$9⁸⁸ ①

WHERE ARE WE GOING!

Penny plays school .. says 11 instructive phrases

$8⁹⁹ without batteries

She encourages pre-schoolers to learn by saying "What time is it?", "Count to 10", "Say your ABC's", plus 8 other sentences. Just push a button to hear her "hi-fi" voice .. order 1 "D" battery below. 19 in. tall, jointed vinyl, with go-to-sleep eyes, rooted hair. With costume, eyeglasses and diploma.
49 N 3404—Wt. 2 lbs. 10 oz.. $8.99

"D" Battery. Shpg. wt. each 4 oz.
49 N 4660....Each 16c; 4 for 60c

Little Miss Echo repeats all you say to her

$22⁸⁸ cash   without batteries   NO MONEY DOWN

Teach her songs, talk with her. Concealed magnetic tape recorder plays back 25 seconds of conversation. Erases when you record again. Order one 9-volt and 2 "D" batteries below. 30 inches tall. Plastic; jointed arms, legs, head. Rooted saran hair.
79 N 3665CM—Wt. 8 lbs.. $22.88

9-volt Battery. Shpg. wt. 4 oz.
79 N 6417M............Each 45c

"D" Battery. Shpg. wt. each 4 oz.
79 N 4660....Each 16c; 4 for 60c

Chatty Cathy dressed in red velveteen bodice, lacy overskirt

1 She is more talkative, but still the same lovable doll playmate. 20 inches tall, with movable arms, legs; rooted Saran hair in pony tails. Shpg. wt. 3 lbs. 4 oz.
49N3560-White Chatty Cathy..$9.88   49N3561-Colored Chatty Cathy..$9.88

Extra Outfits and Accessories for Chatty Cathy

2 **Sunday Visit Outfit.** Nylon sheer ruffled dress, panties. Shoes, socks.
49 N 3569—Shpg. wt. 8 oz.....$2.97

3 **Playtime Outfit.** Cotton denim shorts, shirt. Striped jacket. Sandals, hat.
49 N 3573—Shpg. wt. 8 oz.......$2.23

4 **Sunny Day Set.** Capri 'pants and appliqued blouse. Hat, sandals.
49 N 3571—Shpg. wt. 8 oz.......$1.97

5 **Party Coat.** Velveteen with fuzzy collar and hat. Shoes, socks not incl.
49 N 3572—Shpg. wt. 12 oz......$2.57

6 **Chifferobe.** 4 drawers, shoerack; sliding clothes rack, 6 hangers. Durable plastic, 14x6x14 inches high.
49 N 9278—Shpg. wt. 3 lbs. 8 oz..$5.43

7 **Pencil Post Bed.** Bedspread, canopy cover, pillow. 23x12x20 inches high. Durable plastic. Easy to assemble.
79 N 9277C—Shpg. wt. 4 lbs.....$5.43

8 **Sleepytime Set.** Gets her ready for naptime. Flannel pajamas, matching night cap, fur-like scuffs.
49 N 3570—Shpg. wt. 12 oz......$2.57

Doll not included with any outfit 2 through 8

③ $2²³

② $2⁹⁷

④ $1⁹⁷   ⑤ $2⁵⁷

⑥ $5⁴³   ⑦ $5⁴³

$2⁵⁷ ⑧

10 SEARS 2PCBOL

Chatty Cathy: A page from the 1963 Sears Christmas catalog showing Chatty Cathy with pigtails and some of her clothing and accessories.

Chatty Baby: Two blond Chatty Babies. The doll on the left is wearing a Chatty Baby outfit called Leotard Set and doll on the right is wearing her original outfit. **$65.00 – 90.00** each. Courtesy Carla Marie Cross.

Chatty Baby: In 1962 Chatty Cathy received an 18" little sister, Chatty Baby. Chatty Baby came with either blond or brunette hair. She is marked the same as the pigtailed Chatty Cathy dolls in the previous photo: "CHATTY CATHY®/©1960/CHATTY BABY™/©1961/ BY MATTEL, INC./U.S.PAT. 3,017,187/OTHER U.S. &/FOREIGN PATS. PEND./PAT'D IN CANADA 1962." With original clothing: **$65.00 – 90.00**, lower end if mute, higher end if talking.

Charmin' Chatty: 25" Charmin' Chatty was a pull-string talking doll that talked with the aid of a record inserted into a slot on her side. The blond doll in the photo is in her original outfit and the red haired Charmin' is redressed in non-Chatty clothing. The dolls are marked, "CHARMIN' CHATTY™/©1961 MATTEL, INC./HAWTHORNE, CALIF. USA/U.S.PAT. 3,017,187/ PAT'D IN CANADA 1962/OTHER U.S. & FOREIGN/PATENTS. PENDING" on their backs. All original with glasses: **$75.00 – 150.00** Redressed without glasses: **$25.00 – 40.00**.

Tiny Chatty Baby and Tiny Chatty Brother: Other than their original clothing, the only difference between these two twin dolls is that Tiny Chatty Brother has a definite hair part on the side. The dolls are marked, "TINY CHATTY BABY™/ TINY CHATTY BROTHER™/©1962 MATTEL, INC./HAWTHORNE, CALIF. USA/U.S.PAT. 3,017,187/ OTHER U.S. & FOREIGN/PATENTS. PENDING/PATENTED IN CANADA 1962" on their backs. Tiny Chatty Baby in original clothing: **$35.00 – 50.00**. Tiny Chatty Brother in original clothing: **$45.00 – 65.00**.

Chatty Cathy: In 1970 Chatty Cathy was once again available after an absence of about six years. The reissued version was completely restyled and bore little resemblance to the earlier Chatty Cathy dolls. MIB: **$50.00 – 75.00**. 1971 Sears Christmas catalog.

Sister Belle: Pull-string talker with hard plastic head and stuffed body and limbs. The 16" doll has her voice box inside her head rather than in her body like most dolls. Speaker holes can be found in the back of her head under her yarn hair. Sister Belle is marked, "©MATTEL, INC./HAWTHORNE,/CALIF." on her neck and tagged, "©MATTEL, INC." on her body. **$45.00 – 75.00**.

Matty the Talking Boy: Matty Mattel was the name of the cartoon character mascot used in early television commercials for Mattel toys and often found next to their logo in print ads. Mattel came out with a doll called Matty the Talking Boy, and even though that is the name as it appears on his original box, when he spoke he called himself Matty Mattel. Like Sister Belle, her brother Matty is 16" with yarn hair, hard plastic head, and stuffed body and limbs. He originally came with a felt crown-shaped hat on his head, but rarely do loose dolls still have them. Even though Matty is much harder to find than his sister, not as many collectors had him as children so consequently don't feel the need to include him in their collections. Many collectors purchase him as a companion to Sister Belle more than for nostalgic reasons. **$50.00 – 80.00**. Courtesy Elaine McGrath.

50% Savings

TALKING MATTY MATTEL AND SISTER BELLE

YOUR CHOICE $3.83

I Love You

I'm Matty Mattel

[9] Lovable Casper, the friendly talking ghost, 15 in. tall, in terry cloth costume. Pull the ring, he says 11 different ghostly things like "My name is Casper; I'm a friendly ghost; I don't want to scare you." Stuffed body, plastic head.
48 T 3873—Ship. wt. 2 lbs. **$5.99**

[10] Sister Belle, the lovable talking rag doll, 17 in. tall. Pull the ring, she says "I love you; Sing me a song," and others. With pinafore, yarn hair.
48 T 3872—Ship. wt. 2 lbs. 9 oz. Was $7.67. Now **$3.83**

[11] Matty the Talking Boy wears T-shirt, shorts, shoes, has red hair, stuffed body. Says "I like you; Let's play cowboy," and others when you pull ring.
48 T 3864—Ship. wt. 2 lbs. 4 oz. 17 in. tall. Was $7.67. **$3.83**

[12] Cecil and His Disguises $5.88

TV Favorites

FOR GIRLS AND BOYS

[14] $2.99

[15] $8.99

[16] $6.99

[17] $9.99

[12] Cecil the Seasick Sea-Serpent can disguise himself with 15 different pieces, including a cape, hats, hula skirt, mustaches, a lion's mane, a set of false teeth. Cecil is about 22 in. long, of softest plush with felt nostrils, moving eyes. Wired body can be shaped into many different positions, lets him sit by himself. Ship. wt. 2 lbs.
48 T 6583 . . . . **$5.88**

[13] Smoky Bear. Soft foam rubber stuffed; badge, trousers, plastic shovel. Ship. wt. 1 lb.
48 T 7408 . . . . **$2.97**

[14] Talking Bozo the Clown in his dotted clown suit, comical oversize shoes. Vinyl head, cotton stuffed body. About 18 in. tall.
48 T 7469—Ship. wt. 1 lb. 4 oz. **$2.99**

[15] Talking Cecil the Seasick Sea Serpent—Beany's friend and protector. 18½ in. tall, with movable eyes, felt features, plush body. Pull ring, he says "Hey Beany Boy," "There goes a good kid" and other phrases.
48 T 6585—Ship. wt. 4 lbs. 12 oz. **$8.99**

[16] Beany Boy, Star of TV. He says 11 sentences like "Help, save me," and "I'm Beany Boy." Appealing in Beany-copter hat, shirt, corduroy overalls. Vinyl head, feet, hands. Painted hair, stuffed body.
48 T 3861—About 17½ in. Ship. wt. 3 lbs. **$6.99**

[17] Bugs Bunny—Sassy talking rabbit holds a carrot, says "What's up Doc?" 8 other phrases. Cuddly cutup is cotton stuffed, has plush fur, vinyl face, vinyl hands.
48 T 6586—About 26 in. Ship. wt. 2 lbs. 8 oz. **$9.99**

ALL WARDS ·237·

1963 Montgomery Ward Christmas catalog showing some of the Mattel Talkers available including Sister Belle and Matty Mattel.

Bozo: Pull-string talking clown has a vinyl head with rooted bright orange yarn hair, a stuffed body, and stuffed limbs. The 18" doll is tagged, "Quality Originals by/MATTEL®/BOZO,/the Capital Clown/©Capital Records, Inc./Licensed by Larry/Harmon Pictures Corp./©1963 Mattel, Inc/...Pat.in Canada, 1962/Other Pats.Pend." Talking: **$50.00 – 75.00**.

Shrinkin' Violette: 17" plush pull-string talking doll from the television show *The Funny Company*. The character on the television program had the ability to shrink, thus helping to get her friends out of trouble. The doll says phrases like, "I wish I were brave like you," "I'm just afraid of everything," "It's just awful to be shy." Violette's eyes and mouth move when she talks. She is tagged, "Quality Originals by/ Mattel/Shrinkin'Violette/©1963 The Funny Company." MIB: **$125.00 – 200.00**. Courtesy Joedi Johnson.

Baby Pattaburp and Tiny Baby Pattaburp: These two dolls let out a "burp" when they were patted on the back. The larger doll on the left is Baby Pattaburp. She is 16". She has no markings on her head, but her cloth body is tagged, "QUALITY ORIGINALS BY/MATTEL®/BABY PATTABURP™/©1963 Mattel, Inc./U.S. Pat.Pend./Made in Hong Kong." She is wearing her original dress which is tagged, "BABY PATTABURP™/©1964 MATTEL, INC. JAPAN." Tiny Baby Pattaburp on the right in the photo is 14" and also has no markings on her head. Her body is tagged, "QUALITY ORIGINALS BY/MATTEL®/TINY BABY PATTABURP®/©1965 Mattel, Inc. Hawthorne, Calif, U.S.A./U.S. Patent Pending/Head, Sewn Body and Clothing Made in Japan." The Tiny Baby Pattaburp in the photo has been redressed. Baby Pattaburp: **$35.00 – 45.00**. Tiny Baby Pattaburp, redressed: **$25.00 – 30.00**.

Drowsy

Quite popular in spite of her somewhat homely appearance, talking Drowsy is 16" tall with a vinyl head and hands. Her plush body was designed to look like a flannel sleeper with a buttoned flap in the back. The fabric body of Drowsy when she first came out in1965 was pale pink with cats printed on it, but later the sleeper was changed to the more common dark pink with white polka dots fabric. Most Drowsy dolls came with blond hair, but in 1969 she was also issued in a black version with black hair and a Spanish speaking version as a brunette. Starting in 1974 and continuing through 1976, Drowsy came with plush hands and was 13" tall. Because of the length of time she was available, finding this doll isn't too difficult for the collector.

Drowsy: A Drowsy doll with vinyl hands shown with a 1974 black version Drowsy with plush hands. Although most Drowsy dolls have the talking pull string located on the side of the body, the black doll shown here has it located on the back of the lower neck. This doll also doesn't have the buttoned drawers as many other examples do. The voice box inside this doll is much smaller than the one inside the earlier version. The doll with vinyl hands is unmarked. The black doll is marked, "©MATTEL INC. 1964" on the back of her head. Both dolls have a paper tag with the doll's name, copyright dates and material content. When talking, value can increase **$25.00 – 40.00** for the dolls. White version with vinyl hands, mute: **$30.00 – 45.00**. Reissued black version, mute: **$35.00 – 50.00**.

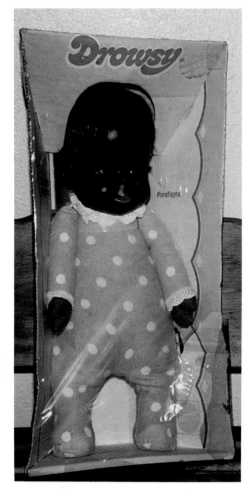

Drowsy: MIB 1974 version with plush hands. MIB: **$75.00 – 125.00**. Courtesy Marcia Fanta.

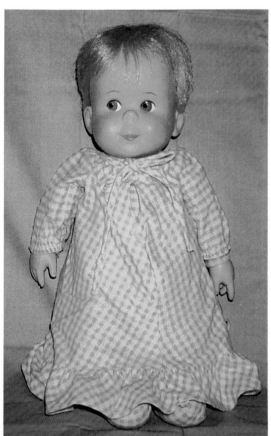

Baby Colleen: This 15" doll has a stuffed body and limbs and a vinyl head and vinyl hands. Under her flannel nightgown Baby Colleen's stuffed body and legs are made to look like a sleeper from matching fabric. **$40.00 – 50.00**. Courtesy Elaine McGrath.

Patootie: This 16" pull-string talking clown originally included an additional mask with a "sad" face on it. When present, the sad mask can add $25 or more to the doll's value. Circa 1967. Doll without mask: **$75.00 – 100.00**. Courtesy Elaine McGrath.

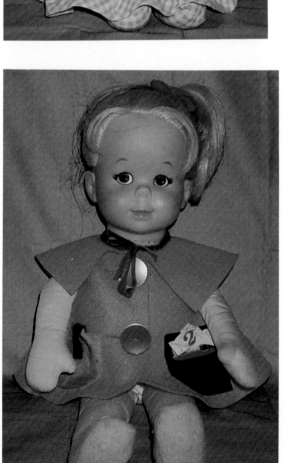

Teachy Keen: 16" pull-string talker with vinyl head and stuffed body and limbs. Her rose-colored jacket was made from felt. Teachy taught children how to button, zipper, tie, and count. **$45.00 – 75.00**. Courtesy Elaine McGrath.

Baby Say 'N See: A 17" pull-string talking doll with cloth body and vinyl arms, legs, and head. The doll's eyes and lips move when she talks. Baby Say 'N See is marked, "©1966 Mattel Inc. U.S.A./U.S. Patent Pending." MIB: **$85.00 – 125.00**. Courtesy Marcia Fanta.

Baby First Step: An 18" battery-operated doll that was issued starting in 1965. In 1966 a Talking Baby First Step joined Baby First Step on the market. She had the same face but a different hair color and style than Baby First Step and not only did she walk, she talked as well. By 1967 both dolls' outfits were updated to a more modern look. The photo shows the first issue Baby First Step in her original pink dress. The doll is marked, "©1964 MATTEL, INC./HAWTHORNE, CALIFORNIA/MADE IN U.S.A./U.S. PATENTS PENDING" on her back. **$40.00 – 55.00**.

Baby First Step: A 1967 Baby First Step wearing the second issue dress. Her hair is a little longer than the first issue Baby First Step. Same markings as first issue doll. **$35.00 – 45.00**.

Baby First Step: 1967 Montgomery Ward Christmas catalog showing Baby First Step and Talking Baby First Step wearing their updated dresses.

167

Baby First Step: In 1968 Mattel issued a restyled Baby First Step with a new face mold and the 19" doll was about an inch taller than the 1964 issue. The restyled Baby First Step is marked, "©1967 MATTEL, INC. U.S.A./U.S. & FOR. PATS. PEND." on her head and "©1964 MATTEL, INC./HAWTHORNE, CALIFORNIA/MADE IN U.S.A./U.S. PATENTS PENDING" on her back. **$25.00 – 35.00**.

Swingy: This battery-operated 18" doll swings back and forth as if dancing. Swingy came with a cardboard 33⅓ RPM record. Starting in 1969, the doll was sold wearing this pink polka-dot dress. The doll is marked, "©1967 MATTEL, INC./U.S. & FOR. PATS.PEND." on her head and "©1964 MATTEL, INC./HAWTHORNE, CALIFORNIA/MADE IN U.S.A./U.S. & FOREIGN PATENTED/OTHER PATENTS PENDING" on her back. MIB: **$75.00 – 95.00**. Courtesy Robin Englehart/Photo by Nancy Jean Mong.

Swingy: Even though the box shows Swingy wearing the polka-dot dress like the one below left, the doll inside came wearing a different style dress. The dress is tagged, "SWINGY©/©1968MATTEL, INC./HONG KONG". **$75.00 – 95.00**.

£3·00

to dance with someone th
will be ready whenever yo
Two HP2 batteries 18p ex

9b

ovable 18"
her up or
he laughs

13 Cirillino A really be
18" baby doll from Italy—

Swingy: Although Swingy dolls in the U.S. have painted eyes, the Swingy doll shown here features inset eyes. She was shown in the 1973 – 74 catalog for Hamleys of Regent Street Ltd. London, and most likely was produced by one of Mattel's foreign licensees.

Baby Small Talk: A 10" pull-string talking doll marked, "©1967 MATTEL INC./HONG KONG" on her head and "©1967 MATTEL. INC./U.S. & FOR. PATS. PEND./HONG KONG" on her back. **$20.00 – 25.00**.

Tiny Swingy: This 11" battery-operated version of Swingy uses the Small Talk face mold. The doll is marked, "©1967 MATTEL, INC./HONG KONG" on her head and "©1967 MATTEL, INC./ U.S. & FOREIGN PATENTED/OTHER PATENTS PENDING/HONG KONG" on her back. Barbie collectors will note that the material used on Tiny Swingy's dress is the same used on Mattel's #1170 Twist 'N Turn Francie doll's swimsuit. The doll shown is missing her original hair band made from the same striped material as her dress. **$30.00 – 40.00**.

Baby Small Talk: Both white and black versions of Baby Small-Talk. Black version: **$30.00 – 45.00**. Courtesy Elaine McGrath.

Storybook Small Talk Dolls: These pull-string talking dolls portrayed fairy tale and nursery rhyme characters Cinderella, Little Bo Peep, Snow White, and Goldilocks. Marks on the dolls vary slightly since the dolls were made in different countries during the years they were produced. The dolls are marked, "©1967 MATTEL INC./HONG KONG" or "©1967 MATTEL INC. JAPAN" on their heads and "©1967 MATTEL. INC./U.S. & FOR. PATS. PEND./HONG KONG" or "©1967 MATTEL. INC./U.S. & FOR./PATS. PEND./MEXICO" on their backs. **$30.00 – 55.00** each.

Storybook Small Talk Cinderella: Talking Cinderella shown in her original box. MIB: **$125.00 – 175.00**. Courtesy Robin Englehart.

Storybook Small Talk Snow White: Talking Snow White shown in her original box. MIB: **$125.00 – 175.00**. Courtesy Robin Englehart/Photo by Nancy Jean Mong.

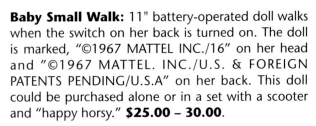

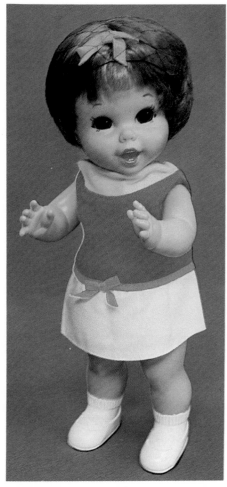

Baby Small Walk: 11" battery-operated doll walks when the switch on her back is turned on. The doll is marked, "©1967 MATTEL INC./16" on her head and "©1967 MATTEL. INC./U.S. & FOREIGN PATENTS PENDING/U.S.A" on her back. This doll could be purchased alone or in a set with a scooter and "happy horsy." **$25.00 – 30.00**.

Baby Small Walk: Baby Small Walk shown with her original box. MIB: **$45.00 – 65.00**. Courtesy Karen Hickey.

Sister Small Talk: 10" pull-string talking doll wearing her original outfit. She is marked, "©1967 MATTEL INC JAPAN" on her head and "©1967 MATTEL INC./U.S. & FOR./PATS PEND./U.S.A" on her back. **$30.00 – 40.00**. Courtesy Elaine McGrath.

Sister Small Talk: Sister Small Talk shown wearing one of her separately sold Big Sister Fashions called Sister's Suities. Doll with outfit: **$30.00 – 40.00**.

Valerie: This 11" Valerie with "Growin' Pretty Hair" has been redressed. She originally wore a yellow and white dress, white socks and shoes. Valerie is marked, "©1967 MATTEL. INC./U.S. & FOR./PATS PEND./HONG KONG" on her back. Redressed: **$25.00 – 30.00**.

Baby Fun: Note the resemblance of Baby Fun's hands, feet, and face to those of Baby Small Talk.

Baby Fun: A 7¼" doll who came with a party noise maker, a horn, balloons, and a bubble pipe. Baby Fun is marked, "©1968 MATTEL INC./HONG/KONG" on her head and "PATENT PENDING /©1968 MATTEL, INC./HONG KONG" on her back. Circa 1973. Without accessories: **$20.00 – 30.00**.

Buffy and Mrs. Beasley: Based on Anissa Jones, the child star who played Buffy on the television program *Family Affair*, and the doll she toted around on the show, Mattel issued a Buffy and Mrs. Beasley doll set in two different sizes. A talking Buffy came in 10" and had the Small Talk body and face. Her companion Mrs. Beasley doll was 4¾". The second set of Buffy/Mrs. Beasley dolls is sometimes associated with the Barbie line since the 6" Buffy had the same body as Tutti and Todd. Values for both these sets of dolls vary tremendously depending on where they are being sold and the completeness of the set. It isn't difficult to find pieces of either set on the doll market. However, finding a mint and complete set is more challenging. Once loose, the tiny Mrs. Beasley dolls almost always lost their square granny glasses. When glasses are present, value would be an additional **$15.00 – 25.00**. The large size Buffy shown in the photo is wearing replaced shoes. Complete loose sets: **$100.00 – 150.00**.

Buffy and Mrs. Beasley: 6" Buffy with the Tutti body. She is missing her original red hair ribbons, and Mrs. Beasley is missing her original glasses. Buffy is marked, "©1965/MATTEL, INC./JAPAN/26" on her back. 3¼" Mrs. Beasley is unmarked. **$100.00 – $150.00** for set.

Buffy and Mrs. Beasley: 6" Buffy and 3¼" Mrs. Beasley in their original box. The back of the box shows a photo of Anissa Jones, the child actress who played the part of Buffy on *Family Affair*, along with the 22" size Talking Mrs. Beasley doll. MIB: **$200.00 – 300.00**. *Courtesy Robin Englehart/Photo by Nancy Jean Mong.*

Talking Buffy and Mrs. Beasley: Buffy and Mrs. Beasley shown in their original box. Like the other boxed set at left, the box shows a photo of Anissa Jones with the 22" size Mrs. Beasley doll used on the show. Buffy is marked, "©1965/MATTEL, INC./U.S. & FOR. PATS.PEND/MEXICO" on her back. Mrs. Beasley is tagged, "MRS. BEASLEY(/"©1967 FAMILY AFFAIR CO./ ©1967/MATTEL, INC./MADE IN HONG KONG/ALL NEW MATERIALS/CONSISTING OF SHREDDED CLIPPINGS 100%" on cloth tag sewn into her skirt. MIB: **$275.00 – 400.00**. *Courtesy Robin Englehart/Photo by Nancy Jean Mong.*

Mrs. Beasley: This 22" pull-string talker is very popular with today's collectors primarily because so many remember it from their childhood. The Mattel doll was based on a doll from the television program *Family Affair*. The talking Mrs. Beasley doll has a vinyl head and hands. Her skirt and collar are removable, so often were lost over the years. Even harder to find today are Mrs. Beasley's original glasses. When they are present, they add $25.00 or more to the value. The doll is tagged, "MATTEL/Mrs. Beasley/©1967 Family Affair Co./ ©1966 Mattel Inc." Mute loose dolls: **$100.00 – 175.00**. Talking and MIB: **$300.00 – 475.00**. Courtesy Marcia Fanta.

Mrs. Beasley: Three different sizes of Mrs. Beasley dolls. The largest size is the 22" talking Mrs. Beasley. The 4¾" Mrs. Beasley is the doll that goes with the Small Talk Buffy, and the 3¼" doll goes with the Tutti-sized Buffy.

Mrs. Beasley: A 10" all-cloth doll was also made of Mrs. Beasley. This version of Mrs. Beasley isn't as common as the other sizes of Mrs. Beasley, but it is also not as popular with collectors so the value is actually lower in spite of its limited availability. The cloth doll was available both in a pull-string talking version and a non-talking version. **$25.00 – 35.00.** 1974 Montgomery Ward Christmas catalog.

Scooba-Doo: Scooba-Doo with black hair, shown in the 1966 Montgomery Ward Christmas catalog.

Scooba-Doo: A beatnik-type pull-string talking doll with a vinyl head and plush body and limbs. The 22" doll was issued with either black or platinum hair. MIB: **$95.00 – 150.00**. Courtesy Joedi Johnson.

Scooba-Doo: A platinum blond Scooba-Doo, shown in the 1965 Montgomery Ward Christmas catalog.

Cheerful-Tearful: This 13" doll pouts when her arm is raised and lowered, and she cries "real" tears. In addition to Cheerful-Tearful, Mattel issued a doll under the name Baby Smile and Frown that was basically the same doll as Cheerful-Tearful, but with auburn hair. The doll on the left is wearing Baby Smile and Frown's original dress and the doll on the right is wearing Cheerful-Tearful's original outfit. Cheerful-Tearful is marked, "©1965 MATTEL, INC./HAWTHORNE, CALIF./ U.S.PATENTS/PENDING/3036-014-3" on her back. **$20.00 – 35.00**.

Baby Cheerful-Tearful: The 6½" version of Cheerful-Tearful pouts and cries when her tummy is pressed. She is shown here in her original crib next to the 13" Cheerful-Tearful. Baby Cheerful-Tearful is marked, "©1966 MATTEL, INC./HONG KONG" on her head and "©1966 MATTEL, INC./MADE IN HONG KONG/U.S.PAT.PENDING" on her lower back. Doll alone: **$15.00 – 20.00**. With crib: **$25.00 – 30.00**.

Tippee Toes: Tippee Toes is a battery-operated doll whose legs move, allowing her to ride her tricycle or horse. Most Tippee Toes dolls came with a tricycle and a horse to ride, but a 1968 Sears exclusive set had the doll available with the two riding toys as well as a baby walker. The walker is very hard to find today. 16" Tippee Toes is marked "JAPAN" on her head and "©1967 MATTEL, INC./HAWTHORNE, CALIFORNIA /MADE IN U.S.A." on her back. The walker has a sticker that reads, "Mattel® Tippee Toes Walkabout™/©1968 Mattel, Inc Hawthorne, Calif./U.S. Pat Pend./Made in U.S.A." It is metal with a clear vinyl seat with flowers printed on it. Tippee Toes' blue plastic tricycle with yellow plastic wheels is marked, "©1967 MATTEL, INC./HAWTHORNE, CALIFORNIA/U.S. PATENT PENDING/MADE IN U.S.A." The yellow horse with pink details and green wheels is marked, "©1967 MATTEL, INC. HAWTHORNE, CALIF. MADE IN U.S.A." Doll only: **$25.00 – 35.00**. Riding Toys: **$20.00 – 25.00** each.

Tippee Toes: 16" Tippee Toes with her "Walkabout." Same markings as above.

Tippee Toes: Tippee Toes with two different hair shades. The outfit on the doll on the right was sold separately for Tippee Toes dolls in a 7-piece clothing and accessory set in the 1968 Sears Christmas catalog.

Baby Go Bye-Bye and her Bumpety Buggy: This doll came with a car that could be programmed to drive in different directions. In 1969, one year earlier than Baby Go Bye-Bye was available, the same doll was sold without a car as Bouncy Baby wearing a different outfit and a different hairstyle. 10½" Baby Go Bye-Bye is marked, "©1968 MATTEL, INC./HONG KONG" on her head and "©1968 MATTEL, INC./MEXICO/U.S. PATENT PENDING" on her lower back. Doll with car: **$50.00 – 75.00**, lower end if car isn't working, higher end if it works. Doll without car: **$15.00 – 20.00**.

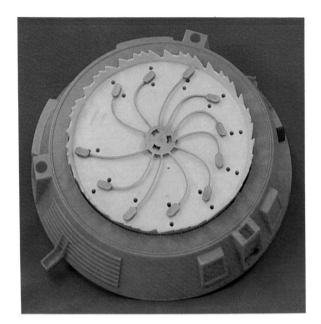

Baby Go Bye-Bye and her Bumpety Buggy: Baby Go Bye-Bye's car has a programmable battery-operated "engine" on which the body of the car is placed. Each of the 11 blue plastic spokes can be placed in one of three holes representing right, straight or left direction. Since this piece is totally separate from the car, it's not unusual to find the car without it. When missing the battery-operated part, the car still displays well for collectors but should not command top value since it is not in working condition.

Doctor Dolittle: This pull-string talking doll representing Rex Harrison in the title role of the movie *Doctor Dolittle.* The 24" doll has a vinyl head and plush body and limbs. The doll is tagged, "©MCM-LXVII/TWENTIETH CENTURY FOX/FILM CORPORATION AND APJAC/©1967 MATTEL INC." MIB: **$125.00 – 150.00.** Courtesy Marcia Fanta.

Doctor Dolittle: A 13" pull-string talking hand puppet was made with the same head mold as the Talking Doctor Dolittle. The puppet is unmarked. Loose and mute: **$25.00 – 35.00.**

★NEW! DOCTOR DOLITTLE and CAPTAIN KANGAROO®

★NEW! DOCTOR DOLITTLE DOLL #5349

From the great new family film! Rex Harrison's likeness! His voice too!

Personable rag doll, authentically recreated from exciting new movie, introduces himself with "How do you do, I'm Doctor Dolittle." Plus nine more phrases in star Rex Harrison's own voice! Removable top hat, coat and vest. 24" tall.

Std. Pack: 6/12 Doz.   Wt: 18 Lbs.

★NEW! TALKING PUSHMI-PULLYU #5225

An animal star from the fabulous movie, "Doctor Dolittle." One head of unique Doctor Dolittle character comically quizzes, "Will you quit pushing me" and the other head replies "Not until you stop pulling me!" 10 phrases, two voices, poseable heads. Plush, 13" tall.
Std. Pack: 6/12 Doz.   Wt: 16 Lbs.

★NEW! CAPTAIN KANGAROO® DOLL #5334

Beloved children's personality kindly reminds, "Do remember to say please and thank you" and nine other phrases in actual TV voice. Removable coat with pockets. 19" tall.
Std. Pack: 6/12 Doz.   Wt: 16 Lbs.

Doctor Dolittle: This 1968 Mattel Toys catalog page shows the company's Talking Doctor Dolittle, a plush talking Pushmi-Pullyu, the two-headed llama-type animal from the *Doctor Dolittle* movie, and a Captain Kangaroo doll. Catalog courtesy Robin Englehart.

TALKING HAND PUPPETS

World of
Puppets

New talking hand puppets featuring famous movie, television and cartoon characters!

OFF TO SEE THE WIZARD FINGER PUPPET

DOCTOR DOLITTLE PUPPET

POPEYE PUPPET

BUGS BUNNY PUPPET

#5364   #5365   #5366   #0376

★ NEW! OFF TO SEE THE WIZARD FINGER PUPPET #5364
"I am Oz, the great and terrible" announces Wizard to Dorothy,
Tin Man and Scarecrow. TV hosts plus a lion on sleeve say
10 phrases. Heads manipulated together or separately. 11½" tall.

★ NEW! DOCTOR DOLITTLE PUPPET #5365
The likeness and voice of Rex Harrison as Doctor Dolittle!
Says "I've talked to animals all over the world" plus nine more
phrases from movie. 14½" tall.

★ NEW! POPEYE PUPPET #5366
In familiar gravel-voice, Popeye chants, "I am strong to
the finish 'cause I eats me Spinach" plus nine other phrases.
Removable pipe can blow bubbles! 12½" tall.

BUGS BUNNY PUPPET #0376
Plush puppet says 11 things like famed, "Eh, what's up, Doc?"
and munches on carrot. Soft, furry robe. 15" tall.
Each in Std. Pack: 6/12 Doz.   Wt: 8½ Lbs.

From the Favorite TV Show!
Pull the talking
ring and listen
WE ALL TALK!

★ NEW! TALKING HAND PUPPET ASSORTMENT # A5362
Twelve puppets in colorful shelf display. Shipped prepacked.
2 ea. BUGS BUNNY PUPPET #0376
4 ea. OFF TO SEE THE WIZARD PUPPET #5364
4 ea. DOCTOR DOLITTLE PUPPET #5365
2 ea. POPEYE PUPPET #5366
Std. Pack: 1 ea. (1 carton) Wt: 21 Lbs.

FREE!
DEMONSTRATION
PUPPET

★ NEW! TALKING HAND PUPPET
ASSORTMENT # A5363
Twelve puppet assortment without display.
Same mix as # A5362.
Std. Pack: 1 ea. (1 carton) Wt: 19 Lbs.

69

"DOCTOR DOLITTLE" ©MCMLXVII Twentieth Century-Fox Film Corporation & Apjac Productions, Inc. ALL RIGHTS RESERVED.
"OFF TO SEE THE WIZARD" ©1967 Metro-Goldwyn-Mayer, Inc.   "POPEYE" ©King Features Syndicate, Inc.   "BUGS BUNNY" ©Warner Bros. Pictures. Inc.

Doctor Dolittle/Mattel Talking Puppets: This 1968 Mattel Toys catalog page shows the company's
Talking Doctor Dolittle puppet as well as their Off to See the Wizard, Popeye, and Bugs Bunny talking
hand puppets. Catalog courtesy Robin Englehart.

Doctor Dolittle: These 5¾" Doctor Dolittle dolls used the same bodies as Mattel's Tutti and Todd dolls. The dolls were made of vinyl with a wire inside the limbs to pose them. Note the two boxed dolls in the photo have the colors on their slacks' design reversed. The dolls are marked, "©1967/MATTEL, INC./JAPAN" on their backs. MIB: **$40.00 – 55.00** each. Courtesy Robin Englehart.

Doctor Dolittle: The 5¾" Doctor Dolittle doll was also available in a set with a Pushmi-Pullyu. MIB: **$65.00 – 80.00.** Courtesy Robin Englehart/Photo by Nancy Jean Mong.

Doctor Dolittle: Back of the Doctor Dolittle and Pushmi-Pullyu set. Courtesy Robin Englehart/Photo by Nancy Jean Mong.

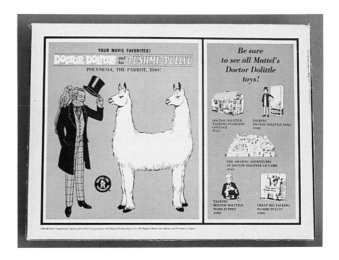

183

Monkees Talking Hand Puppet: Pull-string talking puppet featuring the four members of the Monkees singing group. The puppet is circa 1966. Mute: **$55.00 – 75.00**. Courtesy Elaine McGrath.

Mr. Potts: 22½" cloth pull-string talking doll representing Dick Van Dyke as the character of Mr. Potts from the movie *Chitty Chitty Bang Bang*. On the left is Mattel's Talking Beany doll from the *Beany and Cecil* television cartoon. Mr. Potts: **$55.00 – 75.00**. Courtesy Robin Randall.

Herman Munster: The 21" pull-string talking Herman Munster doll has a vinyl head, vinyl hands, a stuffed body, and stuffed legs. The 12" pull-string talking puppet on the right was made with the same head mold. Doll in working condition: **$200.00 – 300.00**. Puppet in working condition: **$175.00 – 225.00**. Courtesy Elaine McGrath.

Linus the Lionhearted: Both the 21" pull string talking doll and the 12" pull string talking puppet shown here have vinyl faces and felt manes. Doll in working condition: **$50.00 – 75.00**. Puppet in working condition: **$45.00 – $65.00**. Courtesy Elaine McGrath.

Maurice Monkey: 10" pull-string talking puppet who speaks with a French accent. Puppet in working condition: **$30.00 – $45.00**. Courtesy Elaine McGrath.

Tatters: 19" pull-string talking stuffed rag doll with felt eyelids and yellow yarn hair. Tatters has a removable dress, jacket, and pantaloons, but her head scarf is not removable. Mute doll: **$50.00 – 65.00**. Doll in working condition: **$100.00 – 125.00**. Courtesy Robin Randall.

Liddle Kiddles

Ranging in sizes from ¼" to 4", Mattel's Liddle Kiddles have rapidly appreciated in value in the past few years as more and more collectors have rediscovered these childhood favorites. The Kiddles line includes over 100 dolls so only a small sampling is shown here. Values listed include the dolls' very small accessories. Because the tiny accessories so often got lost, in some cases they could be worth more than the dolls themselves, which are more easily located. There really is no one formula for determining value of complete sets of Kiddles versus only the dolls. Some Kiddle dolls are relatively common, so they may be worth only about $15.00. Add their original accessories and the value could shoot up to $60.00 or higher. It is common to find that over the years many Liddle Kiddles have turned green in places from the wires inside them reacting to the vinyl of the doll. Values listed are for Kiddles that have no green color.

First series of Kiddles issued in 1966 include from left to right: Florence Niddle, Howard "Biff" Boodle, Liddle Diddle, Greta Griddle, Lola Liddle, Babe Biddle, Calamity Jiddle, Bunson Burnie, and Millie Middle. Values for these dolls mint and complete can range from **$50.00 – 175.00**.

Second series of Kiddles issued in 1967 include from left to right: Windy Fliddle, Soapy Siddle, Sizzly Friddle, Surfy Skiddle, Beddy Bye Biddle, Trikey Triddle, Freezy Sliddle. Missing from this photo are other Kiddles in the series, Pretty Priddle and Rolly Twiddle. Like the previous Kiddles, values for these dolls mint and complete can range from **$50.00 – 175.00**.

Liddle Diddle: This baby Kiddle named Liddle Diddle is 3" tall. She comes with a crib with a string of beads on the railing, a pink laced trimmed pillow, a flannel blanket, and a yellow duck. Liddle Diddle is marked, "©MATTEL, INC." on the bottom of her head around the neck hole and "©1965/MATTEL, INC./JAPAN/3" on her back. The single digit after "Japan" will vary from doll to doll. Her crib is marked, "LIDDLE KIDDLES ©" on both sides and "JAPAN" on the bottom. It isn't uncommon for people not familiar with Liddle Kiddles to think a crib missing its railings is a pink Liddle Kiddle bed. Mint and complete: **$75.00 – 110.00**.

Freezy Sliddle: This 3½" Kiddle doll comes with a sled. She is marked, "©MATTEL, INC." on the bottom of her head around the neck hole and "©1965/MATTEL, INC./JAPAN" on her back. Her sled is marked, "LIDDLE KIDDLES" with a logo and "MATTEL, INC./TOYMAKERS" with a logo on the back portion of the sled's seat. Underneath the sled is marked, "3516/-173/JAPAN". Mint and complete: **$65.00 – 85.00**.

Bunson Burnie: Bunson Burnie in his original package. The 3" doll is marked, "©MATTEL, INC." on the bottom of his head around the neck hole and "©1965/MATTEL, INC./JAPAN" on his back. His fire truck is marked, "LIDDLE KIDDLES" on the base part of the bumper area and "JAPAN" underneath. MOC: **$175.00 – $250.00**.

187

Shrimpies: Although this doll is not a Liddle Kiddle and was not made by Mattel, it is included here to show the similarities with Mattel Liddle Kiddles. Compare the illustrations on Bunson Burnie's card with the illustrations on the Shrimpies' card and there is no denying they are too similar to be coincidental. Shrimpies were by Blue Box and the dolls are marked, "Made in Hong Kong." If this doll were loose with no accessories it would be valued around **$2.00 – 5.00**, but the package with the similarities to the real Liddle Kiddles holds much appeal to Liddle Kiddle collectors. MOC: **$25.00 – 55.00**.
Courtesy Robin Englehart/Photo by Nancy Jean Mong.

Surfy Skiddle: Surfy often loses her sunglasses and her wave is easily broken, so it is a challenge to the collector to find her complete with all her accessories. Same markings as doll Bunson Burnie. Dressed doll alone: **$20.00 – 35.00**. With all accessories: **$80.00 – 125.00**.

Liddle Red Riding Hiddle: From the Storybook series of Liddle Kiddles, Liddle Red Riding Hiddle is marked, "©MATTEL INC" around the bottom of her head and "©1965/MATTEL, INC./JAPAN" on her back. Dressed doll alone: **$30.00 – 45.00**. Mint and complete set: **$90.00 – 125.00**.

Alice in Wonderliddle: 3½" doll from the Storybook series of Liddle Kiddles. Alice is marked, "©MATTEL INC" around the bottom of her head and "©1965/MATTEL, INC./JAPAN" on her back. Dressed doll alone: **$30.00 – 45.00**. Mint and complete set: **$125.00 – 150.00**.

Heather Hiddlehorse: This 4" Skediddle Kiddle doll could walk with the aid of a "skediddler" pusher or could pedal a riding toy by snapping the button on her back into the button on the riding toy. Many of the Skediddle Kiddles are relatively easy to locate and are often priced in the $25.00 range, but Heather is considerably harder to find and consequently is valued much higher. Heather is marked, "©MATTEL INC 1967 HONG KONG" on her head and "©1967/MATTEL INC./MEXICO/U.S.PAT.PEND." on her back. Fully dressed doll with horse: **$75.00 – 100.00**.

Tessie Tractor: Another hard-to-find Skeddidle Kiddle. Same marks as doll above. Fully dressed doll with tractor: **$75.00 – 100.00**.

Kologne Kiddles and Lucky Locket Kiddles: These 2" tall Liddle Kiddles came packaged inside either a plastic cologne bottle or a plastic locket and could be taken out for play. There were 14 different Locket Kiddles and 9 different Kologne Kiddles. These two lines of Liddle Kiddles are perhaps the ones most 1970s children remember best and the ones most easily found today. Without their original containers, the dolls have a value around $5.00 – 15.00 each. When the dolls are in their original containers, values average around $30.00 and go higher when hang tags and cardboard bases are present on the Kologne bottles or necklace chains are still intact on the Lockets. Locket and Kologne Kiddles are marked, "©M.I." on the back of their heads. In 1975 Mattel reissued six of the Locket Kiddles, but the "Kiddle" name was dropped and they were simply called "Lucky Locket." The dolls were made of a harder vinyl than the earlier Kiddle dolls. They had painted-on panties, unlike the earlier dolls. The reissued Lucky Lockets are worth less than the earlier dolls. Values for the reissued Lockets are at the low end of the range, while the original Locket Kiddles are valued at the higher end. Loose Lockets without chains: **$20.00 – 35.00** each. MOC Lockets: **$40.00 – 75.00.** Kolognes without cardboard bases: **$20.00 – 40.00** each. Kolognes with cardboard bases and hangtags: **$45.00 – 75.00**.

Jewelry Kiddles: The tiny Jewelry Kiddle dolls are approximately 1" in height. They were originally housed in plastic jewelry such as rings, bracelets, pins or necklaces that could be opened so the dolls could be taken out and played with. The jewelry was either shaped like a heart or a flower. The photo shows from the bottom row: flower necklace, heart pin, flower pin, (second row) heart bracelet minus its original chain, flower bracelet minus its original chain, (third row) heart ring, flower ring. Missing from photo is the heart necklace. The bracelets are the easiest to find of the Jewelry Kiddles, and the necklaces are the most difficult to find. Bracelets, rings, or pins with both dolls and jewelry: **$20.00 – 45.00** each. Necklaces with dolls, jewelry, and chains: **$125.00 – 200.00** each.

Dancerina: Dancerina is a 24" battery-operated doll who dances when the center of her crown is pulled up or spins around when the center of her crown is pressed down. She originally came with a small-size 33⅓ rpm record for dancing. Dancerina is marked, "©1968 MATTEL, INC.MEXICO" on her head and "©1968 MATTEL, INC./MADE IN U.S.A./U.S. PATENT PENDING" on her back. MIB: **$125.00 – 200.00**.

Dancerella: Following the success of Dancerina, Mattel issued their 18" Dancerella doll. She too is battery operated with a mechanical crown and works the same way Dancerina. does. Dancerella is marked, "U.S.A./©1972 MATTEL, INC." on her head and "©MATTEL, INC. 1968 1978/ U.S.A." on her back. **$20.00 – 30.00**.

Dancerina and Dancerella: 24" Dancerina shown with 18" Dancerella.

Baby Dancerina: This is an 11" version of Dancerina. The doll came with a blue crown, a blue tutu, and ballet slippers. She also came with a 33⅓" rpm record. **$20.00 – 30.00**. 1970 Sears Christmas catalog.

Baby Whisper: A 17½" doll, this doll tells secrets in a quiet voice. An earlier version of this doll was sold wearing a turquoise and white striped top and turquoise shorts. **$25.00 – 40.00**. 1969 Montgomery Ward Christmas catalog.

Myrtle: Myrtle was step-daughter Dodie's doll on the television show *My Three Sons*. This 14" pull-string talking handpuppet/doll is marked, "©1969 MATTEL INC. MEXICO" on her head, and has a cloth tag sewn in the side of her dress reading, "Quality Originals by/ MATTEL®/Myrtle™/©1969 Columbia/Broadcasting/System, Inc./All Rights Reserved/©1969 Mattel Inc/Hawthorne, Calif./Made in Mexico/U.S. & Foreign Pat'd./Pat'd. Canada 1962/Other Pats.Pend." **$45.00 – 60.00**.

Myrtle: Shown with her original box. MIB: **$175.00 – 200.00**.

Upsy Downsys

Upsy Downsys are small dolls that are colorful, fun, and a bit on the bizarre side. According to the storybook *Welcome to Upsy Downsy Land,* the Upsy Downsys started life as dandelions. A blustery wind blew into town, but the dandelions tickled the wind's nose so he blew them all away. When the dandelions fell back to earth the next morning, some of them drifted through a rainbow and changed into funny little people. They landed right-side-up so they were called the Upsys. Others fell into a storm cloud and came out looking like silly people. When they fell to earth they landed on the ground on their heads and hands, so they were called Downsys. The Upsy are 2½" tall and the Downsys are 3½". They are marked, "©1969 MATTEL, INC./HONG KONG" on their heads. They came with several small accessories as well as a "playland board" that could connect to all the other Upsy Downsy playland boards. There were also storybooks featuring the dolls. The Upsys included Flossy Glossy, Baby So High, Tickle Pinkle, and Pudgy Fudgy. The Downsys included Miss Information, Mother What Now, Downy Dilly, and Pocus Hocus. Courtesy Heidi Neufeld.

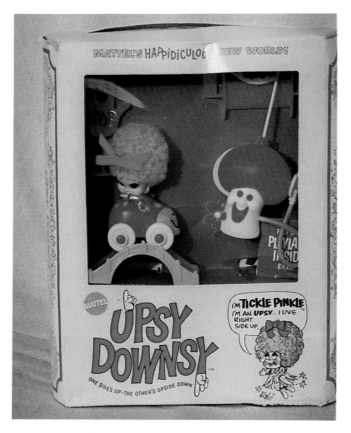

Tickle Pinkle: An Upsy doll that came with a Bugabout car, a mushroom gas pump, a green bridge, a stop sign shaped like a hand, a playland board, and a pink connector. MIB: **$75.00 – 95.00**. Courtesy Robin Englehart.

Miss Information: A Downsy doll that came with a Miss Information Booth car, a sign that said "That Way/This Way/Which Way?", a "Visit the Fall-Up Falls" sign, a playland board, and a pink connector. MIB: **$75.00 – 95.00**. Courtesy Robin Englehart.

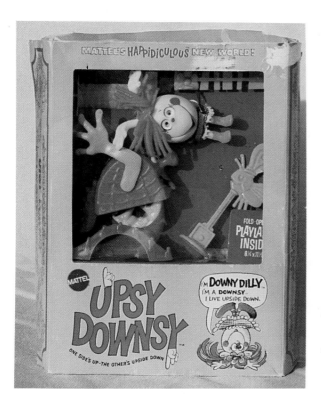

Downy Dilly: A Downsy doll that came with a Footmobile car, a dark orange bridge, a green fence, orange bug street light, a playland board, and an orange connector. MIB: **$75.00 – 95.00**. Courtesy Robin Englehart.

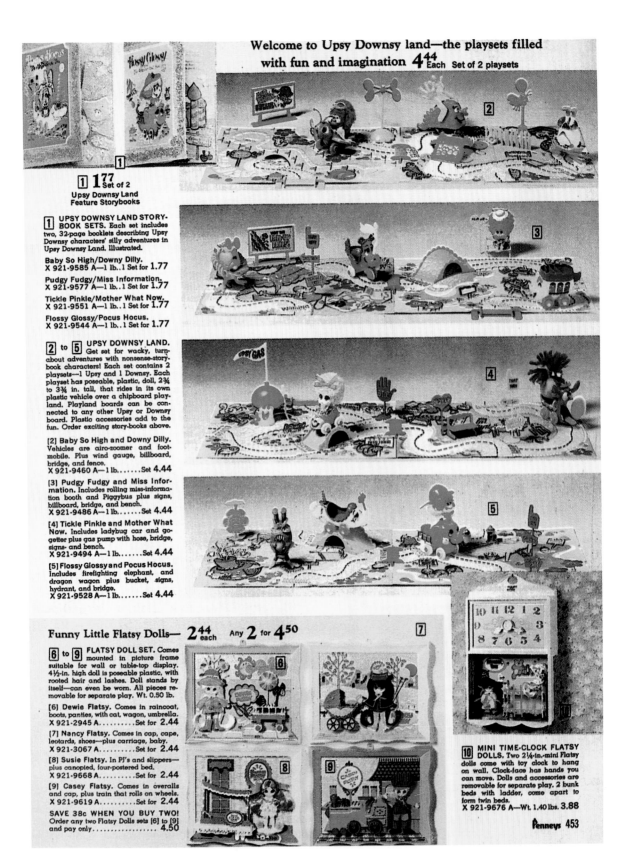

Welcome to Upsy Downsy land—the playsets filled with fun and imagination 4⁴⁴ Each Set of 2 playsets

1 1⁷⁷ Set of 2
Upsy Downsy Land Feature Storybooks

[1] UPSY DOWNSY LAND STORY-BOOK SETS. Each set includes two, 32-page booklets describing Upsy Downsy characters' silly adventures in Upsy Downsy Land. Illustrated.

Baby So High/Downy Dilly.
X 921-9585 A—1 lb..1 Set for **1.77**

Pudgy Fudgy/Miss Information.
X 921-9577 A—1 lb..1 Set for **1.77**

Tickle Pinkle/Mother What Now.
X 921-9551 A—1 lb..1 Set for **1.77**

Flossy Glossy/Pocus Hocus.
X 921-9544 A—1 lb..1 Set for **1.77**

[2] to [5] UPSY DOWNSY LAND. Get set for wacky, turn-about adventures with nonsense-storybook characters! Each set contains 2 playsets—1 Upsy and 1 Downsy. Each playset has poseable, plastic, doll, 2¾ to 3¾ in. tall, that rides in its own plastic vehicle over a chipboard playland. Playland boards can be connected to any other Upsy or Downsy board. Plastic accessories add to the fun. Order exciting story-books above.

[2] Baby So High and Downy Dilly. Vehicles are airo-zoomer and foot-mobile. Plus wind gauge, billboard, bridge, and fence.
X 921-9460 A—1 lb......Set **4.44**

[3] Pudgy Fudgy and Miss Information. Includes rolling miss-information booth and Piggybus plus signs, billboard, bridge, and bench.
X 921-9486 A—1 lb......Set **4.44**

[4] Tickle Pinkle and Mother What Now. Includes ladybug car and go-getter plus gas pump with hose, bridge, signs- and bench.
X 921-9494 A—1 lb......Set **4.44**

[5] Flossy Glossy and Pocus Hocus. Includes firefighting elephant, and dragon wagon plus bucket, signs, hydrant, and bridge.
X 921-9528 A—1 lb......Set **4.44**

Funny Little Flatsy Dolls— 2⁴⁴ each Any 2 for 4⁵⁰

[6] to [9] FLATSY DOLL SET. Comes mounted in picture frame suitable for wall or table-top display, 4½-in. high doll is poseable plastic, with rooted hair and lashes. Doll stands by itself—can even be worn. All pieces removable for separate play. Wt. 0.50 lb.

[6] Dewie Flatsy. Comes in raincoat, boots, panties, with cat, wagon, umbrella.
X 921-2945 A.........Set for **2.44**

[7] Nancy Flatsy. Comes in cap, cape, leotards, shoes—plus carriage, baby.
X 921-3067 A.........Set for **2.44**

[8] Susie Flatsy. In PJ's and slippers—plus canopied, four-postered bed.
X 921-9668 A.........Set for **2.44**

[9] Casey Flatsy. Comes in overalls and cap, plus train that rolls on wheels.
X 921-9619 A.........Set for **2.44**

SAVE 38c WHEN YOU BUY TWO! Order any two Flatsy Dolls sets [6] to [9] and pay only.................**4.50**

[10] MINI TIME-CLOCK FLATSY DOLLS. Two 2¼-in.-mini Flatsy dolls come with toy clock to hang on wall. Clock-face has hands you can move. Dolls and accessories are removable for separate play. 2 bunk beds with ladder, come apart to form twin beds.
X 921-9676 A—Wt. 1.40 lbs. **3.88**

Penneys 453

Upsy Downsys: 1970 J.C. Penney's Christmas catalog showing all the Upsy Downsy dolls.

Quick Curl Casey: This 18½" doll is marked, "©1971 MATTEL INC./HONG/KONG" on her head and "©1971 MATTEL, INC./U.S.A./U.S. PATENT PENDING" on her back. The doll is wearing her original dress but is missing her shoes. **$50.00 – 75.00**.

Best Friend Cynthia: Cynthia uses the same head mold as the 18½" Quick Curl Casey. She is a battery-operated talking doll that works with the help of a record inserted into a slot on her side. Made of plastic and vinyl, the 18½" doll is marked: "©1971 MATTEL INC./HONG/KONG" on her head and "©1971 MATTEL, INC./U.S.A./U.S. PATENT PENDING" on the record button on her back. Redressed and not working, this doll is worth around **$10.00 – 20.00**. In mint condition, all original and working: **$35.00 – 45.00**.

TalkUps: 4½" dolls with bodies that could be pulled away from their heads to make them talk. Their facial features are paper pasted on plastic heads. The paper often peels off or wears off so only dolls with excellent faces can command book value. The TalkUps included Silly Talk (brunette doll), Funny Talk (blond doll), Dressy Talk (doll with orange hair who came with seven different dresses), and Shere. In addition, there were cartoon characters made into TalkUp dolls including Casper the Friendly Ghost, Donald and Daisy Duck and Mickey and Minnie Mouse. The Mattel catalog shown above has Funny Talk's and Silly Talk's names reversed. **$25.00 – 40.00** each. 1972 Mattel catalog.

TalkUps: Funny Talk, Silly Talk, and Dressy Talk. Dressy is hard to find loose and complete with all her outfits. All three TalkUps are marked, "©1971 MATTEL/HONG KONG" on their heads and "©1971 MATTEL INC. HONG KONG" on their bodies. Silly Talk or Funny Talk: **$25.00 – 45.00.** Dressy loose and complete: **$100.00**+. Courtesy Laura Coplen-Miller.

TalkUps: Silly Talk in her original package. MOC: **$125.00 – 200.00.**Courtesy Laura Coplen-Miller.

TalkUps: This TalkUp has a more realistic face than the other dolls. Her name is Shere, but the correct spelling may be Shari, Sheri, or Sherri. She is a rare member of the TalkUps line. **$125.00 – 200.00**. Courtesy Laura Coplen-Miller.

TalkUps: A prototype TalkUps doll with a hand painted face. This doll was acquired from a Mattel designer. Not enough examples to determine a value. Courtesy Laura Coplen-Miller.

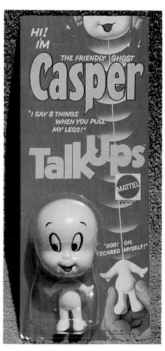

TalkUps: Disney characters Mickey Mouse, Minnie Mouse, Donald Duck, and Daisy Duck came as TalkUps dolls. Not shown in photo is Mickey. Daisy is missing her original dress. The dolls are marked, "©WALT DISNEY PRODUCTIONS/BURBANK TOYS LTD/WELLINGBOROUGH ENGLAND/MADE IN HONG KONG" on their heads and "©1971 MATTEL INC. HONG KONG" on their bodies. **$75.00 – 150.00**. Courtesy Laura Coplen-Miller

TalkUps: Casper the Friendly Ghost was another TalkUps doll. He is shown here in his original package. Casper is marked, "©HARVEY FAMOUS CARTOONS HONG KONG" on his head and "©1971/MATTEL INC./HONG KONG" on his body. MOC: **$200.00 – 250.00**. Courtesy Laura Coplen-Miller.

Talk-A-Littles: Talk-A-Littles pull-string talking rag dolls included 6" Toofums, 7½" Roscoe, and 7" Sassie. **$15.00 – 25.00**. 1972 Mattel catalog.

Small Shots: 5" Small Shots came with roller skates strapped on their feet to race down tracks. In 1972 the line expanded to include the Super Small Shots with jointed waists who came with a riding toy. The Small Shots could be used with Mattel's Hot Wheels tracks. Photo shows the Super Small Shots which included Roarin' Rita and her Wagon, Hasty Harriet and her Skate Crate, Dashin' Dora and her Soapbox, and Reckless Richard and his Go-Cart. **$20.00 – 35.00** each. 1972 Mattel catalog.

Hi Dottie: 17" doll came with a telephone set, one phone doll-sized and the other child-sized. The receiver of the doll-sized phone plugs into Hi Dottie's left hand. When the receiver on the child-size phone is pressed, Hi Dottie talks. She also talks if the button on her left wrist is pressed. The doll is marked, "©1969/MATTEL/INC./MEXICO" on her head and "©1971/MATTEL/INC./MEXICO/U.S. PATENT PEND." on her back. With phone: **$25.00 – 45.00**. 1972 Mattel catalog.

Timey Tell: Timey Tell had a "magic" watch and when her talking ring was pulled, she would tell you the time and say a different phrase for each hour. A matching child-size watch came with the doll. The 16" doll is marked, "©MATTEL, INC. MEXICO" on her head and "©1964 MATTEL, INC./HAWTHORNE, CALIFORNIA U.S.A./PATENTED IN U.S.A. PATENTED/IN CANADA 1962 OTHER/PATENTS PENDING MADE IN MEXICO" on her back. The doll in the photo is missing her shoes, socks, and her watchband. **$20.00 – 25.00**.

Tiny BABY TENDER LOVE
#3188
You'll get the tiniest BABY TENDER LOVE for lots less than you'd expect. She has the same smooth skin, moulded hair. 11½"

Std. Pack: 12
Wt: 9 Lbs.

BABY TENDER LOVE
#3062
Looks and feels so much like a real baby, makes you feel like a real mommy! Bathe her, feed her, change her diaper, too!
14" tall.

Std. Pack: 6   Wt: 16 Lbs.

Living BABY TENDER LOVE
#3163
With movable, poseable arms and legs she seems to be alive! Help her sit. Bathe her, too!
19" tall.

Std. Pack: 6   Wt: 23 Lbs.

Talking BABY TENDER LOVE
#3159
Satin soft, she likes to talk! Says "Nite, nite Mommy!" and 7 things more. Specially constructed voice unit makes it safe for her to bathe. 15" tall.

Std. Pack: 6   Wt: 17½ Lbs.

#3192 Black Tiny BABY TENDER LOVE
Std. Pack: 12   Wt: 9 Lbs.

#3175
Black BABY TENDER LOVE
Std. Pack: 6   Wt: 16 Lbs.

Spanish Speaking BABY TENDER LOVE
#3174
Std. Pack: 6   Wt: 17½ Lbs.

BABY TENDER LOVE Fashions
They're all just as feminine and pretty as you'd expect them to be! Three are for 15 inch dolls. Three for Tiny BABY TENDER LOVE

#A3499 Tiny BABY TENDER LOVE
Playtime Clothes Assortment
#3322 Sweet Sundress (4)
#3323 Snuggletime Suit (4)
#3324 Cuddly Coat (4)

#A3321 BABY TENDER LOVE
Playtime Clothes Assortment Ensembles
#3318 Perky Pinafore (4)   #3320 Romp-A-Rounders (4)
#3319 Beddy-Bye Sleepers (4)

BABY TENDER LOVE Case
#4211
Take your BABY TENDER LOVE doll every place in her sturdy, vinyl, storage and travel case.

Std. Pack: 6
Wt: 9 Lbs

Each size sold in asst. or open stock

Baby Tender Love: This Mattel catalog shows some of the different versions of Baby Tender Love dolls available. They include Tiny Baby Tender Love, Baby Tender Love, Living Baby Tender Love, and Talking Baby Tender Love. Other Tender Love dolls included Tearful Baby Tender Love, Newborn Tender Love, Sweet Sounds Tender Love, Sweet Nature Tender Love, Bless You Baby Tender Love, Happy Birthday Tender Love, Quick Curl Baby Tender Love, and Baby Brother Tender Love. With the exception of Living Baby Tender Love, the limbs of these dolls were not jointed and didn't move. **$20.00 – 35.00** each. 1972 Mattel catalog.

Shoppin' Sheryl: Shoppin' Sheryl is 14½" with a vinyl head and a plastic body and limbs. A magnet inside her right palm and a moveable thumb on her left hand allow Sheryl to hold items. Two buttons on her sides work the moveable thumb. She originally came with a shopping cart, groceries, and display shelves with her name on them. The doll on the left is wearing her original dress but is missing her matching purse, shoes, and socks. Both dolls are marked, "©1970 MATTEL, INC. HONG KONG" on their heads and "©1970 MATTEL, INC./HONG KONG/U.S. PATENT PENDING" on their backs. Dressed doll only: **$25.00 – 30.00**.

Busy Becky: This catalog page shows a Montgomery Ward's exclusive Busy Becky with her Surprise Garden, but a Busy Becky doll in a different outfit was also sold with a housekeeping set. Note the resemblance of this doll to the Shoppin' Sheryl shown above. MIB with accessories: **$65.00 – 80.00**. 1972 Montgomery Ward Christmas catalog.

203

Rock Flowers: 6½" dolls representing hip rock stars. Each doll came with a record that had holes in the center to place a plastic stand in. The doll could then be placed in the stand and would spin around and "dance" to the music when it was played on a record player. Rock Flower dolls have poseable limbs due to a wire inside their vinyl bodies. The original Rock Flower dolls included blond hair Heather, Lilac with red hair, and African-American doll Rosemary. Later Iris and Doug joined the group. These two are harder to find then the first three dolls. Rock Flower dolls are marked, "©MATTEL INC./1970 HONG KONG" on their heads and "HONG KONG/1970 MATTEL, INC./U.S. & FOR. PAT'D//PAT'D IN CANADA" on their backs. The photo shows Heather and Lilac in their original outfits. **$15.00 – 20.00** each.

Rock Flowers: Heather in her original box. MIB: **$35.00 – 50.00**. Courtesy Laura Coplen-Miller.

Rock Flowers: Two different Rosemary dolls in their original boxes. MIB: **$35.00 – 50.00** each. Courtesy Laura Coplen-Miller.

Rock Flowers: Two different Lilac dolls in their original boxes. Note the "Rock Flowers" name on the top of the box near Lilac's name and the slight variation of the design around it from the one on the box on the right. MIB: **$35.00 – 50.00** each. Courtesy Laura Coplen-Miller.

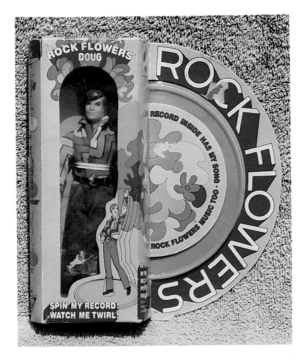

Rock Flowers: Doug shown in his original box. **$40.00 – 55.00**. Courtesy Laura Coplen-Miller

Rock Flowers: Doug shown in a plain cardboard box. Usually dolls in plain boxes like this one are purchased through a mail offer. It is believed this doll was ordered either through some kind of printed advertising offer or as a premium for sending in proofs-of-purchases of some sort. Note the holes in the record where the plastic doll stand would go. **$50.00 – 65.00**. Courtesy Laura Coplen-Miller

Rock Flowers: Iris shown in her original box. **$40.00 – 55.00**. Courtesy Laura Coplen-Miller

Rock Flowers: Toward the end of their "rock star career," Rock Flowers were sold in bags instead of boxes and the "Rock Flowers" name was eliminated from the packaging. The individual dolls' names printed on the package were Doug, Lilac, Heather, and Rosemary. There was no mention of Iris even though she was still available. The photo shows Iris, Doug, and Rosemary. MIP: **$35.00 – 45.00** each. Courtesy Laura Coplen-Miller.

Rock Flowers: Here an unusual "Baggie" Iris includes a record and a Rock Flower fashion that previously was sold separately. **$75.00 – 125.00**. Courtesy Laura Coplen-Miller.

Talking MOTHER GOOSE #5224

Right from nursery land, our snuggly, old Mother Goose recites 10 favorite rhymes. Just pull her talking ring. 20 inches tall, pleasantly plump!

Std. Pack: 6
Wt: 25 Lbs.

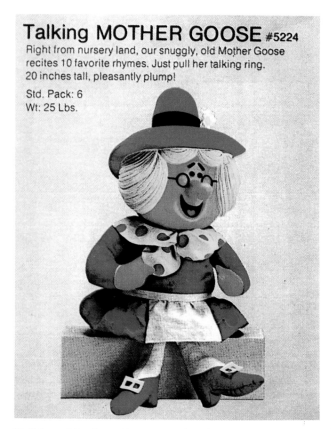

Talking Mother Goose: 20" pull-string talking doll with vinyl head and stuffed body and limbs. **$25.00 – 30.00**. 1972 Mattel catalog.

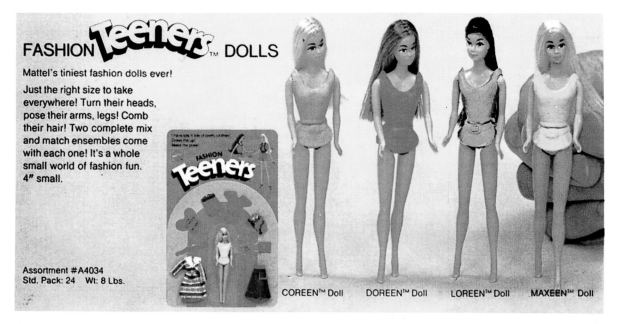

FASHION **Teeners** ™ DOLLS

Mattel's tiniest fashion dolls ever!

Just the right size to take everywhere! Turn their heads, pose their arms, legs! Comb their hair! Two complete mix and match ensembles come with each one! It's a whole small world of fashion fun. 4" small.

Assortment #A4034
Std. Pack: 24   Wt: 8 Lbs.

COREEN™ Doll   DOREEN™ Doll   LOREEN™ Doll   MAXEEN™ Doll

Fashion Teeners: These 4" tiny fashion dolls are often thought to be miniature Barbie dolls since they look quite a bit like Mattel's Malibu Barbie doll. The four different Fashion Teeners include Coreen and Maxeen (both blond), Doreen (red hair), and Loreen (brunette). According to the photo in a 1972 Mattel catalog, it appears Coreen and Maxeen are basically the same doll except Coreen comes dressed in pink and Maxeen comes dressed in yellow. However, the original package on the left in the photo shows a blond doll dressed in yellow with a sticker reading "I'm Coreen" so it's possible Coreen originally came dressed in yellow and Maxeen came dressed in pink. **$5.00 – 10.00** each. 1972 Mattel catalog.

Baby Beans: Mattel made a variety of bean filled dolls in the 1970s. Three different Baby Bean dolls are shown in the photo. The dolls have vinyl heads and hands and "bean" filled bodies and limbs. The two 11½" dolls (measured without their hats) are marked, "©1970 Mattel Inc." on their heads and tagged, "A Quality Original/MATTEL/BABY BEANS©/"©1970 Mattel, Inc./Hawthorne, Calif./Made in Taiwan" along with the material content. The 8" doll on the right is marked, "©1970 Mattel Inc." on his head and tagged, "A Quality Original/MATTEL/ITSY BITSY©/"©1970 Mattel, Inc./Hawthorne, Calif. 90250/Made in Taiwan" along with the material content. **$15.00 – 20.00** each.

Fashion Teeners: This doll is either Coreen or Maxeen from the Fashion Teeners. She is marked, "©1971/MAT-TEL/INC./HONG/KONG" on her lower body. **$5.00 – 10.00**.

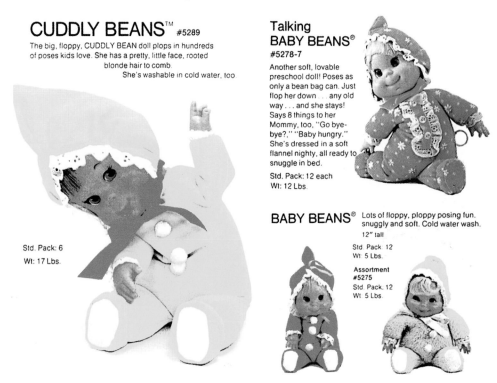

CUDDLY BEANS™ #5289

The big, floppy, CUDDLY BEAN doll plops in hundreds of poses kids love. She has a pretty, little face, rooted blonde hair to comb.
She's washable in cold water, too.

Std. Pack: 6
Wt: 17 Lbs.

Talking BABY BEANS® #5278-7

Another soft, lovable preschool doll! Poses as only a bean bag can. Just flop her down . . . any old way . . . and she stays! Says 8 things to her Mommy, too. "Go bye-bye?," "Baby hungry." She's dressed in a soft flannel nighty, all ready to snuggle in bed.

Std. Pack: 12 each
Wt: 12 Lbs.

BABY BEANS® Lots of floppy, ploppy posing fun, snuggly and soft. Cold water wash.
12" tall

Std. Pack: 12
Wt: 5 Lbs.

Assortment #5275
Std. Pack: 12
Wt: 5 Lbs.

Baby Beans: This 1972 Mattel catalog shows two different Baby Beans dolls as well as Cuddly Beans and Talking Baby Beans. **$15.00 – 20.00** each.

Baby Beans: Five different 12" Baby Beans are shown in this 1973 catalog. **$15.00 – 20.00** each. 1973 Sears Christmas catalog.

BABY BEANS

Soft and squishy bean-bag dolls to cuddle, pamper and pose

1

Give Cry Baby a drink and watch the tears flow each time you tip her head forward

$5⁴⁴

Items 2 thru 5 **$4**⁴⁴ each

(1 thru 5) They'll flip 'n flop into almost any position you want them to. Stuffed with styrene pellets and expanded styrene foam to make 'em super-posable! Vinyl heads and hands. Wash in cold water. Ages 2 to 6.

1 **Cry Baby Beans.** 12 inches tall. Bottle included.
49 C 37004—Wt. 1 lb. 8 oz. $5.44

2 **Biffy Beans.** 12 inches tall.
49 C 37003—Wt. 1 lb. 4 oz. $4.44

3 **Booful Beans.** 12 inches tall.
49 C 35083—Wt. 1 lb. 4 oz. $4.44

4 **Bitty Beans.** 12 inches tall.
49 C 35084—Wt. 1 lb. 4 oz. $4.44

5 **Black Bitty Beans.** 12 in. tall.
49 C 37015—Wt. 1 lb. 4 oz. $4.44

Mama and Baby Beans: There were a number of different versions of Mama and Baby Beans dolls put out by Mattel. Some came with one baby, others came with twin babies. Shown here is the blond version circa 1977. She is 10" tall with Velcro hands. Her baby would have been 3". Mama alone: **$10.00 – 12.00.** With Baby: **$15.00 – 20.00.**

Mama and Baby Beans

5⁸⁸ Set

6 to 9 **Mama and Baby Beans.** Soft, cuddly cotton bodies stuffed with "squooshable" styrene pellet "beans". 10-in. tall Mama's Velcro® hands let her hug and hold her baby. She can pose in lots of different floppy ways. Molded vinyl head with combable rooted hair. She wears a pretty dress and apron. Baby is about 3 in. tall, molded vinyl face and hair, coordinated bunting. Mailable: wt. 1 lb. set.
X 922-0237 A—(6) Blonde 5.88
X 922-0252 A—(7) Brunette 5.88
X 922-0260 A—(8) Black 5.88
X 922-0245 A—(9) Red-Haired 5.88

Mama and Baby Beans: Four versions of Mama and Baby Beans are shown in this 1977 J.C. Penney's Christmas catalog: **$15.00 – 20.00** per set.

Saucy: When you move this 16" doll's left arm up and down, her expression changes to eight different funny faces. The doll is marked, "1972 MATTEL, INC./MEXICO" on her head and "PATENT PENDING" on her back. MIB: **$75.00 – 95.00**. Courtesy Marcia Fanta.

Cathy Quick Curl: A 15" doll with fine copper strands rooted throughout her hair that allow curls to hold quickly and easily. The doll is marked, "©1973 MATTEL, INC. MEXICO." on her head and "©1972 MATTEL, INC./MEXICO/U.S. PATENT PENDING" on her back. **$25.00 – 30.00**.

Peachy and her Puppets: 17" doll came with four puppets. Peachy is marked, "©1972 MATTEL, INC./MEXICO" on her head and "1964 MATTEL,INC./HAWTHORNE, CALIF." on her back. MIB: **$35.00 – 50.00**. Courtesy Marcia Fanta.

Close-up of Peachy's puppets; dog, girl, clown, and monkey. Peachy's puppets are tagged, "Taiwan." **$3.00 – 8.00** each.

Sunshine Family: In 1974 Mattel introduced the Sunshine Family, consisting of the father Steve, the mother Steffie, and baby Sweets. The dolls were available in a set with all three dolls. Steve is 9½", Steffie is 9", and Sweets is 3". Steffie is missing her original apron in the photo. All three dolls are marked, "©1973/MATTEL, INC." on their heads and "©1973/MATTEL, INC./TAIWAN," on their backs. Steffie/Steve: **$15.00 – 20.00** each. Sweets: **$5.00 – 10.00**.

Sunshine Family: In 1978, the last year the Sunshine Family appeared in major department store catalogs, Baby Sweets was issued in an older version and a new baby was added to the line. On the original box the set of four Sunshine Family dolls came in, the only name given for the sister was "Little Sister," but in a booklet that came with the set it refers to her by the name "Sweets." No name is given for the new baby either on the box or in the booklet. The 4¾" Sweets and the 3" baby are not as common as the other earlier dolls since they weren't available as long. The toddler-size Sweets is marked, "©1977/MATTEL, INC. /TAIWAN" on her head and "©Mattel, Inc. 1977/TAIWAN," on her back. The new baby is basically the same baby as the earlier Sweets dolls only he has freckles and comes dressed in the outfit shown in the photo. Sister complete with shoes: **$20.00 – 25.00**. New Baby with original outfit: **$10.00 – 15.00**.

Sunshine Family: Many variations of the dolls in the Sunshine line exist, so a variety of color and styles of each dolls' clothing as well as different hairstyles and textures can be found. Variations of some Steve dolls are shown in this photo. All the dolls in the photo have the same markings, "©1973/MATTEL, INC." on their heads and "©1973/MATTEL, INC./TAIWAN," on their backs. **$15.00 – 20.00** each.

Sunshine Family: A variety of different Steffie dolls is shown in the photo. The three dolls on the right would have had a white apron over their original dresses. All the dolls are marked the same as the Steve dolls at the bottom of the previous page. **$15.00 – 20.00** each.

Sunshine Family: The Sunshine extended family included a 9½" grandfather and a 9" grandmother. Both Grandpa and Grandma Sunshine are marked, "©1975/TAIWAN/MATTEL, INC." on their heads and "©1973/MATTEL, INC./TAIWAN" on their backs. Note the differences in the Grandfather's hair color and style. **$20.00 – 25.00** each.

Honey Hill Bunch: Representing a group of neighborhood kids, these dolls have vinyl heads and stuffed bodies and limbs. They have Velcro strips on their hands to hold their hands together or to hold felt accessories. The dolls were sold either in a play set or separately, and each doll came with an accessory to hold. The photo shows (from left to right) 4" Darlin' (originally came with a purse), 4" Slugger (originally came with a baseball bat), and 3" Li'l Kid (originally came with a dog). The dolls are marked, "©1975/MATTEL, INC./TAIWAN" on their heads and tagged on their bodies, "©Mattel Inc.1975/HAWTHORNE, Calif./90250" along with the material content and license information. **$5.00 – 10.00** each. Courtesy Dal Lowenbein.

Honey Hill Bunch: 4" I.Q. and 4" tall Slugger shown in their original boxes. MIB: **$20.00 – 25.00** each. Courtesy Sharon Wendrow/Memory Lane.

Young Sweethearts: Young Sweethearts, Michael and Melinda, came as a set. Michael is 12" and Melinda is 11½". The tags around their necks are not original to the dolls. MIB: **$30.00 – 50.00**. Courtesy Sharon Wendrow/Memory Lane.

Donny and Marie Osmond: These dolls were issued in 1976 when the *Donny and Marie Show* was on television. Marie is an 11½" Barbie-size doll and is marked, "©MATTEL, INC. /1966/KOREA" on her lower body. Donny is marked, "1088 0500 2/©MATTEL/INC. 1968 HONG KONG" on his back. Loose dolls: **$15.00 – 20.00**. MIB: **$35.00 – 45.00**.

Young Sweethearts: 12" Michael is marked "©1975 MATTEL, INC./TAIWAN" on his head; 11½" Melinda has no markings on her head. Both dolls are marked, "©MATTEL, INC.1975/TAIWAN" on their backs. **$15.00 – 20.00** each.

Donny and Marie Osmond: The two celebrity dolls are shown here in their television studio playset. *Courtesy Patty, Greg, and Michelle Andrews.*

215

Jimmy Osmond: This 10" doll represents the little brother of Donny and Marie. He is not as common as the Donny and Marie dolls. NRFB: **$65.00 – 80.00.** Courtesy Sharon Wendrow/Memory Lane.

Cheryl Ladd/Kate Jackson: These 11½" dolls are often referred to as being Charlie's Angels dolls by collectors, but the dolls are representing the actresses themselves and not the characters they played in the television show *Charlie's Angels* which was very popular at the time the dolls were issued. Their original boxes tout them as "TV's Star Women." Mego made 12¼" dolls of two other Charlie's Angels members, Farrah Fawcett and Jaclyn Smith in 1977, a year before the Mattel dolls came out. Mattel's Kate Jackson doll is marked, "©MATTEL, INC./1978/" on her head and "©MATTEL, INC./1966/14 (off to left)/KOREA" on her lower body. Cheryl has the same markings as Kate on her back, but the markings on her head are very faint as if they were either worn off on the mold or had been removed so they are just barely visible. The dolls in the photo have been redressed. In original clothes: **$25.00 – 35.00** each.

Debby Boone: 11½" Barbie-size doll representing teenage singing sensation of the late 1970s. The doll uses the Barbie body and is marked, "©RESI, INC. 1978/TAIWAN" on her head and "©MATTEL, INC. 1966" on her back. NRFB: **$65.00 – 75.00**. Courtesy Sharon Wendrow/Memory Lane

❀MEGO❀

Mego was the maker of a large number of action figures and dolls representing celebrities and television characters during the 1970s.

Batman & Robin: 8" dolls both with painted on masks. Batman is missing one glove. Both dolls are marked, "N.P.P. INC./ ©1972" on their heads and "©MEGO CORP. 1974/REG.U.S. PAT.OFF./PAT.PENDING/HONG KONG" on their backs. **$50.00 – 65.00** each.

Supergirl & Superman: Both dolls are 8". Supergirl is missing her original shoes. She is much more difficult to find than many of the other 8" Super Hero dolls Mego put out in the 1970s. She is marked, "©N.P.P. INC./1973" on her head and "©MEGO CORP./MGM-LXXII/ PAT.PENDING/MADE IN/HONG KONG" on her back. Superman is marked, "©MEGO CORP. 1974/REG.U.S. PAT.OFF./PAT.PENDING/HONG KONG" on his back. Supergirl: **$90.00 – 125.00**. Superman: **$40.00 – 55.00**.

Spiderman: 8" Spiderman is marked, "©MAR-VEL CO.1972" on his head and "©MEGO CORP. 1974/REG.U.S. PAT.OFF./PAT.PENDING/HONG KONG" on his back. He is easy to find, so his value is lower than many of the other Mego Super Heros. **$20.00 – 25.00**.

Wizard of Oz: 8" dolls from the movie *The Wizard of Oz*. Of the set shown, Dorothy is the easiest to find and the Wicked Witch is the most difficult. The Wizard was included in the Emerald City playset and was also sold separately. **$30.00 – 45.00** each. 1972 Montgomery Ward Christmas catalog.

Dinah-mite: 8" fully poseable fashion doll. Numerous fashions were available separately for her. **$25.00 – 30.00**. 1973 Montgomery Ward Christmas catalog.

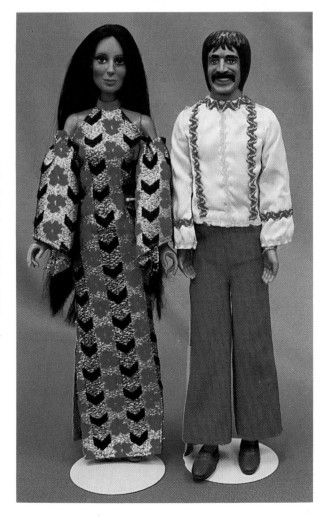

Sonny and Cher: Like many celebrities, singing couple Sonny and Cher were made into dolls. A number of outfits for these 12½" Mego dolls were sold separately for them. Here Sonny is wearing Gypsy King and Cher is wearing her Madame Butterfly dress. Cher is marked, "3906/AF/MEGO CORP. /19©75" on her head and "©MEGO CORP. 1975/MADE IN HONG KONG" on her lower back. Sonny is marked, "MEGO CORP. 1976" on his head and "©MEGO CORP. 1976/MADE IN HONG KONG" on his lower back. In original outfits: **$25.00 – 35.00** each.

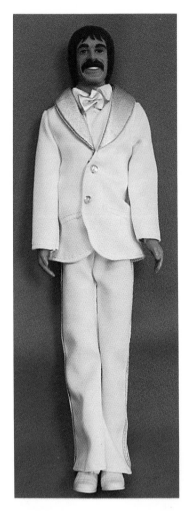

Cher: 12½" doll shown in her original box. MIB: **$40.00 – 50.00**.

Cher: Back of the Cher box showing some of her clothing designed by Bob Mackie.

Sonny: 12½" Sonny wearing his White Tux outfit. With outfit: **$40.00 – 45.00**.

Growing Hair Cher: This doll features shoulder-length hair all around her head with a "growing-hair" section coming out from the top of her head. Pulling on the growing-hair section made it longer. A special key that came with the doll could be inserted into a hole in her back to shorten the hair. This doll is not as common as the previous Cher doll. MIB: **$65.00 – 85.00**.

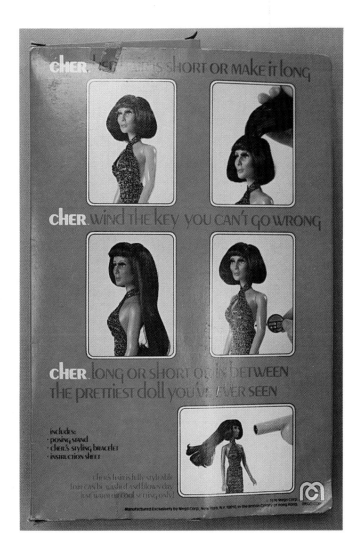

Growing Hair Cher: Back of the Growing Hair Cher box.

Cher: 12½" doll shown in what is often referred to as her Gypsy box. The dolls that came in this box were originally dressed in simple red or blue nylon swimsuits. The bodies of these dolls are made of a lightweight plastic, unlike the earlier dolls that had vinyl bodies. The quality of the doll is not as attractive to collectors as the previous Cher doll, so when loose she is usually not priced as high. However, when the doll is still in her original box, the photo of Cher on the front is enticing enough to collectors to make its value slightly higher than a MIB doll with the orange box. This same doll was also sold in a simple plastic bag with a cardboard hanger at the top. The "baggie" Cher, as she is often referred to, is worth about half the boxed "Gypsy" doll's value if still in her original package. NRFB: **$55.00 – 65.00**. Courtesy Sharon Wendrow/Memory Lane.

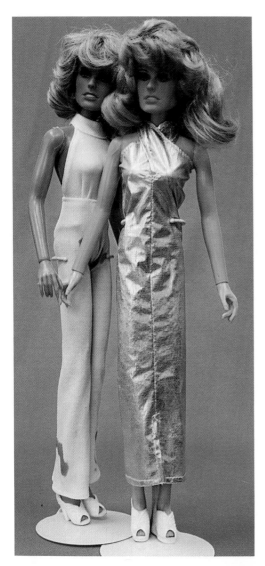

Farrah Fawcett: The doll on the left wearing her original white jumpsuit has hair that is a grayish blond color. It is believed that these grayish hair color dolls are the earlier versions of Farrah. The vinyl skin color on the doll with the grayish-blond hair is a darker tan than the doll's coloring on the right. The doll on the right has been redressed. Both dolls have green eyes and are marked, "©FARRAH" on their heads and "©MEGO CORP. 1975/MADE IN HONG KONG" on their backs. A third version of Farrah was made and sold in a plastic bag with a cardboard label on the top instead of in a box as the two dolls shown here. The "baggie" dolls have hollow legs and cupped hands on hollow arms. The necks on the baggie dolls are shorter than on the boxed dolls. **$25.00 – 40.00** each.

Farrah Fawcett: Close-up of two Farrah dolls showing the difference in their hair colors and slightly different hairstyles.

Diana Ross: 12½" doll made in the image of singer Diana Ross. The doll is marked, "©MOTOWN/RECORD CORPORATION" on her head and "©MEGO CORP. 1975/MADE IN HONG KONG" on her back. NRFB: **$150.00 – 225.00.** Courtesy Sharon Wendrow/Memory Lane.

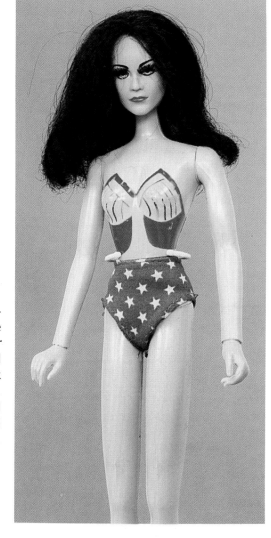

Wonder Woman: This 12½" doll represented actress Lynda Carter who played the title role on the television series *Wonder Woman* starting in 1976. Mego also issued this same doll without the molded-on tank top shown here. She is marked, "D.C. COMICS/INC. 1976" on her head and "©MEGO CORP. 1975/MADE IN HONG KONG" on her lower back. Missing boots, bracelets, and hair band: **$30.00 – 40.00.**

The Waltons: 8" dolls based on characters from the television series *The Waltons*. The dolls came in three different two-doll sets, Mom and Pop, Grandma and Grandpa, and JohnBoy and Ellen (although the character on the show was called Mary Ellen). Mego did not make dolls of the other characters from the show. The dolls are fully jointed and marked, "©1974 LORIMAR INC" on their heads and "©MEGO CORP MCM-LXXII PAT. PENDING MADE IN HONG KONG" on their backs. MIB: **$35.00** each. Courtesy Janet and Mike Lawrence.

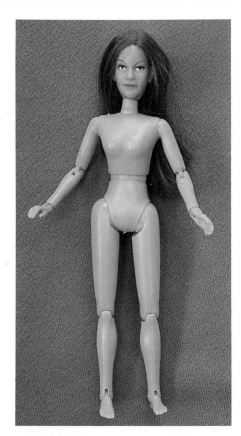

"Ellen" Walton: Photo shows the body construction of the 8" Mego dolls.

❀ MODEL TOYS LTD. ❀

Daisy: Daisy was a popular 9" British fashion doll. Both the doll and her clothing were designed by fashion designer Mary Quant starting in 1973. The doll's name came from Mary Quant's daisy flower logo. Originally Daisy was made exclusively for Flair Toys Limited, however, on the back of the Daisy box in the photo it reads, "Made exclusively for Model Toys Ltd. in the Crown Colony of Hong Kong. Irwin Toy Ltd., 43 Hanna Ave. Toronto, Ontario M6K1X8" so perhaps this particular Daisy is a Canadian issued doll. The Daisy shown in her original box is wearing an outfit called "Dotty." Daisy is marked, "©MODEL TOYS LTD/HONG KONG/P" on her back. MIB: **$70.00 – 95.00.** Courtesy Janet and Mike Lawrence.

Daisy: Daisy shown with a MIP outfit "Miranda 65141." The doll is marked, "©MODEL TOYS LTD/HONG KONG" on her back. Loose doll: **$30.00 – 45.00**. Courtesy Janet and Mike Lawrence.

❀ MY TOY COMPANY ❀

Story Time, Little Red Riding Hood: This doll is similar to Mattel's Liddle Kiddles or Hasbro's Storykin dolls. The outside of the storybook reads, "1968 MY TOY CO., INC. MADE IN HONG KONG." The vinyl doll is 3½" and poseable. She is marked, "MADE IN HONG KONG" on her back. MIP: **$25.00 – 40.00**. Courtesy Robin Englehart/ Photo by Nancy Jean Mong.

❀ PARIS & COMPANY ❀

Happy Hippies: 2½" doll that has a metal loop on top of his head and originally came with a silver chain to wear him as a necklace. His original paper tag reads, "Happy Hippies" on one side and "©PARIS & CO./1968/MADE IN HONG KONG" on the other. Underneath his mustache is a toothy smile. The doll is similar to Mattel Liddle Kiddles and Hasbro Storykins. Happy Hippies came in several different styles. **$20.00 – 25.00.**

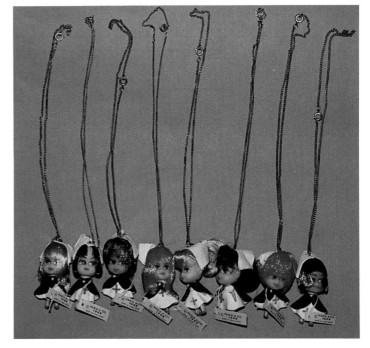

Nurse Dolls (name unknown): 2½" dolls that have metal loops on top of their heads and chains to wear them as necklaces. The dolls are unmarked but have a pink rectangle paper tag that says, "©PARIS & CO./1968/MADE IN HONG KONG." A few of the dolls in the photo also have metal gold tags attached to the rings in their head. The tags are stamped "Paris©". With paper tag and chain: **$10.00 – 12.00 each.** Courtesy Robin Englehart/Photo by Nancy Jean Mong.

❀ PEDIGREE ❀

Pedigree was an English toy company that made many different dolls. In an agreement with the Ideal Toy Company, starting in 1963 Pedigree produced a doll called Sindy just like Ideal's Tammy doll. The early Sindy looked very much like Tammy, and there were numerous similarities between the two dolls as well as many similarities with other members of both lines. Sindy's little sister was Patch, and Patch's friend (who is hard to find today) was Poppet. Tammy's little sister was Pepper, and Pepper's friend (who is hard to find today) was Patti. Sindy had a friend named Mitzi. Tammy had a friend named Misty. The similarities go on and on. By 1966 Tammy was no longer being made, but Sindy is still being manufactured today, now by Hasbro.

England's Pedigree Sindy on the left wearing her "Country Walk" outfit next to America's Ideal Tammy wearing her "Cheerleader" outfit. Both stands have the dolls' respective names printed on them, the shoes they are wearing look to be of the same mold, and both dogs are the same with Sindy's dog being just slightly smaller than Tammy's. Because Sindy and her friends were not initially made for the U.S. market, the Pedigree dolls are much sought after by Sindy and/or Tammy collectors in the U.S. The Sindy doll produced by Marx Toys in the 1970s for the U.S. market is still easily found, so values on those dolls are much lower than the Pedigree dolls. See Marx for other Sindy dolls. Pedigree Sindy with outfit: **$100.00 – 150.00**. Ideal Tammy with outfit: **$50.00 – 65.00**.

Sindy: A variety of early Sindy dolls. The brunette doll on the left is wearing her outfit called Leather Look. She has straight legs. The doll in the middle is wearing her blue bathing suit to Sweet Swimmer. She has bendable legs. The doll on the right also has bendable legs and is wearing the original outfit she was sold in called Weekenders. The dolls are marked, "MADE IN ENGLAND" on their heads. Some pieces of their clothing are tagged, "GENUINE/ Sindy/MADE IN/ENGLAND" with a cloth tag, while other pieces are untagged. Dolls with outfits: **$100.00 – 150.00** each. Courtesy Janet and Mike Lawrence.

Sindy: This Sindy probably dates somewhere from the late 1970s to the mid-1980s. The doll was purchased from Holland, but whether or not it was a doll sold for the Dutch market is unknown. No documentation or information about the doll could be located to determine if she may have been offered through some sort of airline promotion or if the outfit was originally sold separately in stores. The doll is marked, "33055X" on her head and has no markings on her back. **$60.00 – 75.00**. Courtesy Janet and Mike Lawrence.

Sindy: This Sindy is jointed at the neck, shoulders, elbows, waist, hips, and knees. She has rooted eyelashes. In 1971 she was sold as Lovely Lively Sindy, but earlier the outfit was sold separately and was called Lunch Date. This Sindy doll is marked, "3055X" on her head and "MADE IN HONG KONG" on her back with a "P" under it. Doll with outfit: **$60.00 – 75.00**. Courtesy Janet and Mike Lawrence.

Paul: Sindy's boyfriend was Paul. He came with either painted or rooted hair. The painted hair Paul in the photo is shown wearing his original outfit. The shirt is tagged, "GENUINE /Paul/MADE IN/HONG KONG." 12½" Paul is marked "MADE IN HONG KONG" on his back. **$60.00 – 75.00**. Courtesy Janet and Mike Lawrence.

Patch: Patch was Sindy's 9" younger sister. The Patch doll on the left without the headscarf measures only 8½" and has a slightly smaller head than other Patch dolls. There are some Patch dolls, as well as some Sindy dolls, with slightly smaller heads accounting for slightly smaller sized dolls. The doll on the right with the headscarf is 9". Both Patch dolls are marked, "MADE IN HONG KONG" on their backs. Doll in original outfit: **$75.00 – 100.00**. Courtesy Janet and Mike Lawrence.

❀ PRESSMAN TOYS ❀

Small World Dolls: These 8" dolls represented the animated characters from Disney's "It's A Small World" display from the 1964 – 1965 New York World's Fair. The Dutch girl on the right is missing her original hat. Three of the dolls pictured here are marked, "PRESSMAN TOYS/©WALT DISNEY/PROD.1965" on their heads, but the doll third from the left is marked, "PRESS-LIPS DOLL/©WALT DISNEY/PROD.1965." **$20.00 – 35.00** each.

Walt Disney's Small World Dolls

8-inch friends in costumes of far-away lands

$2⁹⁷ each

Adorable dolls in beautifully detailed costumes have bending legs, charming faces. Start a collection.

1 **French Can-Can.** Her skirt's a whirl of red satin and ruffles, her stockings black lace. She wears a glamorous hat of black feathers. 49 N 3623—Shpg. wt. 9 oz....$2.97

2 **Dutch Girl.** Has long blonde braids and bangs, wears a brocaded skirt, embroidered apron. Her hat is white felt, her shoes are plastic. 49 N 3631—Shpg. wt. 9 oz....$2.97

3 **South American.** Full of color, with a basket of fake flowers on her head, a colorful "patchwork" skirt, yellow blouse, contrast trim. 49 N 3628—Shpg. wt. 9 oz....$2.97

4 **African.** Wears a colorful toga, bracelets on wrist and ankles, bright beads on neck, head band. 49 N 3633—Shpg. wt. 9 oz....$2.97

5 **Japanese.** In a flowered silk kimono, with contrasting obi sash and sleeves. Carries a fan. 49 N 3640—Shpg. wt. 9 oz....$2.97

1965 Sears Christmas catalog showing some of Walt Disney's 8" Small World dolls.

❀ REMCO ❀

The Littlechap Family

The Littlechap family of dolls first appeared on the market in 1964. Their biography, which appeared in their fashion booklets and clothing boxes, described them as an upscale American family consisting of the golf-loving father Dr. John, his president-of-the-PTA wife Lisa, their daughter, 17-year-old honor student Judy and their 10-year-old tomboy daughter Libby. Their excellent quality fashions were made in Japan and included many detailed accessories. John Littlechap originally came dressed in a terry cloth robe with a towel around his neck and the three female members of the family came wearing terry cloth wraps. Since the Littlechap dolls were odd sizes, it was difficult for them to share clothing with other fashion dolls on the market at the time, thus creating the need for consumers to purchase Remco Littlechap clothing made specifically for them.

Each Littlechap doll is marked with his or her name and "REMCO INDUSTRIES/1963" in a circle on his or her back. In this photo, Dr. John is shown wearing his original terry cloth robe, Lisa is wearing her Basic Black Dress, Judy is in her Football Outfit, and Libby is shown wearing her Plaid Reefer Coat. Littlechap outfits range from **$20.00 – 75.00**, mint and complete with accessories. Loose dolls wearing their original terry cloth cover-ups range in value from **$20.00 – 40.00**. In the background is a Littlechaps carrying case valued at **$25.00 – 40.00**.

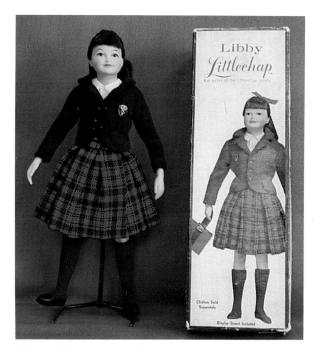

Libby Littlechap: The younger daughter of the Littlechap family with her original box. She originally came wearing a terry cloth cover-up, but here she is redressed in her Three-Piece Blazer outfit. The 10½" doll is marked, "Libby/ Littlechap©/ REMCO INDUSTRIES/1963" in a circle on her back. MIB wearing Littlechap clothing: **$50.00 – 70.00**.

Dr. John Littlechap: The father of the Littlechap family in his original box wearing his original terry cloth robe and towel around his neck. The 15" doll is marked, "Dr./John/ Littlechap©/ REMCO INDUSTRIES/1963" in a circle on his back with a "2" underneath. MIB: **$65.00 – 70.00**.

Judy Littlechap: Most 13½" Judy dolls have brown eyes, but some blue-eyed Judy dolls like the one shown here were also produced. Loose blue-eyed doll: **$40.00 – 75.00**.

Heidi: 5½" Heidi was the first and most popular doll in Remco's line of Pocketbook Dolls. She has a slightly out-of-proportion sized head and a button on her stomach that when pushed springs her hand up to wave. She came housed in a red plastic pocketbook-style case. A rare black version of Heidi was also available. Heidi is marked, "©1964/REMCO IND. INC./K164" on her head (number varies on last line) and "©/REMCO/ INDUSTRIES/INC." on her back. White version with case: **$30.00 – 40.00**. Black version with case: **$75.00 – 125.00**. Courtesy Elaine McGrath.

Jan: Not long after her introduction, Heidi was joined by her 5½" Japanese friend Jan who came in a blue plastic pocketbook-style case. The photo shows two different Jan dolls. Note the doll on the left has a smaller head and lighter lip coloring than the doll on the right. Heidi dolls with smaller heads were also produced. The Jan doll on the left is marked, "©J3/REMCO IND.1966/HONG KONG/22" on her head and "©/REMCO/INDUSTRIES/INC." on her back. The Jan doll on the right is marked, "2/F J22 6/REMCO IND.INC. ©1965" on her head and "©/REMCO/INDUSTRIES/INC." on her back. Loose/no case: **$10.00 – 15.00** each.

This 1966 Montgomery Ward Christmas catalog shows some of the clothing available for the Pocketbook line of dolls.

Heidi's House with Garden That Grows! $9⁸⁹

REAL GRASS GROWS IN THE GARDEN and real vines grow in the window boxes—just plant the seeds, water them and watch—they start growing in just a few days! Seeds, soil and tools included. Garden has a pond you can fill with water and float the 2 plastic ducks.

HOUSE OF STURDY METAL, PLASTIC is easy to assemble—room is gaily decorated in full color, there's a plastic chair and sofa that opens into a bed at night. House, Garden about 38 in. long.
48 HT 11705—House, Garden. (No dolls.) Ship. wt. 5 lbs. 12 oz...$9.89

 $1⁴⁹

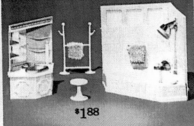 $1⁸⁸

 $2⁹⁹

For the Dinette

BUFFET DOORS OPEN, holds plates, knives, forks, spoons, cups, sugar, creamer, coffee pot, 2 chairs, table with extra leaf.
48HT11406—(No dolls.) Wt. 1 lb. 4 oz. Set $1.49

Her Own Bath Set

SQUEEZE THE BULB and water sprays from shower. Or if she prefers a bath, water comes from the faucet. Vanity with sink, stool, towel rack with 2 real towels.
48 HT 11404—Ship. wt. 1 lb. 2 oz... Set $1.88

For the Bedroom

INCLUDES DOUBLE-DECK BED with ladder, chair, dresser with drawers that open and a real mirror. Lamp on table really lights—use "AA" battery (order Pg. 370).
48 HT 11405—Ship. wt. 2 lbs. 2 oz............Set $2.99

$3⁴⁹

$1⁸⁸

$1⁸⁸

Heidi Shows Slides

FILM PROJECTION SET—slide-film storage rack holds 12 shows—fun and adventure cartoons—192 slides all in color. Screen, projector—use 2 "D" batteries (Order Pg. 370).
48 HT 11707—Ship. wt. 2 lbs. 2 oz.......... Set $3.49

Let's Ride in a Jeep

FUZZY POODLE RIDES IN HEIDI'S JEEP. Phone booth with lift-off receiver. Also includes pretend penny that actually goes into pretend parking meter.
48 HT 11703—Ship. wt. 1 lb. 3 oz........... Set $1.88

Heidi Gets Well

LET'S PLAY NURSE—hospital bed, lamp, reading light, chest of drawers, medicine chest, fever chart, tray, blanket.
48HT11403—Ship. wt. 1 lb. 2 oz. Set $1.88

15 Cycling Fun $2⁹⁹

Heidi's Plane 16 $1⁴⁹

Ponycart Play 17 $1⁴⁹

Time for Tea 18 $1⁹⁹

⑮ MOTORCYCLE WHEELS TURN, rear seat for Jan, Hildy. Hot Dog stand, soda cooler with sliding doors.
48 HT 11706—Ship. wt. 2 lbs. 12 oz........Set $2.99

⑯ POWDER PUFF DERBY PLANE—propeller spins, wheels move. Colorful pilot's scarf included. (No dolls.)
48 HT 11708—Ship. wt. 1 lb. 4 oz. $1.49

⑰ CART HAS ROLLING WHEELS, back steps. Pony detaches for riding—has reins, harness, bridle. (No dolls.)
48 HT 11709—Ship. wt. 1 lb. 4 oz.............$1.49

⑱ TEA SET—includes kimono, sash, fan, shoes. Tea table, 2 cushions, teapot, 2 cups, tray and vase.
48 HT 11704—(No doll.) Ship. wt. 7 oz......Set $1.99

Many accessories were issued for Heidi, Jan, and their friends like those pictured here in the 1966 Montgomery Ward Christmas catalog.

Pocketbook Dolls: Because Heidi and Jan are the two dolls in the Pocketbook line that most people remember from their childhood, they seem to be the two dolls collectors most often want to obtain today. They are also the easiest to find. Later dolls included 4¾" sister Hildy, 4½" brother Herby, 5½" Spunky, and 4¾" Pip. All the dolls in the line came packaged in plastic pocketbook cases. Pictured in front row: Hildy, Herby, Pip; back row: Jan, Heidi, Spunky. The three larger-sized dolls, Jan, Heidi, and Spunky, have buttons on their stomachs that make them wave, while the smaller three dolls do not. The three larger-sized dolls are all marked, "©/REMCO/ INDUSTRIES/INC." on their backs. In addition, Jan is marked, "2/F J22 6/REMCO IND.INC./©1965" on her head. Heidi is marked, "©1964/REMCO IND. INC./K164" on her head. Spunky is marked, "F66/2/REMCO IND. INC./©1966" on her head. It is hard to find Spunky with her original glasses. Heidi's little sister Hildy is marked, "REMCO IND.INC./©1966/F36" on her head. Her body, like the bodies of the other two smaller dolls Herby and Pip, is unmarked. Heidi's little brother Herby is marked, "REMCO IND.INC./©1966/F78" on his head. Pip is marked, "F66/REMCO IND.INC./©1966" on her head. This doll's head mold was later used for Remco's Finger Ding dolls. Pip tends to be harder to find than other members in the line. Mint with case: **$30.00 – 55.00** each.

T.V. Jones and Pussy Meow: These two 5¾" dolls came packaged inside television-shaped cases. Both animals have buttons on their chests that when pushed, turn the dolls' heads. Both animals also make a little squeak noise like a bark and a meow when you push the button. Other characters in the line included Hana Hippo, Ellie Elephant, Patsy Panda, and Mr. and Mrs. Mouse. T.V. Jones in case: **$75.00 – 100.00**. Pussy Meow in case: **$80.00 – 110.00**. Courtesy Elaine McGrath.

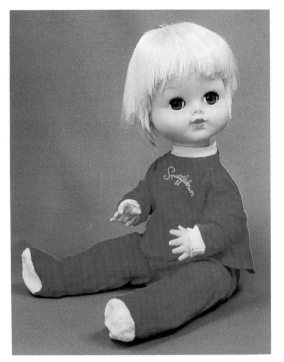

Little Orphan Annie: 16" cloth doll with orange yarn hair. On the belly is written, "KISS 'N HUG ME" along with three hearts. The doll is tagged, "Little Orphan Annie" on one side and "1967/Remco Ind. Inc." on the other. **$20.00 – $30.00**. Courtesy Elaine McGrath.

Snugglebun: This 15" doll originally came with a plastic nightstand containing a lamp and bottle warmer. When the button on her chest is squeezed, her head moves and she cries. The doll is marked, "67/REMCO IND. INC./©1965" on her head and "REMCO IND. INC./©1965/K9" on her back. Doll only: **$15.00 – 20.00**.

Baby Crawl-Along: This 20" doll came with a removable harness, which was attached to a plastic battery case. The doll crawls when a button on the case is pushed. The doll is marked, "R16/REMCO IND.INC./©1967" on the head. Without battery case: **$15.00 – 20.00**. Working/with battery case: **$25.00 – 35.00**.

Tippy Tumbles: 17" doll that does somersaults and handstands with the aid of a plastic "pocketbook" battery case that attaches by cord to a plug in her ankle. Tippy Tumbles originally came wearing blue tights and a sleeveless striped top. The photo shows two variations of Tippy's shirt. In 1977 the Ideal Toy Company also issued a doll called Tippy Tumbles which worked the same way as Remco's doll did. Ideal's Tippy Tumbles doll had blond hair and was dressed in a one-piece jumpsuit. Remco's Tippy is marked, "SM/E51/ REMCO IND.INC./19©69". Without battery case: **$15.00 – 20.00**. Working/with battery case: **$25.00 – 35.00**.

Tumbling Tomboy: 17" Tumbling Tomboy works the same way as Tippy Tumbles, doing somersaults and handstands by pressing the button on a plastic battery case that attaches to her ankle. Some Tumbling Tomboy dolls came with a plastic go-cart that she could ride in when not tumbling around, but other dolls may have been available without the cart. Tumbling Tomboy is marked, "2908/17EYE/NEW/E20/REMCO IND.INC./19©69" on her head. Without battery case: **$15.00 – 20.00**. Working/with battery case: **$25.00 – 35.00**.

Finger Ding Dolls: By placing two fingers inside the legs of these 5½" dolls, a child could make them walk, run, dance, or skate. Without their clothing, Finger Ding Dolls have no legs, only a head, torso, and arms. It is hard for shoes to stay on the dolls' feet without the bulk of fingers inside the tights, so often the shoes that originally came with the dolls are missing. The three Finger Ding Dolls shown here are the most common: Millie Mod, Sally Ice Skater, and Betty Ballerina. All three dolls use the "Pip" face mold from Remco's Pocketbook doll line. The dolls are marked, "2504/REMCO IND.INC./©1966" on their heads and "©1969/REMCO IND. INC./U.S. & FOREIGN/PAT. PEND./JAPAN" on their backs. They are shown with the back of their original box. Loose/without shoes: **$5.00 – 10.00** each.

Finger Ding Dolls: Sally Ice Skater, Betty Ballerina, and Millie Mod shown in their original boxes. MIB: **$35.00 – 55.00** each.

Adventure Boy: In an attempt to appeal to boys, Remco issued a boy version of the Finger Ding Dolls but did not use the name Finger Ding with him. Adventure Boy was marketed more as an action figure than a doll. He came with a snowmobile and a pair of skis. The sleeves of his red jumpsuit are molded as part of his arms and his yellow vinyl vest-front (no back) is stitched onto the jumpsuit. His yellow boots have two holes in the bottoms for attaching the skis. 5½" Adventure Boy is marked, "REMCO IND.INC./19(70" on his head and "©1970/REMCO IND. INC./HARRISON N.J./PAT. PEND./HONG KONG" on his back. MIB: **$40.00 – 55.00**.

Adventure Boy: Another version of Adventure Boy came with a spacecraft. This version is harder to find than the Adventure Boy above. A third version of Adventure Boy available came with a "sky-mobile." Mint and complete: **$30.00 – 45.00**. Courtesy Robin Englehart.

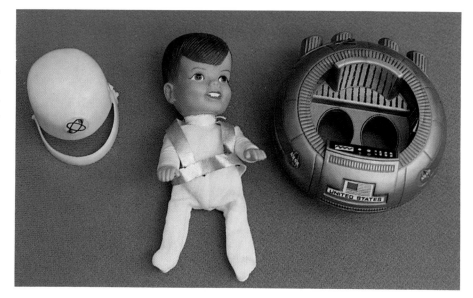

Adventure Boy: Adventure Boy inside his spacecraft. Courtesy Robin Englehart.

Monkees Clever Finger Dolls: This 5" doll represents Davy Jones of the Monkees singing group. Like Adventure Boy, the sleeves of his shirt are molded as part of his arms. Davy is marked with a big "2" on his head and "©1970/REMCO IND. INC./HARRISON N.J./PAT. PEND./HONG KONG" on his back. **$20.00 – 30.00**.

Finger Ding Flower Kids: The Finger Ding Flower Kids were Finger Ding dolls wearing flower petal hats and leaf-shaped collars. The dolls included Li'l Buttercup, Li'l Daisy, and Li'l Rose. Shown in the photo are Li'l Buttercup and Li'l Daisy missing her flower petal hat. Circa 1971. The 5" dolls are marked, "2504/REMCO IND.INC./19©66" on their heads and "©1969/REMCO IND. INC./U.S. & FOREIGN/PAT. PEND./HONG KONG" on their backs. Without shoes: **$15.00 – 20.00** each.

Finger Ding Animals: There are three Finger Ding Animals, Hildy Hen, who came with her own plastic egg, Spunky Monkey, who came with plastic roller skates, and Kitty Kangaroo. These animals are harder to find than the other Finger Ding dolls. Hildy and Spunky are shown in the photo. The 5" dolls are marked, "REMCO IND.INC./19©70" on their backs. Like all the Finger Ding dolls, they often come without their shoes, or in this case, feet. Loose with feet: **$20.00 – 25.00** each.

Finger Ding Animals: Spunky Monkey shown with the original roller skates that attach to the bottom of his feet. **$25.00 – 30.00**. Courtesy Robin Englehart/Photo by Nancy Jean Mong.

Li'l Winking Herby Hippy: 16" doll has a button on his stomach that allows him to wink his right eye. Herby is marked, "REMCO, INC./1968" on his head. **$30.00 – 45.00**. Courtesy Elaine McGrath.

Jumpsy: A 14" battery-operated doll that jumps rope. Jumpsy has molded on shoes and socks. She is marked, "3070/REMCO IND. INC/19©70" on her head and "©1970/REMCO INDUSTRIES INC./HARRISON, N.J./MADE IN USA./PAT.PEND." on her back. MIB: **$45.00 – 65.00**. Courtesy Marcia Fanta.

Sweet April: 5½" Sweet April cries "real" tears after taking her a bottle and having the button on her back pressed. Several playsets as well as additional clothing were sold for Sweet April. This doll is relatively easy to find loose and often can be found for $5.00 – $10.00. Sweet April is marked, "HONG KONG/REMCO IND.INC. 19©71" on her head. Mint in case: **$25.00 – 35.00**.

Sweet April: Sweet April was also produced by Miner Industries, a company who obtained the rights to Remco dolls after Remco went out of business. The Miner Industries Sweet April doll on the right has straighter legs and her torso and limbs are made from a harder vinyl than the Remco doll on the left. The Miner Sweet April is also a deeper tan color than the Remco doll. The Miner Sweet April doll is marked, "HONG KONG/MINER IND. INC/NEW YORK N.Y. 10010" on her head and "MADE IN/ HONG KONG" on her back. Miner Sweet April loose and original: **$5.00 – 10.00**.

Sweet April: This doll was purchased in the early to mid-1980s in a discount store in the U.S. It appears that a Mexican company under license from Miner Industries issued the doll. The doll was called Little Tears Lily going for a stroll and still used the Sweet April logo. MIB: **$15.00 – 20.00**.

Mimi: With the aid of miniature records placed in a compartment in her back, this 20" doll could sing in many languages when a button on her front was pressed. Separate outfits were sold representing various countries. The doll is marked, "HONG KONG/REMCO IND./19©72" on her head, "SOUND DEVICE/MADE IN JAPAN" on the back of her record/battery compartment cover and "©1973/REMCO IND.INC./HARRISON, N.J." on her back. MIB: **$90.00 – 125.00**. Courtesy Marcia Fanta.

Baby This 'n That: This 13" was available both in white and black versions. Originally included with the doll were small accessories to hold in her hand like a toothbrush or a spoon. When one or both of her feet are squeezed, her arms move, her hands rotate, or her mouth moves as if eating. The doll is marked, "MADE IN HONG KONG" on the back of her head under her hairline, "©REMCO 1970/N.Y.N.Y. 10010" on her head and "©1976 REMCO TOYS/NEW YORK, N.Y. 10010/MADE IN HONG KONG/PRO" on her back. White version: **$20.00 – 25.00**. Black version: **$25.00 – 30.00**.

I Dream of Jeannie: This 6½" doll, circa 1976, was released to correspond with the Hanna Barbera animated version of Jeannie that was part of the *The Fred Flintstone and Friends* cartoon show and not the 1960s television show I *Dream of Jeannie* starring Barbara Eden. The doll has posing legs with wire inside. A slightly different 6½" Jeannie doll was issued in a play set that included a genie bottle. The play set Jeannie doll had a slightly bigger head than the Jeannie shown here and hard plastic legs with joints at the knees. She came dressed in a pink version of the blue outfit shown here. Poseable Jeannie doll NRFB: **$65.00 – 100.00**. Courtesy Sharon Wendrow/Memory Lane.

Ronald McDonald: This 7½" doll has a knob on his back which moves his head. Some dolls are marked, "H.K./702" on the head and on the back are three sets of markings that read, "©1976 MCDONALD'S/SYSTEM INC.", "©REMCO 1976/PAT.PEND." and "MADE IN/HONG KONG". Other dolls have no markings on the head and are marked, "©REMCO 1976/Pat.Pend./©1976 McDonalds/System Inc." and "MADE IN/HONG KONG" on the back. **$15.00 – 20.00**.

❀ ROSS PRODUCTS, INC. ❀

Tina Cassini: Two Tina dolls in their original boxes. They have the same markings as the doll on the left. MIB: **$75.00 – 150.00**. Courtesy Janet and Mike Lawrence.

Tina Cassini: Designed by fashion designer Oleg Cassini, this doll was named after his daughter, Tina. Tina Cassini came in various hair colors and dressed in various outfits. Her plastic heart-shaped stands says, "TINA©" on the top and "Made in Hong Kong" on the bottom. The 12" doll is marked, "TINA CASSINI/Made in British/Hong Kong" on her back. MIB: **$75.00 – 150.00**. Courtesy Gloria Telep.

Tina Cassini: A variety of dolls wearing various Oleg Cassini fashions. Outfits are tagged, "MADE IN BRITISH CROWN COLONY OF HONG KONG/DESIGNED BY OLEG CASSINI." Shoes are very much like Ideal's Tammy shoes, however they are marked differently and say, "HONG KONG/MADE IN" on the bottom. Loose dolls: **$50.00 – 90.00** each. Complete outfits: **$25.00 – 75.00**. Courtesy Janet and Mike Lawrence.

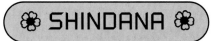
❀ ROYAL DOLL COMPANY ❀

Joy: This sweet large-eyed doll was issued in many different costumes. The 11" doll is marked, "A ROYAL DOLL//19©65" on her head and "©/1961/A ROYAL DOLL" on her back. In ballerina outfit: **$45.00 – 50.00**.

❀ SHINDANA ❀

A division of Operation Bootstrap, Inc. Shindana was primarily known for their black dolls in the 1970s. Their line of dolls included several black celebrity dolls.

Flip Wilson: 16" two-sided stuffed doll representing actor Flip Wilson. On one side of this pull-string talking doll is Flip. On the other side is Geraldine. The doll says things like, "What you see is what you get," and "The devil made me buy this dress." The Flip Wilson doll is tagged "1970 Street Corner Productions, Inc./Operation Bootstrap, Inc./Los Angeles, Calif. 90001/Commonwealth of Pennsylvania Department of Labor and Industry/Stuffed Toys Registration Number/211 APPROVED." Mute: **$25.00 – 40.00**.

"Take life a little easier, woo-we"

NEW
Rodney Allen Rippy

7⁷⁷

He's famous! Everyone knows the little boy that laughs so infectiously as he gives TV commercials! Cute and witty, too. Pull talking ring, hear him say 10 favorite expressions—at random (no batteries needed). Foamstuffed cotton body silk-screened with Rodney in T-shirt and jeans. Abt. 16¾ in. tall. Ship. wt. 2 lbs. 4 oz.

370 WARDS ALL

48 G 10356......7.77

I AM DYN-O-MITE

9⁹⁹

It's J. J.! Hear him say his stuff—in the real J. J.'s voice!

[11] **J. J. the "Dyn-O-Mite!" Talking Doll.** This guy has long floppy arms and legs you can pose in many positions. Kids will enjoy different J. J. sayings when they pull his talking ring. Doll wears turtle neck sweater with decal, jeans, sneakers, and funky hat. Painted face looks just like the real J. J. 23 in. high. Mailable.

X 921-5567 A—Wt. 1 lb... 9.99

©Shindana Toys

J.J.: 23" pull-string talking cloth doll of actor Jimmie Walker who played the character J.J. on the television program *Good Times*. Shindana Toys also made a 14" J.J. doll with a vinyl head and stuffed body. Loose and talking: **$50.00 – 75.00**. 1975 J.C. Penney Christmas catalog J.C. Penney Company, Inc. Used by permission.

Rodney Allen Rippy: 16½" pull-string talking cloth doll of child actor who appeared in a number of television programs and commercials in the early 1970s. Loose and talking: **$40.00 – 65.00**. 1974 Montgomery Ward Christmas catalog.

O.J. Simpson: 9½" action figure/doll of former football player O.J. Simpson. The doll is marked, "Shindana Toys/1975." MIB: **$150.00 – 200.00**. Photos courtesy Pamela Grimes.

O.J. Simpson: Close-up of O.J. Simpson doll. MIB: **$150.00 – 200.00**. Photo courtesy Pamela Grimes.

❀ SKIPPY DOLL CORPORATION ❀

Melody Baby Debbi: This 22" doll came in a plain white cardboard box. Her tag reads, "When you wind up, I slowly move my head to music." Her wind-up knob is on her back. The doll is marked, "SD" on her head. MIB: **$25.00 – $35.00**. Courtesy Gloria Telep.

❀ TRISTAR ❀

Poor Pitiful Pearl: (see also Horsman). Based on a cartoon character by Bill Steig, Tristar put out this 16" version of Poor Pitiful Pearl. MIB: **$65.00 – 85.00**. Courtesy Marcia Fanta.

❀ TOPPER TOYS ❀
(see also Deluxe Redding)

Dawn

Glamorous yet hip dolls, 6" Dawn and her friends were quite popular from 1970 through 1973. Over 30 dolls and close to 100 outfits were offered in the Dawn line. Leftover accessories from Deluxe Redding's Penny Brite were recycled into Dawn accessories. Dawn's bedroom set, kitchen set, and beauty parlor were all sets originally belonging to the larger-sized Penny Brite but were repackaged and changed slightly for Dawn and her friends. The Dawn name was licensed out to other companies to produce items such as paper dolls, Colorforms, lunchboxes, and other products that today are even more desirable to collectors than are the dolls due to their scarcity. A lot of leftover Dawn store stock has turned up over the years, so MIB items aren't too difficult to locate. A common problem of these dolls is green discoloration around their knees from the metal inside reacting to the vinyl. This problem occurs even on NRFB dolls. In the case of NRFB dolls, if the doll is dressed in an outfit that covers the green, the discoloration shouldn't affect the value much as it is so common. Those NRFB dolls dressed in mini dresses where the green is very visible are valued slightly lower than those without it. Loose dolls with green knees are usually valued around **$5.00 – 15.00** depending on the doll.

Dancing Dawn: When this doll's arm is raised and lowered, her head moves and her waist twists as if she is dancing. Dancing Dawn is marked, "©1970/ TOPPER CORP./HONG KONG/P" on her back. The doll also has a number on the back of her head that varies from doll to doll. MIB: **$30.00 – 45.00**.

Dawn: The Dawn doll in the center is wearing her original dress. The dolls on either side of her model just two of the wedding gowns available for Dawn. Markings on the 6½" dolls vary but usually they are marked with a letter, a number, and another letter on the back of their heads and "©1970/ TOPPER CORP./HONG KONG" on their backs. Loose dolls range about **10.00 – $15.00** each. Values for loose wedding outfits range about **$10.00 – 15.00** each.

Dawn Head to Toe: The Head to Toe dolls are not as common as some of the other dolls in the Dawn line. Dawn Head to Toe came dressed in either this silver mini dress or a pink mini dress. NRFB: **$65.00 – 80.00.** Courtesy Sharon Wendrow/Memory Lane.

Dale: The black female member of the Dawn line came with either brown eyes or the more uncommon green eyes. The brown-eyed doll is marked, "4/H80" on her head and the green-eyed doll is marked "4/H50" but these markings may vary from doll to doll. Both dolls are marked "©1970/ TOPPER CORP./HONG KONG/H" on their backs. Both dolls in photo are redressed in Dawn fashions. With brown eyes: **$15.00 – 20.00.** With green eyes: **$20.00 – 25.00.**

Dawn Modeling Agency: Dolls from this group came in elegant outfits and had more elaborate hairstyles than other dolls in the Dawn line. The dolls in the Modeling Agency group included Daphne, Denise, Dinah, Maureen, and Melanie, and each doll was available in two or three different outfits. From left to right in photo are Maureen, Dinah (redressed), MIB Melanie, Daphne, and Denise. The 6½" dolls are marked on the back of their heads with a letter, a number, and another letter and "©1970/ TOPPER CORP./HONG KONG or TAIWAN" on their backs. Loose dolls: **$15.00 – 25.00**. MIB: **$30.00 – 75.00**.

Dawn and Friends: Dawn with just a small sampling of some of her friends. **$10.00 – 20.00** each.

❀ UNEEDA DOLL COMPANY ❀

Dollikin: The fully-jointed hard-plastic Dollikin dolls came out in the late 1950s but continued to be offered into the early 1960s. In the 1970s, vinyl and plastic Dollikin dolls were made in 11½" and 6½" sizes. This 21" hard plastic Dollikin ballerina from 1961 is marked, "Uneeda/2S" on her head. **$150.00 – 200.00**.

Dollikin: This two-doll Dollikin set makes no mention of the baby on the box. The 21" Dollikin mother is hard plastic and is marked, "Uneeda/2S" on her head. The 8" baby has a vinyl head and plastic body and is unmarked. MIB: **$250.00 – 300.00**. Courtesy Gloria Telep.

Dollikins—16 flexible joints allow them to assume hundreds of
different positions, they pose so naturally. Jointed at ankles,
knees, wrists, shoulders, upper arm, elbow, waist and head.

Miss Dollikin—she seems almost
human, she poses so naturally!
Dressed for leisure in dainty white
blouse, plaid tapered slacks in the
latest slim-line style, vinyl shoes. Rooted hair in fluffy bob, sleeping eyes.
Ship. wt. 3 lbs. 4 oz.
48 T 4342—Abt. 20 in. tall **$4.99**

Dollikin Ballerina—duplicates all
the ballet poses—*she seems to
pirouette.* Sleeping eyes, smartly
styled rooted chignon hairdo.
Dressed for the stage in satin and
nylon net tutu, leotards, ballet slippers. Ship. wt. 3 lbs. 4 oz.
48 T 4306—Abt. 20 in. tall. . . . **$7.28**

Mother, Daughter, Baby Brother—*all for only $9.67.* 20-in. Mother wears
cotton suit, blouse, straw hat, shoes. 13-in. Daughter wears outfit that
matches Mommy's—panties, socks, shoes. 8-in. Baby drinks, wets, wears
bunting, carries bottle. All fully jointed, rooted hair, sleeping eyes.
48 T 4304—3 Dolls. Ship. wt. 3 lbs. 4 oz. . . . . Only **$9.67**

This 1961 Montgomery Ward Christmas catalog shows Dollikin dolls available that year, including a ballerina and
a casually dressed doll.

Dollikin: In 1970 an 11½ " Dollikin doll was
introduced. Dollikin came in blond,
brunette, black, and red hair colors. Jointed
at the shoulder, elbow, wrist, thigh, knee,
and foot, these dolls are marked, "©UNEEDA
DOLL CO.INC./MCMLX1X/ MADE IN
HONG KONG" on their heads and "DOL-
LIKIN©/U.S. PAT. #3,010253/OTHER U.S. &
FOR./PAT.PEND." on their backs. **$20.00 –
25.00** each.

Dollikin: Dollikin dolls are fully poseable as illustrated here. This doll comes with long straight hair.

Dollikin: A Dollikin doll with a curly pony-tail. These curly hair dolls have shoes that are hinged on their feet whereas other Dollikin dolls have removable shoes. MIB: **$35.00 – 50.00**.

Pollyanna: 30" doll representing the lead character from the movie *Pollyanna* starring Hayley Mills. Pollyanna is marked, "©WALT DISNEY/PRODS./MFD. BY UNEEDA" on her head. The doll in the photo is missing her original pantaloons. Shoes, socks, and hat not original. **$75.00 – 125.00**.

Toyland Fairy Princess: Character from the movie *Babes in Toyland,* this 30" doll sports the same body as the Pollyana doll shown in the previous photo. She is marked, "©UNEEDA DOLL CO./27" on her head. **$75.00 – 125.00**.

1

TOYLAND FAIRY PRINCESS

32 inch
ONLY $9⁹⁹

Toyland Fairy Princess: 1961 Montgomery Ward Christmas catalog shows the Toyland Fairy Princess wearing the ballerina outfit like the one in the previous photo.

①$15⁷⁷

THE TOYS THAT WALT DISNEY BRINGS TO

ⓒ1961 Walt Disney Productions

① "The Princess" Doll . . famous Babes in Toyland ballerina in a regal pink rayon satin gown, royal blue cape. Silver-color crown. All plastic body, movable arms and legs . .stands by herself. Turning head, go-to-sleep eyes. Rooted acetate hair.
79 N 3606C—32 inch doll. Shpg. wt. 5 lbs. . . .$15.77

② Gun Boat. Cannon "shoots" in any direction. Admiral's head bobs humorously up and down from smokestack as boat rolls along. Bright wood.
49 N 5322 — 7¾x7x5½ in. Shpg. wt. 1 lb. 2 oz.$1.79

314 SEARS FCB

③ Jumping Jack. Crazy clown wildly waves his arms and head as toy rolls on two irregular wheels. Smooth wood, brightly finished.
49 N 5305—8x6x7½ in. Shpg. wt. 1 lb. $1.99

④ Hobby Horse. Spring neck lets head shake as wood horsie rides on 4 irregular wheels. Felt blanket, saddle and stirrups. Yarn mane and tail.
49 N 5321—7x6¼x4¼ in. high. Shpg. wt. 14 oz.$1.69

⑤ Soldier with Cannon. Moves arm to shoot captive out of cannon. Bright wood.
49 N 5307—10x9x4½ in. high. Wt. 1 lb. 8 oz. $2.69

⑥ Soldier on horseback proudly displays American flags. Horse and rider go up and down as toy is pulled. Bright-finished wood.
49 N 5306—9x8x3¾ inches. Shpg. wt. 1 lb. . . .$2.34

⑦ Soldier and Guardhouse. Wooden soldier moves arms up and down to keep the "enemy" away. Stays "at ease" in hardboard guardhouse.
49 N 4521—Soldier, 9 in. high. Wt. 1 lb. 8 oz. . . .$2.39

⑧ Three Soldiers. Can twist into comic poses. Vinyl heads. Cotton uniforms, wire frames.
49 N 3716—About 12 in. tall. Wt. 1 lb. . . . . .Set $2.88

Toyland Fairy Princess: The 1961 Sears Christmas catalog shows the Toyland Fairy Princess doll dressed in a satin gown and cape. It is unknown whether or not this fairy princess outfit actually exists and if it does exist if it was a Sears exclusive.

Plumpees: These roly-poly dolls squeak when you squeeze them. The larger doll is 8" and made of vinyl and is marked, "©UNEEDA DOLL CO. INC./1967" on the head and " 'PLUMPEES'©" on the back. The 6" doll is made of a softer vinyl and is marked, "©UNEEDA/DOLL CO. INC." on the head, "1968 TAIWAN" on the back of the shirt collar and "©UNEEDA/DOLL CO. INC. MCMLXVIII/MADE IN TAIWAN/2C" on the bottom. **$10.00 – 15.00** each.

PeeWee: These 3½" dolls were Uneeda's answer to the tiny doll rage that was taking place in the mid-1960s. Uneeda's dolls were cheap alternatives to the better-made small dolls of the time. There were a large variety of PeeWee dolls sold, sporting many different hairstyles, hair colors, and outfits. In the late 1970s PeeWee dolls were still being sold, but they were different then earlier versions. The '70s PeeWee dolls have stiffer plastic bodies, not pliable ones like the earlier dolls. Unlike the earlier dolls, their feet are not marked. It isn't uncommon for the '70s PeeWee dolls to show up MIB on the collector market at bargain prices. Because they were sold extensively, PeeWee dolls are relatively easy to locate today. While there are currently some PeeWee collectors, their small numbers have so far kept the value of these dolls relatively low. The PeeWee dolls shown in the photo are inside a PeeWee case, which was sold separately. PeeWee dolls are marked, "HONG KONG" on their backs and "PEE-WEES/T.M."on the bottom of their foot or "HONG KONG" on their heads and "PEE-WEES/©U.D.CO. INC./1965/HONG KONG" on their backs. Redressed: **$2.00 – 4.00** each. Originally dressed: **$5.00 – 10.00** each. Courtesy Karen Hickey.

PeeWee: HeeWee dolls were the male version of the PeeWee dolls. They came dressed in all types of uniforms including that of a policeman, a soldier, a sailor, a football player, and a golfer. The photo shows three different HeeWee dolls, a baseball player, a fireman, and a sailor. They are inside a PeeWee case. HeeWee dolls are marked, "1966/©U.D.CO.INC." on the head, "U.D.CO./©/1965" on the bottom of the left foot and "PEE-WEES/T.M."on the bottom of the right foot. **$5.00 – 10.00** each. Courtesy Karen Hickey.

PeeWee: The younger version of PeeWee dolls were called Baby PeeWees. The dolls in the photo are shown inside a PeeWee house. The 3¾" dolls are marked, "HONG KONG/©UNEEDA DOLL CO./IN/1966/BABY/PEEWEE/MADE IN/HONG KONG" on their backs. Redressed: **$2.00 – 4.00** each. Originally dressed: **$5.00 – 10.00** each. Courtesy Karen Hickey.

PeeWee: These two pages from the 1967 J.C. Penney Christmas catalog show some of the dolls in the Pee-Wee line.

PeeWee: This 3½" doll is either a foreign Pee-Wee or a knockoff of one. While she wasn't manufactured by Uneeda, she is included here to show her resemblance to the PeeWee dolls. She is marked "RATTI" on her head and "RATTI/ITALY" on her back. Originally dressed: **$5.00 – 10.00.** Courtesy Janet and Mike Lawrence.

Petal People: These 2½" dolls came inside a 12½" plastic flower-pot stand. The Petal People dolls included Tiny Tulip, Polly Poppy, Dizzy Daisy, Sunny Flower, Rosy Rose, and Daffi Dill. Originally dressed with flower pot stands: **$15.00 – 20.00**. Originally dressed dolls without flower pot stands: **$5.00 – 7.00** each. 1968 Sears Christmas catalog.

Petal People: Polly Poppy shown wearing Rosy Rose's dress. Polly is marked, "HONG KONG" on her back. Loose/redressed in Petal People outfit: **$5.00 – 7.00**.

Granny and Me: 16" doll originally came with a 7" granddaughter doll. The head mold used for Granny was also used on a number of other Uneeda dolls. Granny has a dimple on her chin and painted-on granny-square glasses. She is marked, "UNEEDA DOLL/CO. INC./©1963" on her head. **$18.00 – 22.00.**

Granny and Me: This 1977 J.C. Penney Christmas catalog shows Granny with her 7" granddaughter. Both dolls originally dressed: **$25.00 – 30.00**.

Popeye: 8" doll with vinyl arms and head, stuffed body and legs. The doll is marked, "©U.D.CO.INC./MCMLXXVII/MADE IN HONG KONG" Although the doll is marked with the year 1977, his box is marked "©King Features Syndicate, Inc., 1979." MIB: **$25.00 – 45.00.**

Calico Lassie/Elly May Clampett: Shown here with an original send-away advertising offer, this Calico Lassie doll is better known as the Elly May Clampett doll to collectors. Although in various reference books this doll has been referred to as Elly May Clampett, the character from the television show *The Beverly Hillbillies,* the author has yet to locate anyone who has ever seen this doll MIB or found any original advertising to confirm it actually was sold under the Elly May name. It's possible that she may have simply been dubbed Elly May by collectors because of her resemblance to the character or possibly the same doll was sold both as Calico Lassie and Elly May. In any event, when wearing her blue and white striped shirt and jeans with her rope belt, she has a higher value than when she is wearing any of the other three outfits. The 11½" doll is marked, "UNIQUE" on her head. With jeans outfit: **$50.00 – 85.00.** Other outfits: **$25.00 – 45.00.** Courtesy Janet and Mike Lawrence.

❀ VALENTINE ❀

Doll (name unknown): This pretty 14" doll has a vinyl head and plastic body and limbs. She is marked, "2½ B" on her head and "13-5/V" on her lower back. Her box reads, "A VALENTINE DOLL CREATION" and "I'LL LOVE YOU." No name is mentioned anywhere on the doll or her box. MIB: **$45.00 – 65.00**. Courtesy Gloria Telep.

❀ VOGUE ❀

Brikette: Brikette was available in either 22" or 16" from around 1959 – 1961. She was issued with orange, platinum blond, or brunette hair. She had green eyes, upside-down "V" shaped eyebrows, and a ball-jointed swivel waist. The outfit the doll in the photo is wearing is just one of the many different outfits she originally came in. In 1979 the name Brikette was used again, but these dolls did not have the green eyes, "V" shaped brows, or ball-jointed waists like the earlier dolls. Brikette is marked, "VOGUE INC./19©60" on her head. MIB: **250.00 – 275.00**. Courtesy Robin Randall.

Unknown Brikette-type doll: The resemblance of this doll to Brikette is just too coincidental to believe she wasn't made using the Brikette mold. She is 20" tall with vinyl head and arms, and plastic torso and legs. Her facial features and hands are the same as Brikette's. Unlike Brikette, this doll has curved eyebrows, doesn't have a swivel waist, and has no markings. Several doll authorities could not identify this doll, and until another doll like her turns up MIB, her identity remains a mystery. It is possible she could have been made by another company who purchased the Brikette molds from Vogue. No other examples of her have been found to comparatively determine a value, but because she would appeal to Brikette collectors, she would likely command a value of **$45.00 – 75.00**.

Unknown Brikette-type doll: This 18" doll not only has the same face as Brikette but also orange hair and green eyes like Brikette. Even her blue dress with a red and white striped V-neck front imitates Brikette's. Unlike Brikette, this doll has curved eyebrows. Her arms, legs, and body are made of lightweight plastic. She is unmarked. Brikette imitators such as this one are a bit more common than the previous doll. **$35.00 – 55.00**.

Unknown Brikette-type dolls: The two Brikette imitators are shown side-by-side for comparison.

Miss Ginny: Vogue's 8" Ginny doll which was so popular in the 1950s continued to be made in both plastic and vinyl throughout the 1960s into the 1970s. A more sophisticated Ginny doll called Miss Ginny started out as a 16" doll in 1962 and later came both in 12" and 15" sizes. This 15" Miss Ginny is marked, "VOGUE DOLL/©1974" on her head. **$25.00 – 40.00**.

Little Miss Ginny: Little Miss Ginny was a 12" doll who began in 1965 and continued throughout the 1970s. This 12" size Ginny was issued in various outfits including 12 different costumes of Far-Away Lands. Here Little Miss Ginny represents Spain. With tag: **$30.00 – 45.00.** Courtesy Marcia Fanta.

Ginny: This 8" Ginny is from the Far-Away Lands Series. She is missing her original hat. The doll is marked, "VOGUE DOLLS/(GINNY(/1977" on her head and "VOGUE DOLLS ©1972/MADE IN HONG KONG/3" on her back. **$20.00 – 25.00.**

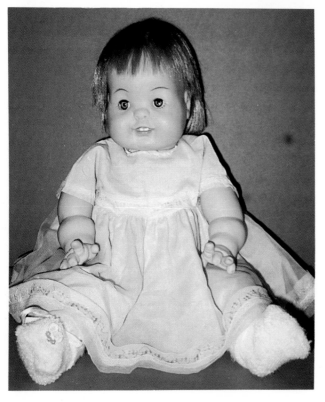

Baby Dear One: 25" doll designed by popular children's illustrator Eloise Wilkins to represent a life-like one-year-old baby. The doll has a vinyl head and limbs and a cloth body. She is a heavy doll weighing more than four pounds. Circa 1962. Baby Dear One is marked, "©/1961/E.Wilkin/Vogue Dolls/Inc." on her head and "VOGUE DOLLS/INC." on her back. **$175.00 – 225.00.** Courtesy Dawn Thomas.

Too Dear: 23" doll designed by illustrator Eloise Wilkins to represent a two-year-old version of the above Baby Dear One doll. The doll is all vinyl. Circa 1963. Too Dear is marked, "©/1963/E.Wilkin/Vogue Dolls" on her head. **$175.00 – 225.00**. Courtesy Dawn Thomas.

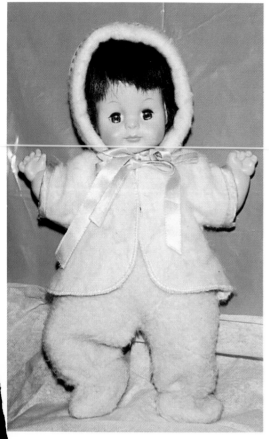

Baby Dear: A redesigned 12" Baby Dear. **$25.00 – 40.00**. Courtesy Marcia Fanta.

Baby Dear One: A redesigned 24" Baby Dear One doll with vinyl head and limbs and stuffed body. **$25.00 – 40.00.** ©1974 JCPenney Catalog, J.C. Penney Company, Inc. Used by permission.

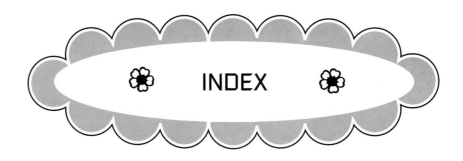

INDEX

Almost from the time she stopped playing with dolls, Cindy Sabulis began collecting them. Her doll collection officially started when she received her first Madame Alexander doll at age 11. When her first four Madame Alexander dolls were not being played with, they sat on display on the windowsill in her bedroom. Those well-loved dolls are worth more sentimentally than monetarily, yet they hold the honor of being responsible for sparking Cindy's interest in collecting dolls.

Today Cindy is involved in many aspects of doll collecting. She and her husband Steve are owners of Toys of Another Time, a business specializing in dolls from the 1950s – 1970s. They sell at doll shows, through mail order, and via the Internet. Over the past 14 years Cindy has written dozens of articles for doll and collectibles publications. She is co-author of the book, *The Collector's Guide to Tammy, the Ideal Teen* and is also an advisor/contributor for *Schroeder's Collectible Toys Garage Sale & Flea Market Annual,* and *Flea Market Trader,* providing information and values on Tammy, Liddle Kiddles, Tressy, Littlechaps, and many other dolls. A summa cum laude graduate in computer science from Sacred Heart University, she worked professionally as a computer programmer as well as a freelance writer and editor. In 1993 after several years of selling in her spare time, she left the corporate world to devote full time to the doll business.